The Complete Idiot's Reference Card

HTML Codes for Cool Characters

Symbol	Character Code	Entity Name	Symbol	Character Code	Entity Name	Symbol	Code	Name
Space	 		H	H		p	p	
!	!		I	I		q	q	
"	"	"	J	J		r	r	
#	#		K	K		s	s	
$	$		L	L		t	t	
%	%		M	M		u	u	
&	&	&	N	N		v	v	
'	'		O	O		w	w	
(	(		P	P		x	x	
)	)		Q	Q		y	y	
*	*		R	R		z	z	
+	+		S	S		{	{	
,	,		T	T				|	
-	-		U	U		}	}	
.	.		V	V		~	~	
/	/		W	W		N/A	&#127;	
0	0		X	X			€	
1	1		Y	Y		N/A		
2	2		Z	Z		,	‚	
3	3		[	[		ƒ	ƒ	
4	4		\	\		„	„	
5	5		]	]		…	…	
6	6		^	^		†	†	
7	7		_	_		‡	‡	
8	8		`	`		ˆ	ˆ	
9	9		a	a		‰	‰	
:	:		b	b		Š	Š	
;	;		c	c		‹	‹	
<	<	<	d	d		Œ	Œ	
=	=		e	e		N/A		
>	>	>	f	f		Ž	Ž	
?	?		g	g		N/A		
@	@		h	h		N/A		
A	A		i	i		'	‘	
B	B		j	j		'	’	
C	C		k	k		"	“	
D	D		l	l		"	”	
E	E		m	m		♦	•	
F	F		n	n		– (en dash)	–	
G	G		o	o		— (em dash)	—	
						~	˜	

ALPHA

Symbol	Character Code	Entity Name	Symbol	Character Code	Entity Name	Symbol	Character Code	Entity Name
™	&#153;		»	&#187;	&raquo;	N/A	&#222;	&THORN;
š	&#154;		¼	&#188;	&frac14;	ß	&#223;	&szlig;
›	&#155;		½	&#189;	&frac12;	à	&#224;	&agrave;
œ	&#156;		¾	&#190;	&frac34;	á	&#225;	&aacute;
N/A	&#157;		¿	&#191;	&iquest;	â	&#226;	&acirc;
ž	&#158;		À	&#192;	&Agrave;	ã	&#227;	&atilde;
Ÿ	&#159;		Á	&#193;	&Aacute;	ä	&#228;	&auml;
Non-breaking space			Â	&#194;	&Acirc;	å	&#229;	&aring;
			Ã	&#195;	&Atilde;	æ	&#230;	&aelig;
¡	&#161;	&iexcl;	Ä	&#196;	&Auml;	ç	&#231;	&ccedil;
¢	&#162;	&cent;	Å	&#197;	&Aring;	è	&#232;	&egrave;
£	&#163;	&pound;	Æ	&#198;	&AElig;	é	&#233;	&eacute;
N/A	&#164;	&curren;	Ç	&#199;	&Ccedil;	ê	&#234;	&ecirc;
¥	&#165;	&yen;	È	&#200;	&Egrave;	ë	&#235;	&euml;
¦	&#166;	&brvbar;	É	&#201;	&Eacute;	ì	&#236;	&igrave;
§	&#167;	&sect;	Ê	&#202;	&Ecirc;	í	&#237;	&iacute
¨	&#168;	&uml;	Ë	&#203;	&Euml;	î	&#238;	&icirc;
©	&#169;	&copy;	Ì	&#204;	&Igrave;	ï	&#239;	&iuml;
ª	&#170;	&ordf;	Í	&#205;	&Iacute;	N/A	&#240;	&eth;
¬	&#172;	&not;	Î	&#206;	&Icirc;	ñ	&#241;	&ntilde;
Soft hyphen	&#173;	&shy;	Ï	&#207;	&Iuml;	ò	&#242;	&ograve;
			Ð	&#208;	&ETH;	ó	&#243;	&oacute;
®	&#174;	&reg;	Ñ	&#209;	&Ntilde;	ô	&#244;	&ocirc;
¯	&#175;	&macr;	Ò	&#210;	&Ograve;	õ	&#245;	&otilde;
°	&#176;	&deg;	Ó	&#211;	&Oacute;	ö	&#246;	&ouml;
±	&#177;	&plusmn;	Ô	&#212;	&Ocirc;	÷	&#247;	&divide;
²	&#178;	&sup2;	Õ	&#213;	&Otilde;	ø	&#248;	&oslash;
³	&#179;	&sup3;	Ö	&#214;	&Ouml;	ù	&#249;	&ugrave;
´	&#180;	&acute;	×	&#215;	&times;	ú	&#250;	&uacute;
µ	&#181;	&micro;	Ø	&#216;	&Oslash;	û	&#251;	&ucirc;
¶	&#182;	&para;	Ù	&#217;	&Ugrave;	ü	&#252;	&uuml;
·	&#183;	&middot;	Ú	&#218;	&Uacute;	ý	&#253;	&yacute;
¸	&#184;	&cedil;	Û	&#219;	&Ucirc;	N/A	&#254;	&thorn;
¹	&#185;	&sup1;	Ü	&#220;	&Uuml;	ÿ	&#255;	&yuml;
º	&#186;	&ordm;	Ý	&#221;	&Yacute;			

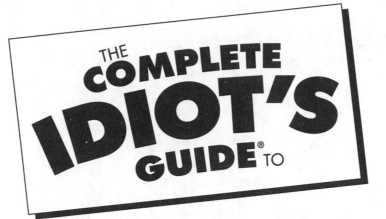

THE COMPLETE IDIOT'S GUIDE® TO

Creating a Web Page

Fifth Edition

by Paul McFedries

ALPHA

A Pearson Education Company

Copyright © 2002 by Pearson Education, Inc.

International Standard Book Number: 0-02-864316-X

Library of Congress Catalog Card Number: 2001099416

04   03   02   8   7   6   5   4   3   2   1

Interpretation of the printing code: The rightmost number of the first series of numbers is the year of the book's printing; the rightmost number of the second series of numbers is the number of the book's printing. For example, a printing code of 02-1 shows that the first printing occurred in 2002.

Printed in the United States of America

Publisher: *Marie Butler-Knight*
Product Manager: *Phil Kitchel*
Managing Editor: *Jennifer Chisholm*
Acquisitions Editor: *Eric Heagy*
Development Editor: *Clint McCarty*
Production Editor: *Katherin Bidwell*
Copy Editor: *Susan Aufheimer*
Technical Editor: *Don Passenger*
Illustrator: *Chris Eliopoulos*
Cover/Book Designer: *Trina Wurst*
Indexer: *Tonya Heard*
Layout/Proofreading: *Gloria Schurick, Kimberly Tucker*

Contents at a Glance

Contents

Introduction

Creating a web page sounds like tough stuff, doesn't it? I mean, have you ever *seen* the code that comprises a web page? It looks as though someone took a bunch of letters, numbers, and symbols, put them through some kind of linguistic blender, and then poured the result onto the web. It's ugly, it's messy, and it's downright intimidating. But it's also one more thing:

It's easy.

Yes, you read that right: Creating web pages is really quite easy. Actually, let me qualify that: Creating web pages is easy *if* you approach it in the right way. What's the right way? Starting at the very beginning with the most basic structure of a page, and then slowly working step-by-step through the rest of it, tacking on bits and pieces as you go along. This way you slowly build your HTML knowledge until, before you know it, you have your very own web page for all to see.

The good news is that this step-by-step, piece-by-piece method is exactly the approach I use in this book. To that end, this book doesn't assume you have any previous experience with web page production. All the information is presented in short, easy-to-digest chunks that make building a page fun and easy on the brain.

Sounds great! But why are you calling me an idiot?

Well, when it comes to producing content for the World Wide Web, a "complete idiot" is someone who, despite having the normal complement of gray matter, wouldn't know HTML from H. G. Wells. This is, of course, perfectly normal and, despite what many so-called Internet gurus may tell you, it does not imply any sort of character defect on your part.

So I might as well get one thing straight right off the bat: The fact that you're reading *The Complete Idiot's Guide to Creating a Web Page, Fifth Edition* (my, that is a mouthful, isn't it?) does *not* make you an idiot. On the contrary, it shows that …

- ◆ You don't take yourself—or any of this web page malarkey—too seriously, so you're willing to have a little irreverent fun as we go along.
- ◆ You're determined to learn this HTML thing, but you don't want to be bothered with a lot of boring, technical details.
- ◆ You realize it doesn't make sense to learn absolutely everything about HTML. You just need to know enough to get your web page up and running.
- ◆ You're smart enough not to spend your days reading five bazillion pages of arcane (and mostly useless) information. You do, after all, have a life to lead.

How This Book Is Set Up

I'm assuming you have a life away from your computer screen, so *The Complete Idiot's Guide to Creating a Web Page*, is set up so you don't have to read it from cover to cover. If you want to know how to add a picture to your web page, for example, just turn to the chapter that covers working with images. (Although, having said that, beginners will want to read at least Chapter 2, "Laying the Foundation: The Basic Structure of a Web Page" before moving on to more esoteric topics.) To make things easier to find, I've organized the book into half a dozen more or less sensible sections:

Part 1: "Creating Your First Web Page"

After dipping a toe into the web publishing waters with some introductory material in Chapter 1, "A Brief HTML Primer," you then dive right into the hurly-burly of web page construction. The next five chapters here in Part 1 take you step-by-step, piece-by-piece through the process of building a spanking new web page. These chapters build your knowledge of basic HTML slowly and with lots of examples. Then Chapters 7, "The Host with the Most: Choosing a Web Hosting Provider," and 8, "Publish or Perish: Putting Your Page on the Web," show you how to successfully negotiate the big moment: getting your page on the web for your friends and family to admire.

Part 2: "A Grab Bag of Web Page Wonders"

Part 2 takes you beyond the basics by presenting you with a hodgepodge of web page topics. You get oh-so-simple instructions on web page knickknacks such as image links (Chapter 9, "Images Can Be Links, Too"), tables (Chapter 10, "Table Talk: Adding Tables to Your Page"), multimedia (Chapter 11, "Making Your Web Pages Dance and Sing"), forms (Chapter 12, "Need Feedback? Create a Form!"), and frames (Chapter 13, "Fooling Around with Frames").

Part 3: "High HTML Style: Working with Style Sheets"

Style sheets are the wave of the future in web page design, so Part 3 devotes no less than three chapters to mastering them. I explain the basics in Chapter 14, "A Beginner's Guide to Style Sheets," and then I show you how to wield styles for fonts, colors, and backgrounds (Chapter 15, "Sheet Music: Styles for Fonts, Colors, and Backgrounds"), as well as dimensions, borders, and margins (Chapter 16, "The Box Model: Styles for Dimensions, Borders, Margins, and More").

Part 4: "Working with JavaScripts and Java Applets"

The three chapters in Part 4 show you how to add tiny little programs to your web pages to give them that interactive boost. Chapter 17, "The Programmable Page: Adding JavaScripts to Your Pages," tells you all about this JavaScript thing that everyone always blathers on about. It also gives you quite a few examples of scripts that you can plop right inside your pages. Chapter 18, "More JavaScript Fun," takes the JavaScript ball and runs with it by showing you a whack of other examples that do all kinds of amazingly useful things. Chapter 19, "Caffeinating Your Pages: Adding Java Applets," turns your attention to Java and the applets that it creates.

Part 5: "Rounding Out Your HTML Education"

This part of the book features some chapters that help increase your webmaster IQ. You learn a about a few more web page tricks to stuff up your sleeve (Chapter 20, "Web Page Doodads You Should Know About"), you get some hints on proper web page style (Chapter 21, "The Elements of Web Page Style"), and some Internet resources that help you create great pages (Chapter 22, "Some HTML Resources on the Web").

Part 6: "Show Me the Money: Turning Your HTML Skills Into Cash"

Most web welders are happy just to put up their pages and leave it at that. But a few want to generate some extra cash from their hard work, and that's what I show you how to do in this section. You learn how to get started as a professional web designer (Chapter 23, "Turning Pro: Becoming a Paid Web Designer"), how to make money from putting ads and links to affiliate programs on your site (Chapter 24, "Joint Ventures: Working with Ads and Affiliate Programs"), and how to sell things from your site (Chapter 25, "Selling Stuff Online").

You Want More? You've Got It!

Happily, there's more to this book than 25 chapters of me yammering away. To put a feather in your HTML cap and to make your page publishing adventures a bit easier, I've included a few other goodies:

◆ **Tear-out Card: HTML Codes for Cool Characters**   This page (it's located after the inside front cover of the book, in case you missed it on the way in) lists all the HTML codes you can use to incorporate characters such as ¢ and © in your web page. (This is all explained in more detail in Chapter 3.)

◆ **Appendix A: Speak Like a Geek Glossary**   You can find this section near the back of the book. It's a glossary of Internet, World Wide Web, and HTML terms that should help you out if you come across a word or phrase that furrows your brow.

◆ **Appendix B: Frequently Asked Questions About HTML**   This section runs through a few dozen of the most common questions asked by beginning webmasters and, of course, offers simple solutions to each problem.

◆ **The CD: The Webmaster's Toolkit**   The book's major bonus is the CD that's glued onto the back cover. This little plastic Frisbee contains a complete Webmaster's Toolkit with tons of HTML-related doodads, including all the HTML examples I use in the book, some sample web pages, HTML programs, lots of graphics you can put in your web page, and tons more.

♦ **The Complete Idiot's HTML Tag Reference**   This is also on the CD, and it gives you a complete list of all the HTML tags in the known universe.

♦ **The Complete Idiot's Style Sheet Reference**   This CD reference runs through all the available style sheet properties, tells you which browsers support them, lists all the possible values, and gives you lots of examples.

♦ **Bonus web chapters**   These chapters on my site show you a few ways to make this stuff a bit easier. Specifically, I show you how to wield several tools that take some of the drudgery out of putting together a web page, including Netscape Composer, the Office HTML tools, and more. I give you my web address later in this introduction.

Also, as you're trudging through the book, look for the following features that point out important info:

Webmaster Wisdom

These boxes contain notes, tips, and asides that provide you with interesting and useful (at least theoretically!) nuggets of web page lore.

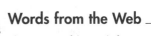

Words from the Web

This type of box defines words and phrases that every budding webmaster needs to know.

Page Pitfalls

These boxes contain web page cautionary tales that warn you of traps to avoid and hurdles to jump over.

What's New in This Edition

Sending a book out to market is a little like watching one of your kids leave home. Will they be okay? Will other people accept them? Will they be successful in their chosen field? Will they be displayed prominently at the front of the store? (Well, okay, we probably don't want our kids displayed prominently in the front of stores.) I'm happy to report that *The Complete Idiot's Guide to Creating a Web Page* has been a resounding success in its first four ventures into the cold, cruel world. I've received a lot of comments from people saying they liked the book and really enjoyed the approach. Thanks!

The only complaints I heard were from people who wanted more! Well, you got it. This fifth edition includes the same easy-to-digest methods for setting up a web page, but also includes the following tidbits:

♦ Updated coverage of the basic HTML codes to include the latest and greatest enhancements

♦ Lots of new tips and traps sprinkled throughout the book

♦ Much more extensive coverage of style sheets

♦ How to add a search feature to your site

♦ How to add a chat room or bulletin board

♦ The details of using server-side includes (SSI)

♦ Fully revised and updated links to all the web-based resources mentioned in the book

♦ How to make money by selling ads on your site

♦ How to sell goods and services online

♦ An updated HTML tag reference

♦ An updated style sheet reference

♦ An expanded list of Frequently Asked Questions about HTML

♦ Lots of new programs on the CD

Online Resources for Readers

All the stuff that's crammed into this book is only the beginning. I've also set up a few online resources you can use to get more info and continue your HTML education.

This Book's Home Page

For starters, there's the World Wide Web home of *The Complete Idiot's Guide to Creating a Web Page*, which is at the following address: www.mcfedries.com/CreatingAWebPage.

Here you get book info, extra material not found in the book, HTML updates, new and changed HTML resources, and much more.

Links to Readers' Web Pages

I was mighty impressed by the pages being cobbled together by the readers of the first edition, so I decided to let other people know about them. To that end, I set up a showcase page that features links to the web pages created by readers. Here's the address: www.mcfedries.com/CreatingAWebPage/links.html.

When you have your own page up and running on the web, make sure you add it to the list!

The CIGHTML Mailing List

There's nothing like the give-and-take of a mailing list to not only learn more about a topic, but also to foster a sense of community among people who share a common interest. The readers of *The Complete Idiot's Guide to Creating a Web Page* share a common interest in stitching together web pages, so I created a mailing list just for them. To join in our discussions of HTML and web page design, send an e-mail message to the following address: listmanager@mcfedries.com.

Include just the following command in the Subject line: join cightml.

You'll get back a welcome message that gives you instructions on participating in the list. If you'd like to check out what's happened previously on the list, head for the CIGHTML mailing list archives: www.mcfedries.com/CreatingAWebPage/list/.

Let Me Know How You're Doing!

Hey, you paid good money for this book, so it's only reasonable that you should be able to get in touch with its author, right? Sure! So, as long as you have something nice to say (complaints will be acknowledged only grudgingly), why not drop me a line and let me know how your web page is coming along or, heck, just tell me what you thought of the book. If your page is ready to go, send me its web address and I'll surf over and take a look. Here's my e-mail address: webpages@mcfedries.com.

If you'd like to drop by my own home page, here's the address: www.mcfedries.com.

See you in cyberspace!

Acknowledgments (The Giving Credit Where Credit Is Due Department)

The job of editor in a publishing house is the dullest, hardest, most exciting, exasperating, and rewarding of perhaps any job in the world.

—Maxwell Perkins

The wonderful editors at Alpha Books have taken all of these qualities and harnessed them into whipping this book into literary shape. That's good news for you because it means you get a book that has no fluff, chaff, or anything else that isn't bookworthy. That takes skillful editing, and the following folks had the necessary skills to get the job done: Acquisitions Editor Eric Heagy, Development Editor Clint McCarty, Production Editor Katherin Bidwell, Copy Editor Susan Aufheimer, and Technical Editor Don Passenger.

The members of the editorial team aren't the only people who had their fingers in this publishing pie. Flip back a few pages and you'll find a list of the designers, illustrators, indexers, and other professionals who worked long and hard to produce this book. I tip my authorial hat to all of them. I'd also like to thank the thousands and thousands of readers who have written to me over the years to offer compliments and suggestions. If this is the best edition yet (and I lack just enough humility to think that it is), it's thanks in no small measure to my readers' willingness to offer a couple of cents' worth.

Special Thanks to the Technical Reviewer

The Complete Idiot's Guide to Creating a Web Page, Fifth Edition, was reviewed by an expert who double-checked the accuracy of what you'll learn here, to help us ensure that this book gives you everything you need to know about creating a web page. Special thanks are extended to Don Passenger.

Don Passenger has been computing from the punch card mainframe day to present (including Fortran, Basic, WordStar, and even Osborn and Tandy computers). He ventured into HTML in 1995 armed with a simple text editor and a copy of the first edition of this book.

Passenger holds an AA from Grand Rapids Community College, a BSNR from the University of Michigan, and a JD from Notre Dame Law School. He is an adjunct member of the Davenport University faculty teaching in both the Legal Studies and Computer Information Systems departments, including several HTML courses.

Trademarks

All terms mentioned in this book that are known to be or are suspected of being trademarks or service marks have been appropriately capitalized. Alpha Books and Pearson Education, Inc., cannot attest to the accuracy of this information. Use of a term in this book should not be regarded as affecting the validity of any trademark or service mark.

Part 1

Creating Your First Web Page

I know you must be chomping at the bit to get started creating a web page to call your own. Well, I'm happy to say, your big moment is just around the corner. The eight chapters here in Part 1 will take you through the entire web page production process, from go to whoa. You'll see that it's really not all that hard to get a page from in here (your computer) to out there (the World Wide Web). When the dust settles, you'll have an actual, honest-to-goodness, "Look, ma, I'm in cyberspace!" web page. You will be, in short, a full-fledged member of the Royal Order of webmeisters and the envy of all your pathetically pageless friends.

Chapter 1

A Brief HTML Primer

In This Chapter

- What in the name of blue blazes is HTML?
- A look at what kind of havoc you can wreak with HTML
- Answers to pressing HTML questions
- A veritable cornucopia of web page examples that show HTML in its best light

Before you go off half-cocked and start publishing pages willy-nilly on the World Wide Web, it helps to have a bit of background on HTML. After all, you wouldn't try to set up shop in a new country without first understanding the local geography and customs and learning a few choice phrases, such as "I am sorry I insulted your sister" and "You don't buy beer, you rent it!"

This chapter gives you a handle on the HTML hoo-ha that seems to be such an integral part of web page construction. What is HTML? Why bother with it? What can you do with it? Why does it sound so darned scary? Will it turn your brain to mush? This chapter answers all these questions and more.

Okay, so just what is HTML?

I have some good news, and I have some bad news. The bad news is that HTML stands for—brace yourself—*HyperText Markup Language*. (I'll pause for a sec to let you get the inevitable jargon-induced shudders out of the way.)

The good news, however, is that HTML doesn't stand for Hard To Master Lingo. HTML is, in fact, really a sheep in wolf's clothing: It looks nasty, but it's really quite tame. (And, no, it won't turn even a small part of your brain to mush.) Learning basic HTML—which is what 90 percent of all web pages use—isn't much tougher than reciting the alphabet, and it's way easier than programming your VCR. (This is, I'm sure, good news for those of you who sport that scarlet letter of modern technology: The flashing 12:00 on your VCR clock.)

That's all well and good, Author Boy, but HyperText Markup Language isn't exactly a phrase that trips lightly off the tongue; it really sounds intimidating.

Well, you're right, it does. So, in the spirit of self-help books everywhere, you need to face your fears and look HTML squarely in the eye. Specifically, you need to examine what each element of HyperText Markup Language means in plain English:

♦ **HyperText**   As I'm sure you know, a *link* is a special word or phrase in a web page that "points" to another web page. When you click one of these links, your browser transports you immediately to the other page, no questions asked. The eggheads who invented the web actually used the highfalutin term *hypertext link* for this special text (the prefix *hyper-* means "beyond"). Because these hypertext links are really the distinguishing feature of the World Wide Web, web pages are often known as *hypertext documents.* So, HTML has the word "HyperText" in it because you use it to create these hypertext documents. (It would be just as accurate to call it WPML— Web Page Markup Language.)

♦ **Markup**   My dictionary defines "markup" as (among other things) "detailed stylistic instructions written on a manuscript that is to be typeset." For our purposes, I can rephrase this definition as follows: "detailed stylistic instructions typed into a text document that is to be published on the World Wide Web." That's HTML in a nutshell. It has a few simple codes for detailing things such as making text bold or italic, creating bulleted lists, inserting images, and, of course, defining links. You just type these codes into the appropriate places in an ordinary text document, and the web browser software does the dirty work of translating the codes. The result? Your page is displayed the way you want, automatically.

♦ **Language**   This word might be the most misleading of them all. Many people interpret this to mean that HTML is a programming language, and they wash their hands of the whole thing right off the bat. "You mean I gotta learn programming to get my two cents worth on the web?" Not a chance, Vance. HTML has nothing, I repeat, *nothing*, whatsoever to do with computer programming. Rather, HTML is a "language" in the sense that it has a small collection of two- and three-letter combinations and words that you use to specify styles such as bold and italic.

What can you do with HTML?

All right, so HTML isn't the Hideous, Terrible, Mega-Leviathan that its name might suggest, but rather a Harmless, Tame, Mini-Lapdog. What can you do with such a creature? Well, lots of things, actually. After all, people aren't flocking to the web because it's good for their health. Just the opposite, in fact. They're surfing 'til they drop because the web presents them with an attractive and easily navigated source of information and entertainment (or *infotainment*, as the wags like to call it). It's HTML that adds the attractiveness and ease of navigation. To see what I mean, the next few sections take you through examples of the basic HTML elements.

You can format text.

A high Jolts Per Minute (JPM) count is what turns the crank of your average web-surfing dude and dudette. However, nothing generates fewer jolts (and is harder on the eyes to boot) than plain, unadorned text. To liven things up, you need to use different sizes and styles of type for your web page text. Happily, HTML is no slouch when it comes to dressing up text for the prom:

Words from the Web

Creating something (such as a web page) for no other reason than the sheer fact that you *can* create it is called **inverse vandalism**.

- ◆ You can display your web prose as bold.
- ◆ You can emphasize text with italics.
- ◆ You can make text look as though it was produced by a typewriter.
- ◆ You can display text using different colors, such as red, white, and blue.
- ◆ You can use different font sizes for words and even individual characters.

Figure 1.1 shows examples of each kind of style. (I show you how to use HTML to format web page text in Chapter 3, "From Buck-Naked to Beautiful: Dressing Up Your Page."

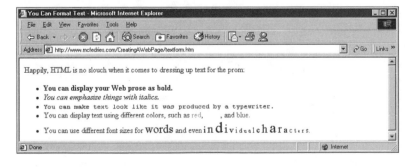

Figure 1.1

Some examples of HTML text styles.

You can create lists of things.

If you're presenting information on your web page, it helps if you can display your data in a way that makes sense and is easy to read. In some cases, this means arranging the data in lists, such as a numbered list or a bulleted list (see Figure 1.1 for an example of the latter). I fill you in on how to use HTML to create these and other kinds of lists in Chapter 4, "The Gist of a List: Adding Lists to Your Page."

You can set up links to other pages.

Web sessions aren't true surfin' safaris unless you take a flying leap or two. I'm speaking, of course, of selecting links that take you to the far-flung corners of the web world.

You can give the readers of your web pages the same kicks by using HTML to create links anywhere on a page. You can set up three kinds of links:

◆ Links to another of your web pages.

◆ Links to a different location in the same web page. (This is useful for pages that contain several sections; you could, for example, put a "table of contents" at the top of the page that consists of links to the various sections in the document.)

◆ Links to any page anywhere on the web.

Plenty of sites exist only to provide a web "mouse potato" (like a couch potato, only with a computer) with huge lists of links to pages that are informative, entertaining, or simply "cool." For example, Figure 1.2 shows a page from the Yahoo! website, which boasts tens of thousands of links arranged in dozens of categories (Yahoo! is a good place to go if you're looking for websites on a particular subject). In this case, the page shows a few links to some "useless" web pages. ("Beard research"!? "thoughts of cabbage"!?) You find out how to use HTML to sprinkle links all over your web pages in Chapter 5, "Making the Jump to Hyperspace: Adding Links."

Figure 1.2

This page from Yahoo! shows a few links to some, uh, unusual sites.

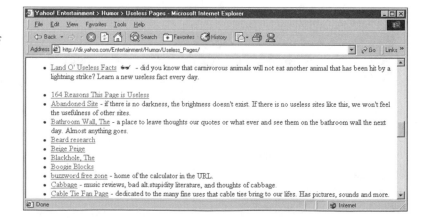

You can insert images.

Fancy text effects, lists, and lotsa links go a long way toward making a web page a hit. But for a real crowd-pleasing page, you want to throw in an image or two. It could be a picture of yourself, a drawing the kids made, some clip art, or any of the images that are on this book's CD. As long as you have the image in a graphics file, you can use HTML to position the image appropriately on your page. I give you the details (as well as info on the types of graphics files you can use) in Chapter 6, "A Picture Is Worth a Thousand Clicks: Working with Images."

Figure 1.3 shows an example page with an image. This is a page from my site, and the image is used to illustrate a point from the text.

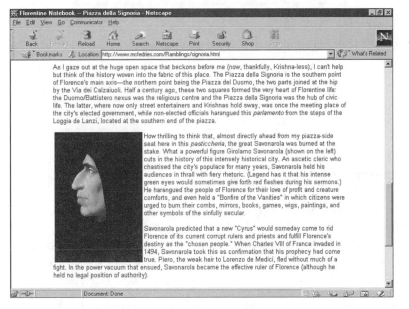

Figure 1.3

A well-chosen image or two can do wonders for otherwise drab web pages.

You can format information in tables.

If your web page needs to show data formatted in rows and columns, you could try using tabs and spaces to line things up all nice and neat. However, you'll groan in disappointment when you view the page in a browser. Why? Because HTML reduces multiple spaces to a single space, and it ignores tabs completely! This sounds like perverse behavior, but it's just the way HTML was set up.

You're not out of luck, though. You can use HTML to create tables to slot your data into slick-looking rows and columns. Figure 1.4 shows an example of a table. I tell you how to use HTML to construct tables in Chapter 10, "Table Talk: Adding Tables to Your Page."

Figure 1.4

Tables: a blessing for neat freaks everywhere.

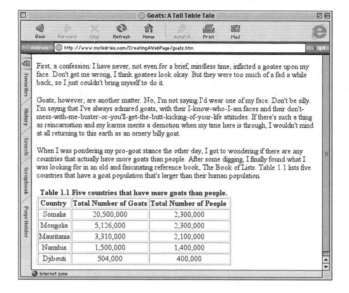

Pages from All Walks of Web Life

Now that you've got some idea of what HTML can do, wouldn't you like to see the rabbits various web magicians have pulled from their HTML hats? To that end, the next few sections present some real-world examples of web pages that show you what you can do with a little HTML know-how. In fact, all of the pages featured in these sections were created by a reader of previous editions of *The Complete Idiot's Guide to Creating a Web Page!*

Of course, these examples represent only the smallest subset of the web world. There are millions of web pages out there, and each one is like a digital fingerprint—a unique expression of its creator's individuality.

The Personal Touch: Personal Home Pages

The simplest, and probably the most common, type of web page is the personal home page. This is a page that an individual sets up to tell the web world a little bit about herself. They're the web equivalent of those "Hi! My Name is …" stickers that people wear at parties and receptions. They range from warm and fuzzy ("Welcome, friend, to my home page"), to downright vainglorious ("Let me tell you everything there is to know about me"), to frighteningly personal ("Dear diary …"). Figure 1.5 shows an excellent personal home page created by a reader named, more than a little appropriately, Gordon Reeder.

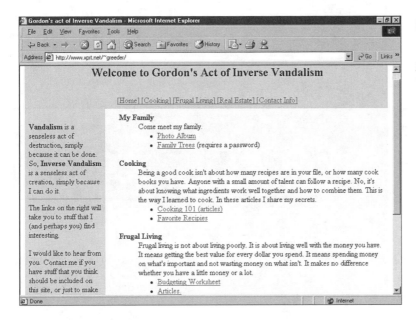

Figure 1.5

The humble home page is perhaps the most common web page variety.

Hobbyists do it themselves with HTML.

Sometimes the hardest thing about putting together a web page is thinking of something to say. (Although there are plenty of garrulous guys and gals out there for whom this is definitely not a problem!) So, what's a body to do about a bad case of web writer's block? Well, lots of people go with what they know: They talk about their hobbies and interests.

Hey, it makes sense. You're more likely to sound enthusiastic and excited about a topic you're keen on, so you're also more likely to hold your reader's interest. You can do lots of things to fill up your page—introduce the hobby to novices, talk about how you got started, show some samples of your work (depending on the hobby, of course), include links to related web pages, and much more.

Words from the Web

A website that's run by an expert in a particular field and that contains lots of useful, accurate information is called a **guru site**.

As you might imagine, there's no shortage of hobby-related pages on the World Wide Web. You can find info on everything from amateur radio to beekeeping to woodworking. Figure 1.6 shows a gardening page put together by reader Paula Graham.

Figure 1.6

Hobby pages abound on the web.

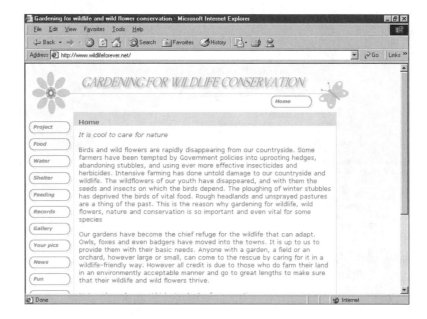

Not for Bathroom Reading: Electronic Magazines

The web's marriage of text and graphics meant it was only a matter of time before someone decided to "publish" a web-based magazine. Now it seems that new electronic magazines (they're usually called either webzines or e-zines) hit the web's newsstands every few days. The quality, as you might expect, runs the gamut from professional to prosaic, from slick to sick. But the good ones are very good, with well-written articles, handsome graphics, and some unique approaches to the whole magazine thing. There are, literally, hundreds of e-zines out there, so there's no shortage of reading material. John Labovitz maintains a list of e-zines at www.meer.net/johnl/e-zine-list/index.html.

Figure 1.7 shows the home page for Shock Value, a webzine published by reader C.J. Cauley.

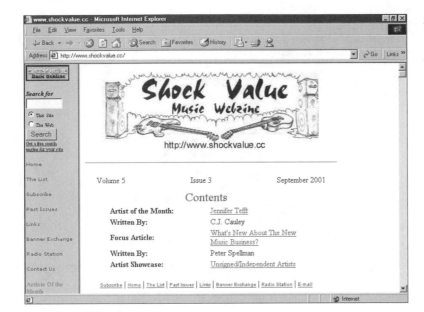

Figure 1.7

Shock Value: *an electronic magazine.*

Corporate culture hits the web.

In the late 1990s, one of the biggest engines that drove the growth of the web was the influx of businesses scrambling to get a "presence" in cyberspace. Companies from mom-and-pop shops to Fortune 500 behemoths set up on the web in anticipation of, well, *something.* Nobody was quite sure why they needed a website, but they were happy to put one up, just in case something *big* happened one of these days. Hey, who can blame them? With all the Internet hype that was floating around, no self-respecting CEO was going to be caught with his or her pants down.

Many readers of the previous editions have leveraged their new HTML skills to build pages for their companies. (And a few even managed to get paid to create sites for other companies!) Naturally enough, readers who have their own businesses also become their own site designers. For example, Figure 1.8 shows a nice website crafted by reader Beth Lins for her Gentle Valley Soaps business.

Figure 1.8

If you run your own business, put up your own business web page.

Helping Hands: Government and Public Service Pages

While Big Business was rushing to get on the web, you better believe Big Brother wasn't going to be left behind. Yes, governments—local, state, and federal—have put up web pages to beat the band. Granted, many of these sites are quite useful. You can use them to contact representatives, read government reports and studies, do research, renew your license, and even file taxes. Some of the pages are even—gasp!—creative.

There are also many pages devoted to public service organizations, nonprofits, and other institutions that are in the business of helping people. A good example is Parent Help U.S.A., a site designed by reader Nancy Palmer and shown in Figure 1.9.

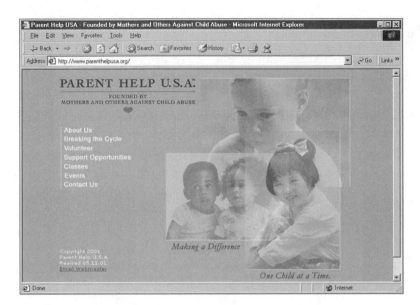

Figure 1.9

The home page for Parent Help U.S.A.

From Student to Savant: Professional Web Designers

The biggest compliment a teacher can get is to have a student take up the teacher's subject as a career. This tells the teacher that (a) they taught the student well, and (b) they inspired the student to learn more about the subject. Over the years, I've had a number of readers go on to become professional web designers and have gone on to do some remarkable work. One of those is Patsy West, and her WebsiteWiz page is shown in Figure 1.10.

Figure 1.10

WebsiteWiz is the home of professional web designer Patsy West.

The Least You Need to Know

◆ HTML: It's no big whoop. HTML sounds evil, but it's really just a relatively small collection of codes that tell the browser how to display text, where to put images, set up links, and so on.

◆ HTML is versatile. With HTML, you can format text using bold, italics, colors, and sizes, create lists and links, insert images, and build tables.

◆ You can do it, too! Tens of thousands of my readers have cobbled together hand-some and creative pages of their own, so there's no reason in the world that *you* can't do it, too.

Laying the Foundation: The Basic Structure of a Web Page

In This Chapter

- A laundry list of things you need to get started
- A quick course on tags, the building blocks of HTML
- The basic blueprint for all web pages
- How to add a title, toss in some text, and split your prose into paragraphs
- Your field guide to the most fundamental of HTML flora and fauna

This book's goal is to help you create your own web pages and thus lay claim to a little chunk of personal cyberspace real estate: a home page away from home, if you will. Before you can live in this humble abode, however, you have to "pour the concrete" that serves as the foundation for the rest of your digital domicile. In this chapter, I show you a few HTML basics that constitute the underlying structure of all web pages.

Getting Started

As you saw in Chapter 1, "A Brief HTML Primer," some web pages look truly spectacu-lar. To achieve these impressive effects, you might think you need to stretch a fancy word processing or page layout program to its limits. Or you might think you have to rush out and spend big bucks for some kind of highfalutin "HTML generator" that's designed specifically for cranking out web pages. Nah, you're way off. All you really need for creat-ing a basic page is a lowly text editor. Yes, even a brain-dead program such as Windows Notepad is more than adequate for doing the HTML thing.

Surely a plain old run-of-the-mill text editor won't let me create anything resembling those beau-tiful pages I see on the web.

Yes, it will—and stop calling me Shirley. The vast majority of all the web pages in the world are really just simple text files.

So why in the name of Sam Hill do those pages look so good? Text files I've seen have been ugly with a capital Ugh!

The web's beauty secret is that it's actually the web browsers that determine how a page looks. When you surf to a web page, the browser reads the text, scours the file for HTML markings, and then displays the page accordingly. So, for example, you can mark inside your text file that you want a certain word to appear as bold. When the browser comes to that part of the document, it goes right ahead and formats the word in a bold font. The browser handles all this dirty work behind the scenes, and you never have to give it a sec-ond thought (or even a first thought, for that matter).

First, crank out a new text file.

So, to get to the point at long last, the first thing you need to do is fire up your favorite text editor:

- ◆ For most versions of Windows, you start the Notepad text editor by selecting **Start, Programs, Accessories, Notepad.**

- ◆ If you have Windows XP, you launch Notepad by selecting **Start, All Programs, Accessories, Notepad.**

- ◆ Mac fans can use the SimpleText program, the icon for which is in the **Macintosh HD:Applications** folder.

- ◆ If you have another text editor, launch it the way you normally do.

Both Notepad and SimpleText display a brand-new text document automatically when you start each program. If you ever need to start a new document by hand, select the **File, New** command.

If you prefer, it's okay to use a word processor such as WordPad, the program that comes with most versions of Windows, or Microsoft Word. Again, launch the program and a new document will be staring at you in a few seconds (or choose **File, New** to do it yourself). If you take the word processor route, please keep the following caveats in mind:

♦ **Don't use the program's commands to format the document in any way (such as adding italics or centering paragraphs).** Not only do you run the risk of having a browser choke on these extra formatting codes, but every web browser on the face of the Earth will completely ignore your efforts. Remember, the only way to make a browser do your bidding and display your web page properly is to use the appropriate HTML codes.

♦ **Don't save the file in the word processor's native format.** Be sure to save the file as pure text, sometimes referred to as ASCII text. More on this in a sec.

(Of course, that isn't to say there aren't other, equally important, accouterments you might need. For me, a good, strong cup of coffee is a must. Other optional HTML accessories include the appropriate mood music—something by The Spinners, perhaps?—a copy of *Feel the Fear and Do It Anyway*, and semi-important things such as your creativity and imagination.)

Webmaster Wisdom

Speaking of word processors, Word 97, 2000, and 2002 all have HTML capabilities built right into the program. To find out more, see the bonus chapters on my website: www.mcfedries. com/CreatingAWebPage.

Notes About Saving HTML Files

While slaving away on the text file that will become your web page, make sure you practice safe computing. That is, make sure you save your work regularly. However, from the thousands of notes that I've received from readers, I can tell you that the number-one thing that trips up wet-behind-the-ears webmeisters is improperly saving their HTML files. To help you easily leap these saving hurdles, here are a few notes to pore over:

♦ **The Save command.** You save a file by selecting the program's **File, Save** command. The first time you do this with a new file, the Save As dialog box shows up for work. You use this dialog box to specify three things: the filename, the file type, and the file's location on your hard disk. The next few notes discuss some tidbits about the name and type.

Webmaster Wisdom

Many new HTMLers get confused about whether to use .htm or .html when naming their files. Actually, you're free to use either one because it doesn't make any difference. Note, though, that if you're still using Windows 3.x, you must use .htm.

◆ **Use the right file extension.** Most web browsers know how to deal only with files that end with either the .htm or the .html file extension (for example, mypage.html). Therefore, when you name your file, be sure to specify either .htm or .html.

◆ **Use lowercase filenames only.** The majority of web servers (computers that store web pages) are downright finicky when it comes to uppercase letters versus lower-case letters. For example, the typical server thinks that index.html and INDEX. HTML are two different files. It's dumb, I know. So, to be safe, always enter your filenames using only lowercase letters.

Webmaster Wisdom

You can see that Windows is a bit stupid when it comes to file extensions. I'll show you how to over-come this later in this chap-ter. See the section titled "Help! The browser shows my tags!"

◆ **Don't use spaces.** Most versions of Windows and the Mac are all happy to deal with filenames that include spaces. Internet Explorer, too, is space savvy. However, Netscape gets *really* confused if it comes upon any filename that has one or more spaces. So, to be safe, avoid using spaces in your filenames. If you want to separate words in file and directory names, use an underscore (_) or a hyphen (-).

◆ **Use the right file type.** While in the Save As dialog box, you need to select the correct "file type" for your HTML file (Mac users don't have to bother with this). How you do this depends on what program you're using:

If you're using Notepad: Use the **Save as type** list to select **All Files (*.*).** This ensures that Notepad uses your .htm or .html extension (and not its normal .txt extension).

If you're using Windows WordPad: Use the **Save as type** list to select **Text Document.** You also need to surround your filename with quotation marks (for example, "index.html") to ensure that WordPad uses your .htm or .html extension.

If you're using Microsoft Word: Use the **Save as type** list to select **Text Only (*.txt).** Again, you need to surround your filename with quotation marks.

◆ When you've done all that, click **Save** in the Save As dialog box to save the file. (If you're using WordPad, the program might ask if you're sure you want to save the file in "Text-Only format." Say "Duh!" and click **Yes.**)

The Edit-Save-Browse Cycle

By now you've probably figured out the biggest problem associated with fashioning a web page out of a text file: There's no way to know what the page will look like after it's been foisted on to the web! Fortunately, all is not lost. Most browsers are more than happy to let you load a text file right from the confines of your computer's hard disk. This means you can test drive your page without first having to put it on the web. So here's the basic cycle you'll use to build your pages:

Webmaster Wisdom

When you run the **File, Open** command, the Open dialog box probably won't show your HTML files. To see them, use the **Files of type** list to select **All Documents (*.*)** (some programs use **All Files (*.*)**, instead).

1. In your text editor or word processor, either start a new file (if one isn't started for you already) or use the **File, Open** command to open an existing file. (If you're opening an existing HTML file in Microsoft Word, you need to select the **View, HTML Source** command to see the tags.)

2. Add some text and HTML stuff (I'll define what this "stuff" is in the next section) to your file.

3. Select the program's **File, Save** command to save the file using the points I mentioned above.

4. Load the file into your browser of choice to see how things look. As a public service (it's a tough job but, hey, somebody's gotta do it), here are the appropriate instructions for loading a file from your hard disk using the Big Two browsers:

   ◆ In Internet Explorer for Windows, select the **File** menu's **Open** command (or press **Ctrl+O**), click the **Browse** button in the Open dialog box that appears, and then pick out the file you need. You can reload the file by selecting the **View** menu's **Refresh** command, or by pressing **F5**.

   ◆ In Internet Explorer for the Mac, select the **File, Open File** command (or press ⌘**+O**) and then use the Open dialog box to choose your file. You can reload the page by selecting **View, Refresh,** or pressing ⌘**+R**.

   ◆ In Netscape Navigator 4, pull down the **File** menu, select the **Open Page** command (or you can press **Ctrl+O**), click the **Choose File** button, and then find the file by using the Open dialog box that appears. To reload the file, pull down the **View** menu and select **Reload** (or press **Ctrl+R**).

   ◆ In Netscape 6, select **File, Open File** (or press **Ctrl+O**) and then use the Open File dialog box. To reload, select **View, Reload,** or **Ctrl+R**.

Page Pitfalls

If you find that Netscape stubbornly refuses to update your edited page, give Netscape a kick in the pants by exiting the program and then restarting it. Alternatively, hold down the **Shift** key and click the Reload button.

5. Lather. Rinse. Repeat steps 2 and 3. Note that after the file is loaded in the browser, you need only choose the program's **Reload** command to see the effects of your changes.

Tag Daze–Understanding HTML's Tags

As I mentioned earlier, the magic of the web is wrought by browser programs that read text files and then decipher the HTML nuggets that you've sprinkled hither and thither. These HTML tidbits are markers—called *tags*—that spell out how you want things to look. For example, if you want a word on your page to appear in bold text, you surround that word with the appropriate tags for boldfacing text.

In general, tags use the following format:

```
<TAG>The text to be affected by the tag</TAG>
```

The *TAG* part is a code (usually a one- or two-letter abbreviation, but sometimes an entire word) that specifies the type of effect you want. You always surround these codes with angle brackets <>; the brackets tell the web browser that it's dealing with a chunk of HTML and not just some random text.

For example, the tag for bold is <B>. So if you want the phrase "BeDazzler Home Page" to appear in bold, you type the following into your document:

```
<B>BeDazzler Home Page</B>
```

The first <B> says to the browser, in effect, "Listen up, Browser Boy! You know the text that comes after this? Be a good fellow and display it in bold." This continues until the browser reaches the </B>. The slash (/) defines this as an *end tag*, which lets the browser know it's supposed to stop what it's doing. So the </B> tells the browser, "Okay, okay. Ixnay on the oldbay!" As you'll see, there are tags for lots of other effects, including italics, paragraphs, headings, page titles, links, and lists. HTML is just the sum total of all these tags.

> **CAUTION**
>
> **Page Pitfalls**
>
> One of the most common mistakes rookie web weavers make is to forget the slash (/) that identifies a tag as an end tag. If your page looks wrong when you view it in a browser, a missing slash is the first thing you should look for. The second thing you should look for is another common error: using the backslash (\). Zees ees verboten in zee HTML!

And Now, Some Actual HTML

Okay, you're ready to get down to some brass HTML tacks. (Halle-freakin'-lujah, I hear you saying.) You'll begin by cobbling together a few HTML tags that constitute the underlying skeleton of all web pages.

Your HTML files will always lead off with the <HTML> tag. This tag doesn't do a whole heckuva lot except tell any web browser that tries to read the file that it's dealing with a file that contains HTML knickknacks. Similarly, the last line in your document will always be the corresponding end tag: </HTML>. You can think of this end tag as the HTML equivalent for "The End." So each of your web pages will start off with this:

```
<HTML>
```

and end with this:

```
</HTML>
```

The next items serve to divide the page into two sections: the header and the body. The header section is like an introduction to the page. Web browsers use the header to glean various types of information about the page. Although a number of items can appear in the header section, the only one that makes any real sense at this early stage is the title of the page, which I talk about in the next section.

To define the header, add a <HEAD> tag and a </HEAD> tag immediately below the <HTML> tag you typed in earlier. So, your web page should now look like this:

```
<HTML>
<HEAD>
</HEAD>
</HTML>
```

Webmaster Wisdom

It makes absolutely no difference if you enter your tag names in uppercase letters or lowercase letters. Uppercase letters are easier to read and to distinguish from regular text, so that's the style I use in this book. Note, however, that the latest HTML standard suggests that all HTML tags be entered using lowercase letters. For this reason, you might want to get into the habit of using lowercase letters in your tags.

The body section is where you enter the text and other fun stuff that the browser will actually display. To define the body, you place a <BODY> tag and a </BODY> tag after the header section (that is, below the </HEAD> tag), as follows:

```
<HTML>
<HEAD>
</HEAD>
<BODY>
```

Page Pitfalls

Another very common page error is to include two or more copies of these basic tags (particularly the <BODY> tag). For best results, make sure you use each of these six basic structural tags only once in each page.

```
</BODY>
</HTML>
```

Hmm. It's not exactly a work of art, is it? On the excitement scale, these opening moves rank right up there with watching the grass grow and tuning in to C-SPAN on a slow news day. Let's just file this stuff in the "Necessary Evils" section and move on to more interesting things.

A Page by Any Other Name: Adding a Title

If you try loading your web page into a browser, you'll just get a whole lot of nothingness because you haven't given the browser anything meaty that it can sink its teeth into. The first snack you can offer a hungry browser program is the title of the web page. The page's title is just what you might think it is: the overall name of the page (not to be confused with the name of the file you're creating). When a person views the page, the title appears in the title bar of the browser's window.

The ‹TITLE› Tag

To define a title, you surround the title text with the <TITLE> and </TITLE> tags. For example, if you want the title of your page to be "My Home Sweet Home Page," you enter it as follows:

```
<TITLE>My Home Sweet Home Page</TITLE>
```

Note that you always place the title inside the head section, so your basic HTML document now looks like so:

```
<HTML>
<HEAD>
<TITLE>My Home Sweet Home Page</TITLE>
</HEAD>
<BODY>
</BODY>
</HTML>
```

Figure 2.1 shows this document loaded into the Windows version of Internet Explorer. Notice how the title appears in the window's title bar.

Webmaster Wisdom

To relieve some of the inevitable boredom of these early stages of web page creation, you'll find some help on the CD that comes with this book. I've included a file named **skeleton. htm** that contains all the tags that make up the bare bones of a web page. You can use this file as a template each time you start a new web page.

The page title

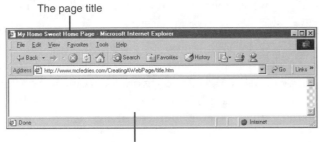

The body text will appear here.

Fugure 2.1

Most Windows web browsers display the title in the title bar (duh).

Title Do's and Don'ts

Here are a few things to keep in mind when thinking of a title for your page:

◆ Do make sure your title describes what the page is all about.

◆ Don't make your title too long. If you do, the browser might chop it off because there's not enough room to display it in the title bar. Fifty or sixty characters are usually the max.

◆ Do use titles that make sense when someone views them out of context. For example, if someone really likes your page, that person might add it to his or her list of favorites or bookmarks (hey, it could happen). The browser displays the page title in the favorites list, so it's important that the title makes sense when that person looks at the bookmarks later on.

◆ Don't use titles that are cryptic or vague. Titling a page "Link #42" or "A Page" might make sense to you, but your readers might not appreciate it.

Fleshing Out Your Page with Text

With your page title firmly in place, you can now think about putting some flesh on your web page's bones by entering the text you want to appear in the body of the page. For the most part, you can simply type the text between the <BODY> and </BODY> tags, like so:

```
<HTML>
<HEAD>
<TITLE>My Home Sweet Home Page</TITLE>
</HEAD>
<BODY>
This text appears in the body of the Web page.
</BODY>
</HTML>
```

Before you start typing willy-nilly, however, there are a few things you should know:

♦ You might think you can line things up and create some interesting effects by stringing together two or more spaces. Ha! Web browsers chew up all those extra spaces and spit them out into the nether regions of cyberspace. Why? Well, the philosophy of the web is that you can use only HTML tags to lay out a document. So, a run of multiple spaces (or white space, as it's called) is ignored. (There are a couple of tricks you can use to get around this, however. I tell you about them in the next chapter.)

♦ Tabs also fall under the rubric of white space. You can enter tabs all day long, but the browser ignores them completely.

♦ Another thing that browsers like to ignore is the carriage return. It might sound reasonable to the likes of you and me that pressing **Enter** starts a new paragraph, but that's not so in the HTML world. I talk more about this in the next section.

♦ If HTML documents are just plain text, does that mean you're out of luck if you need to use characters such as ©, ™, ¶? Luckily, no, you're not. HTML has special codes for these kinds of characters, and I talk about them in the next chapter.

♦ Word processor users, it bears repeating here that it's not worth your bother to format your text using the program's built-in commands. The browser cheerfully ignores even the most elaborate formatting jobs because, as usual, browsers understand only HTML-based formatting. (And besides, a document with formatting is, by definition, not a pure text file, so a browser might bite the dust trying to load it.)

> **CAUTION**
>
> **Page Pitfalls**
>
> Note, too, that the angle bracket characters < and > can't be displayed directly in HTML pages because the browser uses them to identify tags. Again, if you need to use them, I show you some special codes in the next chapter that get the job done.

How to Do Paragraphs

As I mentioned earlier, carriage returns aren't worth a hill of beans in the World Wide Web. If you type one line, press **Enter,** and then type a second line, the browser simply runs the two lines together, side by side.

If a new paragraph is what you need, you have to stick the browser's nose in it, so to speak, by using the <P> tag. For example, consider the following text:

```
<HTML>
<HEAD>
<TITLE>My Home Sweet Home Page</TITLE>
```

```
</HEAD>
<BODY>
This text appears in the body of the Web page.
This is the second line (not!).
<P>
This is the third line.
</P>
</BODY>
</HTML>
```

Figure 2.2 shows how this text looks in the browser. As you can see, the first two lines appear beside each other, despite the fact that they're on separate lines in the original text. However, the third line sits nicely in its own paragraph thanks to the <P> tag that precedes it. Note, too, that I used the </P> end tag to finish the paragraph.

Figure 2.2

You need to use the <P> tag to create paragraphs in HTML.

Help! The browser shows my tags!

When you view your HTML file in the browser, you might be dismayed to see that it shows not only your page text, but all the HTML tags, as well (see Figure 2.3).

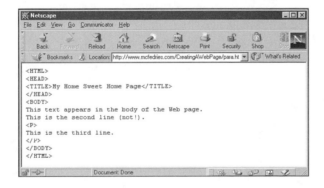

Figure 2.3

The browser might show your tags along with your text.

This kind of problem is almost always caused by one of the following:

♦ The file isn't a pure text file but is, rather, in a word processor format. As I mentioned earlier, if you're using a word processor to create your HTML files, make sure that when you save the file, you save it as a text file.

♦ The file doesn't have a .htm or .html extension. If you're using Windows and saving a file as text, Windows has a perverse tendency to always want to add the .txt extension to the end of the filename. Even if you specify the .htm or .html extension when you save the file, Windows just adds the .txt extension anyway (so you end up with something like index.htm.txt).

Assuming the latter is the problem, you saw earlier how you can overcome it by surrounding your filename with quotes in the Save As dialog box. To avoid that hassle, tell Windows to display file extensions. That way, the system always honors the extensions you enter by hand and won't force documents saved as text to always use the .txt extension. Here's how you do it:

1. Select **Start, Programs, Windows Explorer.**
2. Pull down the **View** menu and select the **Options** command (or the **Folder Options** command, depending on which version of Windows you're using).
3. In the Options dialog box (you might need to select the **View** tab, again depending on which flavor of Windows you have), deactivate the **Hide MS-DOS extensions for the file types that are registered** check box.
4. Click **OK.**

After that's done, you're able to add the .htm or .html extension to the end of your filenames without having to use quotation marks.

Note, too, that you should check your existing HTML files to see if they have .txt extensions. For example, you might have files named index.htm.txt, or whatever. If so, edit the filename to remove the .txt at the end.

The Least You Need to Know

◆ At last, a purpose in life for text editors. You can create perfectly good web pages using a lowly text editor such as Notepad (Windows) or SimpleText (Mac).

◆ Be careful when using a word processor. If you prefer to use WordPad, Word, Microsoft Works, or some other word processor, don't use the program's formatting commands and be sure to save the file as a text file.

◆ Web page filename tidbits. When naming your files, use the .htm or .html extension, use only lowercase letters, and avoid spaces like the plague.

◆ The bare bones. Always start your page with the following eight tags:

```
<HTML>
<HEAD>
<TITLE>
</TITLE>
</HEAD>
<BODY>
</BODY>
</HTML>
```

◆ Text goes in the body. Other than the page title, the text and tags that you want other folks to see goes inside the body section (that is, between the <BODY> and </BODY> tags).

◆ <P> stands for paragraph. To start a new paragraph in your page, plop the <P> tag at the point where you want the paragraph to begin. At the end of the paragraph, don't forget the </P> end tag.

Chapter 3

From Buck-Naked to Beautiful: Dressing Up Your Page

In This Chapter

◆ HTML tags for formatting characters
◆ How to create impressive-looking headings
◆ Miscellaneous text tags
◆ How to insert special characters in your page
◆ A complete makeover for your web page text

In the early, pretext stages of the web page production process, your page is essentially naked. It passes its days exposed to the elements, shivering and teeth-chatteringly cold. Brrr! To put some color in your page's cheeks and prevent it from catching its death, you need to clothe it with the text you want everyone to read, as described in Chapter 2, "Laying the Foundation: The Basic Structure of a Web Page."

These new text garments might be warm, but they aren't much to look at. I mean, face it, a plain-text web page just doesn't present your prose in the best light. I'm definitely talking Worst Dressed List here.

However, this really doesn't matter for those times when you're just kicking around the web house. At this stage, you're the only one who sees your web page, so you usually don't care how it looks. But what about when it's time to go out on the town? What do you do when you want the rest of the web world to see your creation? Heck, you can't send your web page out into cyberspace looking like *that!*

Before your page has its coming-out party, you need to dress it up in apparel appropriate for the occasion. In short, you need to format your text so it looks its best. This chapter is your web page fashion consultant as it examines the various ways you can use HTML to beautify your words.

Sprucing Up Your Text

The first of our web page makeover chores is to examine some tags that alter the look of individual words and phrases. The next few sections fill you in on the details.

Some Basic Text Formatting Styles

The good news about text formatting is that most browsers support only four basic kinds: **bold**, *italic*, <u>underline</u>, and `monospace`. The bad news is that HTML has about a billion different tags that produce these styles. However, I'll take mercy on you and only let you in on the easiest tags to use. Table 3.1 shows the tags that produce each of these formats.

Table 3.1 The Basic Text Formatting Tags

Text style	Begin tag	End tag
Bold	<B>	</B>
Italic	<I>	</I>
<u>Underline</u>	<U>	</U>
`Monospace`	<TT>	</TT>

Here's a sample HTML document (bookstor.htm on this book's CD) that shows each of these styles in action. Figure 3.1 shows how the styles look when viewed with Internet Explorer.

```
<HTML>
<HEAD>
```

```
<TITLE>Some Basic Text Formatting Styles</TITLE>
</HEAD>
<BODY>
<U>Supply Without the Demand</U>
<P>
<TT>Print-on-demand</TT> is new system that lets bookstores print out a book
whenever a customer asks for one. It's <I>really</I> slick. Recently, I was in
a store called <b>The Book "Seller"</B> and it had a service called <B>Print-
On-Non-Demand</B> featuring books that <I>very</I> few people would ever
order, much less print out. The titles included <I>The Complete Idiot's Guide
to Village Idiocy</I> and <I>The 10-Minute Guide to Butt-Scanning</I>.
</P>
</BODY>
</HTML>
```

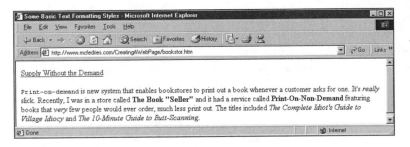

Figure 3.1

A web page showing the four basic text formatting styles.

Webmaster Wisdom

Just in case you're a glutton for punishment, here's a rundown of some alternative tags you can use for these text styles:

Text style	Alternative tags
Bold	<STRONG>
Italic	<EM> or <CITE> or <ADDRESS>
Monospace	<CODE> or <KBD>

(Note that, to keep things simple, I've left out the corresponding end tags, such as </STRONG> and </EM>.) I should also mention here that you might want to think twice (or even three times) before using the <U> tag for underlining. As you can see in Figure 3.1, underlined text looks suspiciously like a link, which will only serve to confuse your readers.

Keep in mind that this book's CD includes all the HTML examples you read about in the book. (For more about the CD, see Appendix C, "The CD: The Webmaster's Toolkit.") This helps make your web-building chores easier because you can use the examples to get started with your own pages. To get your mitts on the example I used previously, look for the file named bookstor.htm on the CD. If you don't have a CD-ROM drive on your computer, or if the CD is damaged, you can get the examples from my website at the following URL: www.mcfedries.com/CreatingAWebPage/examples.html

Combining Text Formats

You should note, as well, that all modern browsers are perfectly happy to let you combine these text styles. So, for example, if you need bold italic text, you can get it by throwing the <B> and <I> tags together, like so:

```
<B><I>This'll give you, like, bold italic text</I></B>
```

Accessorizing: Displaying Special Characters

You might think that because HTML is composed in text-only documents (documents that include only the characters and symbols you can peck out from your keyboard), non-standard characters such as ¢ and ¥ would be taboo. It's true that there's no way to add these characters to your page directly, but the web wizards who created HTML thought up a way around this limitation. Specifically, they came up with special codes called *character entities* (which is surely a name only a true geek would love) that represent these and other oddball symbols.

These codes come in two flavors: a *character reference* and an *entity name*. Character references are basically just numbers, and the entity names are friendlier symbols that describe the character you're trying to display. For example, you can display the registered trademark symbol ® by using either the ® character reference or the ® entity name, as shown here:

Page Pitfalls

To ensure that all browsers render your characters properly, use only lowercase letters when typing the entity names.

```
Print-On-Non-Demand&#174;
```

or

```
Print-On-Non-Demand&reg;
```

Note that both character references and entity names begin with an ampersand (&) and end with a semicolon (;). Don't forget either character when using special characters in your own pages.

Table 3.2 lists a few other popular characters and their corresponding codes. You'll find a more complete list in the tearout card in the front of this book.

Table 3.2   A Few Common Characters

Symbol	Character Reference	Entity name
<	&#060;	&lt;
>	&#062;	&gt;
Nonbreaking space		
¢	&#162;	&cent;
£	&#163;	&pound;
¥	&#165;	&yen;
©	&#169;	&copy;
®	&#174;	&reg;
°	&#176;	&deg;
$\frac{1}{4}$	&#188;	&frac14;
$\frac{1}{2}$	&#189;	&frac12;
$\frac{3}{4}$	&#190;	&frac34;
×	&#215;	&times;

Webmaster Wisdom

The table contains a bizarre entry called a "nonbreaking space." What's up with that? Remember in Chapter 2 when I told you that HTML simply scoffs at white space (multiple spaces and tabs)? Well, you use the nonbreaking space thinga-majig when you want to force the browser to display white space. For example, if you want to indent the first line of a paragraph by three spaces, you'd start it like so:

```
   This line appears indented by three spaces.
```

You can also use the nonbreaking space to position images, line up text, and much more.

A Few Formatting Features You'll Use All the Time

This section takes you through five more formatting tags that should stand you in good stead throughout your career as a web engineer. You use these tags for adding headings, aligning paragraphs, displaying "preformatted" text, inserting line breaks, and displaying horizontal lines. The next few sections give you the details.

Sectioning Your Page with Headings

Many web designers divide their page contents into several sections, like chapters in a book. To help separate these sections and thus make life easier for the reader, you can use headings. Ideally, headings act as minititles that convey some idea of what each section is all about. To make these titles stand out, HTML has a series of heading tags that display text in larger, bold fonts. There are six heading tags in all, ranging from <H1>, which uses the largest font, down to <H6>, which uses the smallest font.

What's with all the different headings? Well, the idea is that you use them to outline your document. As an example, consider the headings I've used in this chapter and see how I'd format them in HTML.

The overall heading, of course, is the chapter title, so I'd display it using, say, the <H1> tag. The first main section is the one titled "Sprucing Up Your Text," so I'd give its title an <H2> heading. That section contains three subsections, "Some Basic Text Formatting Styles," "Combining Text Formats," and "Accessorizing: Displaying Special Characters." I'd give each of these titles the <H3> heading. Then I come to the section called "A Few Formatting Features You'll Use All the Time." This is another main section of the chapter, so I'd go back to the <H2> tag for its title, and so on.

Webmaster Wisdom

Notice that I force the browser to display a less-than sign (<) by using the character code <, and to display a greater-than sign (>) by using the code >.

The following HTML document (look for headings.htm on the CD in this book) shows how I'd format all the section titles for this chapter, and Figure 3.2 shows how they appear in Internet Explorer on the Mac. (Notice that I don't need to use a <P> tag to display headings on separate lines; that's handled automatically by the heading tags.)

```
<HTML>
<HEAD>
<TITLE>Some Example Headings</TITLE>
</HEAD>
<BODY>
<H1>From Buck-Naked to Beautiful: Dressing Up Your Page</H1>
<H2>Sprucing Up Your Text</H2>
<H3>Some Basic Text Formatting Styles</H3>
<H3>Combining Text Formats</H3>
<H3>Accessorizing: Displaying Special Characters</H3>
<H2>A Few Formatting Features You'll Use All the Time</H2>
<H3>Sectioning Your Page With Headings</H3>
<H3>Aligning Paragraphs</H3>
<H3>Handling Preformatted Text</H3>
<H3>Them's the Breaks: Using &lt;BR&gt; for Line Breaks</H3>
```

```
<H3>Inserting Horizontal Lines</H3>
<H2>Textras: Fancier Text Formatting</H2>
<H3>The &lt;FONT&gt; Tag I: Changing the Size of Text</H3>
<H3>The &lt;BASEFONT&gt; Tag</H3>
<H3>The &lt;FONT&gt; Tag II: Changing the Typeface</H3>
<H3>Changing the Color of Your Page Text</H3>
<H3>The &lt;FONT&gt; Tag III: Changing the Color</H3>
<H3>The Dreaded &lt;BLINK&gt; Tag</H3>
</BODY>
</HTML>
```

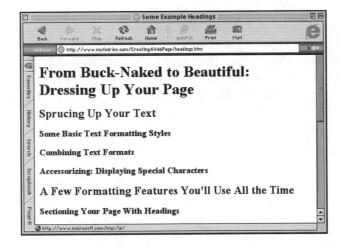

Figure 3.2

Examples of HTML's heading tags.

Aligning Paragraphs

Centering text and graphics is a time-honored way to give reports and brochures a professional look and feel. To provide the same advantage to your web pages, the <CENTER> tag gives you centering capabilities for your page headings, paragraphs, lists, and even graphics. Here's how <CENTER> works:

```
<CENTER>
[Headings, text, and graphics that you want centered go here.]
</CENTER>
```

The <CENTER> tag is a nice, simple way to shift things to the middle of a page. However, you can also use the <P> tag and the heading tags by shoehorning some extra text inside the tag. This extra text is called an *attribute* and it tells the browser to modify how it normally displays the tag.

For example, to center a paragraph, you use the following variation on the <P> tag theme:

```
<P ALIGN="CENTER">
```

When the browser stumbles upon the ALIGN attribute, it knows that it's going to have to modify the behavior of the <P> tag in some way. The exact modification is supplied by the value of the attribute, which is "CENTER" in this case. This orders the browser to display the entire contents of the following paragraph centered in the browser window.

Similarly, you can center, say, an <H1> heading like so:

```
<H1 ALIGN="CENTER">
```

The advantage to this approach is that you can also use either LEFT or RIGHT with the ALIGN attribute to further adjust your paragraph alignment. The LEFT value aligns the text on the left side of the window (that is, the normal alignment), and the RIGHT attribute aligns the text on the right side of the window.

> **CAUTION**
>
> **Page Pitfalls**
>
> Always surround attribute values with quotation marks, like so:
>
> ```
> <P ALIGN="RIGHT">
> ```
>
> And if your page doesn't display properly when you view it in the browser, immediately check to see if you left off either the opening or closing quotation mark.

Handling Preformatted Text

In the previous chapter, I told you that web browsers ignore white space (multiple spaces and tabs) as well as carriage returns. Well, I lied. Sort of. You see, all browsers normally *do* spit out these elements, but you can talk a browser into swallowing them whole by using the <PRE> tag. The "PRE" part is short for "preformatted," and you normally use this tag to display preformatted text exactly as it's laid out. Here, "preformatted" means text in which you use spaces, tabs, and carriage returns to line things up.

Let's look at an example. The following bit of code is an HTML document (look for pre.htm on this book's CD) in which I set up two chunks of text in a pattern that uses spaces and carriage returns. The first bit of doggerel doesn't make use of the <PRE> tag, but I've surrounded the second poem with <PRE> and </PRE>. Figure 3.3 shows the results. Notice that the lines from the first poem are strung together, but that when the browser encounters <PRE>, it displays the white space and carriage returns faithfully.

```
<HTML>
<HEAD>
<TITLE>The &lt;PRE&gt; Tag</TITLE>
</HEAD>
<BODY>
<H3>Without the &lt;PRE&gt; Tag:</H3>
          Here's
        some ditty,
      specially done,
    to lay it out all
  formatted and pretty.
```

```
Unfortunately, that is all
  this junk really means,
    because I admit I
     couldn't scrawl
       poetry for
         beans.
<H3>With the &lt;PRE&gt; Tag:</H3>
<PRE>
       Here's
     some ditty,
   specially done,
 to lay it out all
formatted and pretty.
Unfortunately, that is all
  this junk really means,
    because I admit I
     couldn't scrawl
       poetry for
         beans.
</PRE>
</BODY>
</HTML>
```

Webmaster Wisdom

You'll notice one other thing about how the browser displays text that's ensconced within the <PRE> and </PRE> tags: It formats the text in an ugly monospaced font. The only way to get around this is to use something called a "style sheet" to specify the font you want the browser to use with the <PRE> tag. I show you how this works in Part 3, "High HTML Style: Working with Style Sheets."

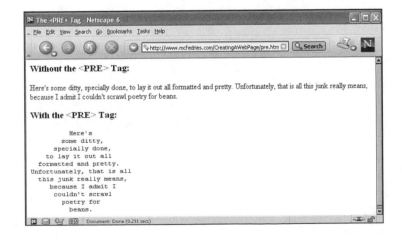

Figure 3.3

How preformatted text appears in Netscape 6.

Them's the Breaks: Using <BR> for Line Breaks

As you saw in the previous chapter, you use the <P> tag when you need to separate your text into paragraphs. When a browser spies a <P> tag, it starts a new paragraph on a separate line and inserts an extra, blank line after the previous paragraph. However, what if you don't want that extra line? For example, you might want to display a list of items with each item on a separate line and without any space between the items. (Actually, there are better ways to display lists than the method I show you here; see Chapter 4, "The Gist of a List: Adding Lists to Your Page.")

Well, you could use the <PRE> tag, but your text would appear in that ugly, monospaced font. A better solution is to separate your lines with <BR>, the line break tag. A browser starts a new line when it encounters <BR>, but it doesn't toss in an extra blank line. Here's an example (it's the file named breaks.htm on the CD):

```
<HTML>
<HEAD>
<TITLE>Line Breaks</TITLE>
</HEAD>
<BODY>
<H2>Supply Without the Demand</H2>
<HR>
<TT>Print-on-demand</TT> is new system that lets bookstores print out a book
whenever a customer asks for one. It's <I>really</I> slick. Recently, I was in
a store called <b>The Book "Seller"</B> and it had a service called <B>Print-
On-Non-Demand</B>&#174; featuring books that <I>very</I> few people would ever
order, much less print out. The titles included the following
<P>
The Complete Idiot's Guide to Village Idiocy<BR>
The 10-Minute Guide to Butt-Scanning<BR>
Baby's First Book of Java<BR>
Leashes Unleashed<BR>
Programmer's Guide to Basic Hygiene<BR>
Teach Yourself the Presidency in 4 Years
</P>
</BODY>
</HTML>
```

In the list of books, I added the <BR> tag to the end of each line (except the last one; I don't need it there). As you can see in Figure 3.4, Internet Explorer dutifully displays each line separately, with no space in between.

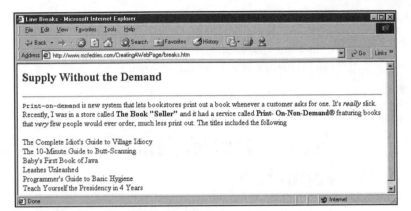

Figure 3.4

Use the <BR> tag to force a line break in your text.

Inserting Horizontal Lines

If you're particularly eagle-eyed, you might have noticed a horizontal line extending across the browser screen shown in Figure 3.4. What gives? Well, while you weren't looking, I surreptitiously inserted an <HR> tag into the HTML text. <HR>, which stands for "horizontal rule," produces a line across the page, which is a handy way to separate sections of your document.

If you use <HR> by itself, you get a standard line that goes right across the page. However, there are various attributes associated with the <HR> tag that enable you to change the line's size, width, alignment, and more. Table 3.3 shows a rundown.

Table 3.3   Extra Attributes for the <HR> Tag

<HR> Extension	What It Does
<HR WIDTH="*x*">	Sets the width of the line to *x* pixels
<HR WIDTH="*y*%">	Sets the width of the line to *y* percent of the window
<HR SIZE="*n*">	Sets the thickness of the line to *n* pixels (where the default thickness is 1 pixel)
<HR ALIGN="LEFT">	Aligns the line with the left margin
<HR ALIGN="CENTER">	Centers the line
<HR ALIGN="RIGHT">	Aligns the line with the right margin
<HR NOSHADE>	Displays the line as a solid line (instead of appearing etched into the screen)

Webmaster Wisdom

The <HR> tag draws a plain horizontal line. You might notice some web pages have fancier lines that use color and other neat texture effects. Those lines are actually images; I show you how to add images to your page in Chapter 6, "A Picture Is Worth a Thousand Clicks: Working with Images."

Note that you can combine two or more of these attributes in a single <HR> tag. For example, if you want a line that's half the width of the window and is centered, then you'd use the following tag:

```
<HR WIDTH="50%" ALIGN="CENTER">
```

Textras: Fancier Text Formatting

As you saw a bit earlier in this chapter, you can display your text in a different font size by using one of the heading tags (such as <H1>). Unfortunately, you can't use heading tags to adjust the size of individual characters because headings always appear on a line by themselves. To fix this, you use two tags: <FONT> and <BASEFONT>, which I discuss in the next couple of sections. I'll also show you how to change the color of your text.

The ‹FONT› Tag, Part I: Changing the Size of Text

The <FONT> tag adjusts (among other things) the size of any text placed between <FONT> and its corresponding end tag, </FONT>. Here's how it works:

```
<FONT SIZE="size">Affected text goes here</FONT>
```

The *size* part is a number that pinpoints how big you want the text to appear. You can use any number between 1 (tiny) and 7 (gargantuan); 3 is the size of standard-issue text. Here's an example (see fontsize.htm on the CD in this book):

```
<HTML>
<HEAD>
<TITLE>Changing the Size of Text</TITLE>
</HEAD>
<BODY>
<H1>Changing Font Size with the &lt;FONT&gt; Tag</H1>
<HR>
<FONT SIZE="7">This text uses a font size of 7.</FONT><BR>
<FONT SIZE="6">This text uses a font size of 6.</FONT><BR>
<FONT SIZE="5">This text uses a font size of 5.</FONT><BR>
<FONT SIZE="4">This text uses a font size of 4.</FONT><BR>
<FONT SIZE="3">This text uses a font size of 3 (normal).</FONT><BR>
<FONT SIZE="2">This text uses a font size of 2.</FONT><BR>
```

```
<FONT SIZE="1">This text uses a font size of 1.</FONT><BR>
<HR>
<FONT SIZE="7">Y</FONT>ou can mix and match sizes:
<BR>
Here at Shyster & Son Brokerage, you'll see your investments
<FONT SIZE="7">s</FONT><FONT SIZE="6">h</FONT><FONT SIZE="5">r</FONT>
<FONT SIZE="4">i</FONT><FONT SIZE="3">n</FONT><FONT SIZE="2">k</FONT>
while our commissions
<FONT SIZE="4">g</FONT><FONT SIZE="5">r</FONT><FONT SIZE="6">o</FONT>
<FONT SIZE="7">w!</FONT>
</BODY>
</HTML>
```

Figure 3.5 shows the results as they appear with Internet Explorer.

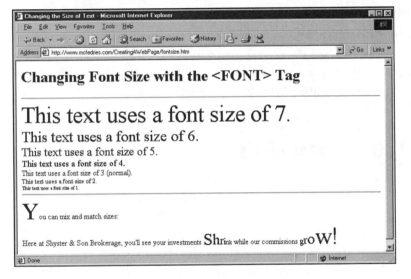

Figure 3.5

Use the <FONT> tag to adjust the size of your web page text.

The <BASEFONT> Tag

I mentioned earlier that the standard font size in a web page is 3. This is called the *base font*, and you'll be interested to know that it's not set in stone. To change it, use the <BASEFONT> tag:

```
<BASEFONT SIZE="size">
```

Once again, *size* is a number between 1 and 7 that specifies the base font size you want. For example, if you enter **<BASEFONT="7">** at the top of your document (that is, immediately after the <BODY> tag), then all the text will appear with font size 7.

You might be wondering what the heck's the big deal with <BASEFONT>. After all, couldn't you just insert a <FONT SIZE="7"> tag at the top of the document? Good point. (Gee, you *are* paying attention, aren't you?) The beauty (if beauty is the right term) of base fonts is that they enable you to set up relative font sizes. A relative font size is one that's so many sizes larger or smaller than the base font. Here's an example:

```
<BASEFONT="6">
This text is displayed in the base font size. However
<FONT SIZE="-2">these three words</FONT> were displayed in
a font size that's two sizes smaller than the base font.
```

The <FONT SIZE="-2"> tag tells the browser to display the text in a font size that's two sizes smaller than the base font (to get larger fonts, you'd use a plus sign (+), instead). Therefore, because I specified a base font of 6, the text between the <FONT> and </FONT> tags appears with a font size of 4.

Why not simply use <FONT SIZE="4">, instead? Well, suppose you plaster your document with dozens of font changes and then, when you display it in the browser, the fonts appear too small. If you're using explicit font sizes, you have to painstakingly adjust each <FONT> tag. However, if you're using relative font sizes, you only have to change the single <BASEFONT> tag.

The ‹FONT› Tag, Part II: Changing the Typeface

By default, the browser uses a plain typeface to render your pages. However, you can change that by shoehorning the FACE attribute into the <FONT> tag, like so:

```
<FONT FACE="typeface">
```

Here, *typeface* is the name of the typeface you want to use. The following page (it's typeface.htm on this book's CD) shows a few FACE-enhanced <FONT> tags in action, and Figure 3.6 shows what Internet Explorer 6 thinks of the whole thing.

```
<HTML>
<HEAD>
<TITLE>Changing the Typeface</TITLE>
</HEAD>
<BODY>
<H1>The &lt;FONT&gt; Tag Can Also Do Different Typefaces</H1>
<HR>
<FONT SIZE="6">
This is the default browser typeface (Times New Roman).<BR>
<FONT FACE="Arial">This is the Arial typeface.</FONT><BR>
<FONT FACE="Courier New">This is the Courier New typeface.</FONT><BR>
<FONT FACE="Comic Sans MS">This is the Comic Sans MS typeface.</FONT><BR>
<FONT FACE="Whatever">Doh! This is NOT the Whatever typeface!</FONT>
```

```
</FONT>
<BODY>
<HTML>
```

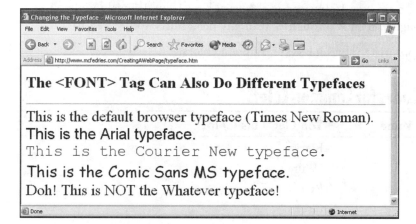

Sounds easy, right? Not so fast, bucko. The problem with the FACE attribute is that it works only if the typeface you specify is installed on the user's computer. If it's not, you're out of luck because the browser will just use its default typeface. In the previous example, notice that the browser doesn't render anything for the Whatever typeface because it's not installed. (It doesn't even exist because I just made up the name!)

To increase your chances, however, you're allowed to add multiple typeface names to the FACE attribute:

```
<FONT FACE="Arial, Verdana, Helvetica">
```

If Arial's not installed, the browser will try Verdana, instead; if Verdana's not installed, the browser tries Helvetica; if that's a no go, the default typeface is used.

Some Notes About Working with Colors

The next couple of sections show you how to change text colors. You'll find that you often have to work with colors when constructing web pages, so it's probably a good idea to take a minute or two now and get the HTML color techniques down pat.

Most of the time, you specify a color by entering a six-digit code that takes the following form:

#rrggbb

This sure looks weird, but there's method in its mathematical madness. Here, *rr* is the red part of the color, *gg* is the green part, and *bb* is the blue part. In other words, each code represents a combination of the three primary colors, and it's this combination that produces the final color. These are called *RGB values*.

The truly nerdish aspect of all this is that each two-digit primary color code uses *hexadecimal* numbers. These are base 16 (instead of the usual base 10 in decimal numbers), so they run from 0 through 9, then A through F. Yeah, my head hurts, too.

Table 3.4 lists the appropriate values for some common colors.

Table 3.4   RGB Codes for Common Colors

If You Use This Value	You Get This Color
#000000	Black
#FFFFFF	White
#FF0000	Red
#00FF00	Green
#0000FF	Blue
#FF00FF	Magenta
#00FFFF	Cyan
#FFFF00	Yellow

Rather than working with these bizarre RGB values, you might prefer to use the standard HTML color names, which are supported by Internet Explorer 3.0 and later, as well as Netscape Navigator 3.0 and later. These color names use nice English words such as "Blue" and "Tan" (as well as plenty of bizarre words such as "Bisque" and "Orchid"). A complete list of the color names, their corresponding RGB values, and a swatch that shows the color are available in the file x11color.htm on the CD in this book (see Figure 3.7 for a black-and-white version of that document).

Figure 3.7

The colors, color names, and their RGB equivalents.

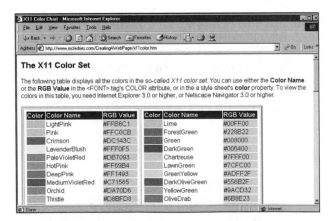

Changing the Color of Your Page Text

Browsers display your text in basic black, which is readable but not all that exciting. To put some color in your text's cheeks, let's look at a few extra goodies.

For starters, the <BODY> tag has a TEXT attribute:

```
<BODY TEXT="color">
```

Here, color is either a color name or an RGB value that specifies the color you want to use.

Webmaster Wisdom

Because you can change the color of your page's background, links, and text, it's very important that you choose a color combination that makes for easy reading. Light yellow text on white, or bright green text on red, can be a little hard on the eyes.

Changing the Color of Your Links

There are also ways to specify colors for the links you include in your page. Here's how they work:

```
<BODY LINK="color" VLINK="color" ALINK="color">
```

Use LINK to specify the color of new links (links the reader has never clicked before); use VLINK to set up a color for visited links (links the reader *has* clicked before); use ALINK to set up a color for active links. (An *active link* is a link you've clicked, but the other page hasn't showed up yet.)

The ‹FONT› Tag, Part III: Another Way to Change Text Color

The problem with these <BODY> tag attributes is that they affect the entire page. What if you only want to change the color of a heading, a word, a link, or even a single letter? For that you need to return to our old friend the <FONT> tag, which also supports a COLOR attribute:

```
<FONT COLOR="color">
```

Here's an example:

```
<FONT COLOR="#FF0000">This text is red.</FONT>
```

CAUTION **Page Pitfalls**

The HTML elements I discussed in this chapter (and many of the ones I talk about in subsequent chapters) can make a web page actually look worse if you misuse or overuse them. If you're interested in making your pages look their best, be sure to read Chapter 21, "The Elements of Web Page Style," where I discuss the do's and don'ts of web page design.

The Least You Need to Know

♦ The basic styles. Use the <B> tag for bold text, <I> for italics, <U> for underlining, and <TT> for monospace.

♦ Headings, galore. The heading tags run from <H1> (the largest) through <H6> (the smallest). Remember, too, that text between heading tags always appears in a separate paragraph.

♦ Modifying tag behavior with attributes. Many tags can take one or more attributes that change the way the browser handles the tag. When specifying attributes, always surround the values with quotation marks.

♦ Alignment options. To align your text, the <P> tag and the heading tags accept the ALIGN attribute, which can take any of three values: LEFT, CENTER, and RIGHT.

♦ Other useful formatting tags. Use the <PRE> tag to force the browser to display white space; use <BR> to insert a line break; and use <HR> to insert a horizontal line.

♦ The hard-working <FONT> tag. To format text, use the <FONT> tag's various attributes, including SIZE (to change the size of the text), FACE (to change the typeface), and COLOR (to change the color).

♦ Doing your page's colors. You'll most often specify a color using the code #*rrggbb*, where *rr* is the red value, *gg* is the green value, and *bb* is the blue value. Each value is a hexadecimal number that runs from 00 to FF.

Chapter 4

The Gist of a List: Adding Lists to Your Page

In This Chapter

- ◆ Creating numbered lists on your web page
- ◆ How to set up bulleted lists
- ◆ Cobbling together a definition list
- ◆ More list examples than you can shake a stick at

Are you making a list and checking it twice? Gonna find out who's naughty and … oops, drifted off to the North Pole for a second! But if you do want to include a list in your web page, what's the best way to go about it? You saw in the previous chapter how you can use the
 (line break) tag to display items on separate lines. That works well enough, I guess, but hold your list horses—there's a better way. HTML has a few tags that are specially designed to give you much more control over your list-building chores. In fact, HTML offers no less than three different list styles: numbered lists, bulleted lists, and definition lists. This chapter takes you through the basics of each list type and provides you with plenty of examples.

Putting Your Affairs in Order with Numbered Lists

If you want to include a numbered list of items—it could be a top-ten list, bowling league standings, or any kind of ranking—don't bother adding in the numbers yourself. Instead, you can use HTML ordered lists to make the web browser generate the numbers for you.

Ordered lists use two types of tags:

♦ The entire list is surrounded by the <OL> (ordered list) and </OL> tags.

♦ Each item in the list is preceded by the <LI> (list item) tag and is closed with the </LI> end tag.

The general setup looks like this:

```
<OL>
<LI>First item.</LI>
<LI>Second item.</LI>
<LI>Third item.</LI>
<LI>You get the idea.</LI>
</OL>
```

Here's an example (see numlist1.htm on the CD in this book):

```
<HTML>
<HEAD>
<TITLE>Numbered Lists - Example #1</TITLE>
</HEAD>
<BODY>
<H3>My Ten Favorite U.S. College Nicknames</H3>
<OL>
<LI>Missouri-Kansas City Kangaroos</LI>
<LI>Delaware Fightin' Blue Hens</LI>
<LI>Texas Christian Horned Frogs</LI>
<LI>Coastal Carolina Chanticleers</LI>
<LI>Kent State Golden Flashes</LI>
<LI>Marshall Thundering Herd</LI>
<LI>Idaho Vandals</LI>
<LI>Purdue Boilermakers</LI>
<LI>South Carolina Fighting Gamecocks</LI>
<LI>Wake Forest Demon Deacons</LI>
</OL>
</BODY>
</HTML>
```

Notice that I didn't include any numbers before each list item. However, when I display this document in a browser (see Figure 4.1), the numbers get inserted automatically. Pretty slick, huh?

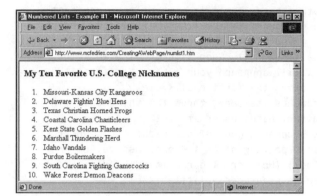

Figure 4.1

How the numbered list appears in Internet Explorer.

Webmaster Wisdom

Your list items don't have to be just plain text, so you're free to go crazy and insert other HTML tags. For example, you could use <B> and </B> to boldface a word or two in the item, you could use the <FONT> tag to change the font size or typeface of the item, or you could make an item a hypertext link to another web page. Just make sure to start each line with the <LI> tag. (I discuss this linking stuff in the next chapter.)

The items you toss into your numbered lists don't have to be short words and phrases, however. For example, if you're explaining how to perform a certain task, a numbered list is the perfect way to take your readers through each step. Here's a more involved example (it's numlist2.htm on this book's CD) that uses a numbered list to explain how to juggle:

```
<HTML>
<HEAD>
<TITLE>Numbered Lists - Example #2</TITLE>
</HEAD>
<BODY>
<H3>The Complete Idiot's Guide to Juggling</H3>
<HR>
Here are the basic steps for the most fundamental of juggling
moves&#151;the three-ball cascade:
<OL>
<LI>Place two balls in your dominant hand, one in front of the other,
and hold the third ball in your other hand. Let your arms dangle
naturally and bring your forearms parallel to the ground (as though
you were holding a tray).</LI>
<LI>Of the two balls in your dominant hand, toss the front one towards
your left hand in a smooth arc. Make sure the ball doesn't spin too
much and that it goes no higher than about eye level.</LI>
<LI>Once the first ball has reached the top of its arc, you need to
```

```
release the ball in your other hand. Throw it towards your dominant
hand, making sure it flies <I>under</I> the first ball. Again, watch
that the ball doesn't spin or go higher than eye level.</LI>
<LI>Now things get a little tricky (!). Soon after you release the
second ball, the first ball will approach your other hand (gravity
never fails). Go ahead and catch the first ball.</LI>
<LI>When the second ball reaches its apex, throw the third ball (the
remaining ball in your dominant hand) under it.</LI>
<LI>At this point, it just becomes a game of catch-and-throw-under,
catch-and-throw-under. Keep repeating steps 1-5 and, before you know
it, you'll be a juggling fool. (However, I'd recommend holding off on
the flaming clubs until you've practiced a little.)</LI>
</OL>
</BODY>
</HTML>
```

As you can see, most of the items are quite long; and it's kind of hard to tell where each <LI> item begins and ends. However, as shown in the Figure 4.2, the list looks pretty good when viewed in a web browser.

Figure 4.2

Numbered lists are perfect for outlining the steps in a procedure.

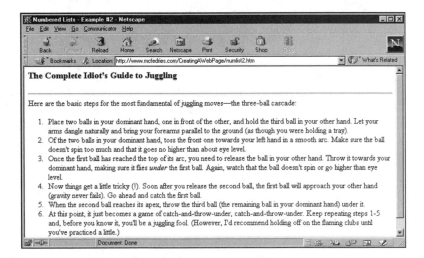

Using a Different Numbering Scheme

That <OL> tag's TYPE attribute enables you to define a different numbering scheme. Here's how it works:

```
<OL TYPE="type">
```

Here, *type* is one of the characters shown in Table 4.1.

Table 4.1   The ‹OL› Tag's TYPE Attribute Values

Type	Numbering scheme	Example
1	Standard numbers	1, 2, 3
a	Lowercase letters	a, b, c
A	Uppercase letters	A, B, C
i	Small Roman numerals	i, ii, iii
I	Large Roman numerals	I, II, III

Here's an example (see oltype.htm on this book's CD):

```
<HTML>
<HEAD>
<TITLE>The TYPE attribute</TITLE>
</HEAD>
<BODY>
<B>TYPE="a":</B>
<OL TYPE="a">
<LI>First</LI>
<LI>Second</LI>
<LI>Third</LI>
</OL>
<B>TYPE="A":</B>
<OL TYPE="A">
<LI>Win</LI>
<LI>Place</LI>
<LI>Show</LI>
</OL>
<B>TYPE="i":</B>
<OL TYPE="i">
<LI>Gold</LI>
<LI>Silver</LI>
<LI>Bronze</LI>
</OL>
<B>TYPE="I":</B>
<OL TYPE="I">
<LI>Miss America</LI>
<LI>First runner-up</LI>
<LI>Second runner-up</LI>
</OL>
</BODY>
</HTML>
```

Webmaster Wisdom

Another useful <OL> tag attribute is START, which enables you to define the starting point of the list number. For example, if you use <OL START="100">, the first item in your numbered list will be 100, the second will be 101, and so on.

Figure 4.3 shows how Internet Explorer handles the various types of lists.

Figure 4.3

The <OL> tag's TYPE attribute in action.

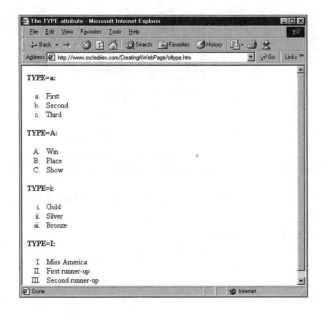

Scoring Points with Bulleted Lists

Numbered lists, of course, aren't the only kinds of lists. If you just want to enumerate a few points, a bulleted list might be more your style. They're called "bulleted" lists because a web browser displays a cute little dot or square (depending on the browser) called a *bullet* to the left of each item.

The HTML tags for a bulleted list are pretty close to the ones you saw for a numbered list. As before, you precede each list item with the same <LI> tag, but you enclose the entire list with the <UL> and </UL> tags. Why "UL"? Well, what the rest of the world calls a bulleted list, the HTML powers-that-be call an *unordered list*. Yeah, that's real intuitive. Ah well, here's how they work:

```
<UL>
<LI>First bullet point.</LI>
<LI>Fifty-seventh bullet point.</LI>
<LI>Sixteenth bullet point.</LI>
<LI>Hey, whaddya want-it's an unordered list!</LI>
</UL>
```

Here's an HTML document (look for bulleted.htm on the CD in this book) that demonstrates how to use the bulleted list tags:

```
<HTML>
<HEAD>
<TITLE>Bulleted List Example</TITLE>
</HEAD>
<BODY>
<H3>Famous Phobias</H3>
<UL>
<LI>Augustus Caesar &#151; Achluophobia (fear of sitting in the dark)</LI>
<LI>Sigmund Freud &#151; Siderodromophobia (fear of trains)</LI>
<LI>Arnold Sch&#246;nberg &#151; Tridecaphobia (fear of the number 13)</LI>
<LI>John Cheever &#151; Gephyrophobia (fear of crossing bridges)</LI>
<LI>Sid Caesar &#151; Tonsurphobia (fear of haircuts)</LI>
</UL>
</BODY>
</HTML>
```

Figure 4.4 shows how the Internet Explorer browser renders this file—little bullets and all.

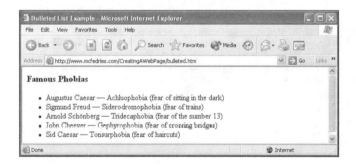

Figure 4.4

A typical bulleted list.

Changing the Bullet Type

The basic bulleted-list bullet is a small circle. However, most browsers also support an extra TYPE attribute that modifies the bullet:

```
<UL TYPE="type">
```

In this case, *type* can be either disc (the standard bullet), circle, or square. (Note that you must use lowercase values here.) Here's a for-instance (look for ultype.htm on this book's CD):

```
<HTML>
<HEAD>
<TITLE>Bulleted List Extensions</TITLE>
</HEAD>
```

```
<BODY>
<H3>Using the &lt;UL TYPE="<I>type</I>"&gt; Tag</H3>
<HR>
<UL TYPE="disc">
<LI>Compact disc</LI>
<LI>Disc jockey</LI>
<LI>Disc brake</LI>
</UL>
<UL TYPE="circle">
<LI>Circle the wagons!</LI>
<LI>Circle all that apply</LI>
<LI>Chalk Circle</LI>
</UL>
<UL TYPE="square">
<LI>Square root</LI>
<LI>Three square meals</LI>
<LI>Times square</LI>
</UL>
</BODY>
</HTML>
```

And Figure 4.5 shows how it looks from Internet Explorer's point of view.

Figure 4.5

The <UL> tag's TYPE attribute enables you to choose from any of three different bullet styles.

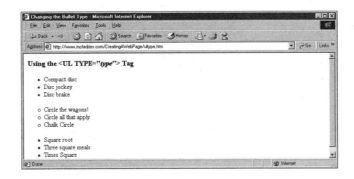

Webmaster Wisdom

The best way to get a custom bullet, in my not-so-humble opinion, is to insert a graphic that has a cool bullet-like image. I show you how this is done in Chapter 6, "A Picture Is Worth a Thousand Clicks: Working with Images."

Defining Definition Lists

The final type of list is called a *definition list*. Originally, people used it for dictionary-like lists where each entry had two parts: a term and the definition of the term. As you'll see, though, definition lists are useful for more than just definitions.

To mark the two different parts of each entry in these lists, you need two different tags. The term is preceded by the <DT> tag, and the definition is preceded by the <DD> tag, like so:

```
<DT>Term</DT><DD>Definition</DD>
```

You can, if you like, put the <DT> part and the <DD> part on separate lines, but I prefer this style (and either way, they end up looking the same in the browser). You then surround the whole list with the <DL> and </DL> tags to complete your definition list. Here's how the whole thing looks:

```
<DL>
<DT>A Term</DT><DD>Its Definition</DD>
<DT>Another Term</DT><DD>Another Definition</DD>
<DT>Yet Another Term</DT><DD>Yet Another Definition</DD>
<DT>Etc.</DT><DD>Abbreviation of a Latin phrase that means "and so forth."</DD>
</DL>
```

Webmaster Wisdom

People often use definition lists for things other than definitions. Some web welders like to use the term (the <DT> part) as a section heading and the definition (the <DD> part) as the section text. You can also leave out the term and just use the <DD> tag by itself. This is handy for those times when you need indented text (say, if you're quoting someone at length).

Let's look at an example. The HTML document shown next (it's on this book's CD in the file named defnlist.htm) uses a definition list to outline a few words and phrases and their definitions. (Notice that I've applied bold face to all the terms; this helps them stand out more when the browser displays them.)

```
<HTML>
<HEAD>
<TITLE>Definition List Example</TITLE>
</HEAD>
<BODY>
<H3>Some Techno-Terms You Should Know</H3>
<DL>
<DT><B>Barney Page</B></DT><DD>A Web page that tries to capitalize on a
current craze.</DD>
<DT><B>Bit-Spit</B></DT><DD>Any form of digital correspondence.</DD>
<DT><B>Byte-Bonding</B></DT><DD>When computer users discuss things that
nearby noncomputer users don't understand. See also <I>geeking out</I>.</DD>
<DT><B>Clickstreams</B></DT><DD>The paths a person takes as she negotiates
various Web pages.</DD>
```

```
<DT><B>Cobweb Page</B></DT><DD>A Web page that hasn't been updated in a
while.</DD>
<DT><B>Geek</B></DT><DD>Someone who knows a lot about computers and very
little about anything else.</DD>
<DT><B>Geeking Out</B></DT><DD>When <I>geeks</I> who are <I>byte-bonding</I>
start playing with a computer during a noncomputer-related social event.</DD>
</DL>
</BODY>
</HTML>
```

Figure 4.6 shows how the definition list appears in the Internet Explorer for the Mac scheme of things.

Figure 4.6

A few definitions arrayed, appropriately enough, in a definition list.

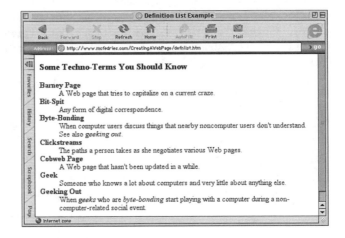

Combining Lists Inside Lists

These three types of HTML lists should serve you well for most of your web page productions. However, you're free to mix and match various list types to suit the occasion. Specifically, it's perfectly legal to plop one type of list inside another (this is called *nesting lists*). For example, suppose you have a numbered list that outlines the steps involved in some procedure. If you need to augment one of the steps with a few bullet points, you can simply insert a bulleted list after the appropriate numbered list item.

As an example, I'll take the definition list from the last section and toss in both a numbered list and a bulleted list. Here's the result (I've lopped off some of the lines to make it easier to read; you can find the full document on this book's CD in the file named combo.htm):

```
<DL>
<DT><B>Barney Page</B><DD>A Web page that tries to capitalize on a
current craze. Here are some recent Barney page subjects:
```

```
<UL>
<LI>Star Wars: The Phantom Menace</LI>
<LI>Survivor</LI>
<LI>Scooters</LI>
</UL>

</DD>
<DT><B>Bit-Spit</B><DD>Any form of digital correspondence.
<DT><B>Byte-Bonding</B><DD>When computer users discuss things that
nearby noncomputer users don't understand. Here are the three stages
of byte-bonding that inevitably lead to <I>geeking out</I>:

<OL>
<LI>&quot;Say, did you see that IBM ad where the nuns are talking about
surfing the Net?&quot;</LI>
<LI>&quot;Do you surf the Net?&quot;</LI>
<LI>&quot;Let's go surf the Net!&quot;</LI>
</OL>

</DD>
...
</DL>
```

After the first definition list entry—the one for Barney Page—I've inserted a bulleted list that gives a few examples. (I've added blank lines above and below the bulleted list to make it stand out better. Note that I added these lines for cosmetic purposes only; they don't affect how the page appears in the browser.) Then, after the third definition list entry—Byte-Bonding—I've put in a numbered list. Figure 4.7 shows how all this looks when a browser gets hold of it.

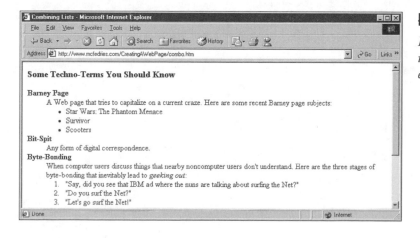

Figure 4.7

HTML is more than happy to let you insert lists inside each other.

The Least You Need to Know

 ◆ Numbered lists. Use the <OL> and </OL> tags and surround each list item with <LI> and </LI>.

 ◆ Changing the number type. Add the TYPE attribute to the <OL> tag and set it to one of the following values: a, A, i, or I.

 ◆ Bulleted lists. Use the <UL> and </UL> tags and surround each list item with <LI> and </LI>.

 ◆ Changing the bullet type. Add the TYPE attribute to the <UL> tag and set it to one of the following values: disc, circle, or square.

 ◆ Definition lists. Use the <DL> and </DL> tags. For each list item, surround the term with <DT> and </DT> and the definition with <DD> and </DD>.

 ◆ Nested lists. The browser won't mind in the least if you insert one type of list inside another.

Chapter 5

Making the Jump to Hyperspace: Adding Links

In This Chapter

- Some URL fundamentals
- Creating links to other web pages
- Creating links to other locations in your web page
- Creating links that send e-mail messages
- Easy hypertext help that'll have your web pages fully linked in no time flat

As a would-be web page publisher, you've gotta give the people what they want, right? And what today's modern surfer wants more than anything else is to *interact* with a web page. Unfortunately, truly interactive pages require a bit more effort to create. (I'll talk about interaction a bit more in Part 2, "A Grab Bag of Web Page Wonders," and Part 4, "Working with JavaScripts and Java Applets.")

However, there is a way to throw at least a small interactive bone to the readers of your web creations: Give 'em a few links that they can follow to the four corners of the web world (or even just to another part of your own cyberspace plot). It's an easy way to give your pages a dynamic feel that'll have people coming back for more. This chapter explains links and shows you how to put the "hypertext" into HTML.

The URL of Net: A Cyberspace Address Primer

Before the hypertext festivities commence, there's a bit of background info I need to slog through for you. As I mentioned in Chapter 1, "A Brief HTML Primer," a *hypertext link* is a special word or phrase in a web page that, when the user clicks it, takes him or her to a different web document (or to an FTP site, or whatever). Each web page (and, indeed, any Internet resource) has its own address, which is called a *Uniform Resource Locator* (or URL, for short).

When you combine these two factoids, you realize that for a link to work properly, you need to know the correct address of the resource to which you're linking. To do that, you need to understand the anatomy of these URL things. Unfortunately, the whole URL concept seems to have been invented by some insane Geek of Geeks who never believed normal human beings would actually use the darn things. They're long, they're confusing, they're messy, and they're almost impossible to type correctly the first time. Not to worry, though. I've gone *mano-a-mano* with this URL foofaraw, and I've come up with a plan that's designed to knock some sense into the whole mess.

The idea is that, like journalists and their five Ws (who, what, where, when, and why), you can reduce any URL to three Ws (who, what, and where) and an H (how). So, the basic form of any URL ends up looking like this:

> *How://Who/Where/What*

Hmm. I'm definitely talking serious weirdness here, so let's see what the heck I mean by all that:

- **How**   The first part of the URL specifies how the data is going to be transferred across Net lines. This is called the *protocol* and, luckily, mere mortals like you and I don't need to concern ourselves with the guts of this stuff. All you need to know is which protocol each resource uses, which is easy. For example, the World Wide Web uses something called HTTP (I tell you which protocols other resources use later in this chapter). So, the "how" part of the URL is the protocol, followed by a colon (:) and two slashes (//). (I told you this stuff was arcane; it makes alchemy look like *The Cat in the Hat*.) So, a web page URL always starts like this (lowercase letters are the norm, but they're not necessary): http://.

- **Who**   Calling the next part the "who" of the URL is, I admit, a bit of a misnomer because there's no person involved. Instead, it's the name of the computer where the resource is located—in geek circles, this is called the *host name*. (This is the part of an Internet address that has all those dots you're always hearing, such as ncsa. uiuc.edu or www.yahoo.com.) For example, this book's home page is located on a computer named www.mcfedries.com. You just tack this "who" part onto the end of the "how" part, as shown here: http://www.mcfedries.com.

◆ **Where**   The next part of the address specifies where the resource is located on the computer. This generally means the directory in which the resource is stored; the directory might be something like /pages or /pub/junk/software. This book's home page is in its own directory, which is /creatingawebpage/. (To get your own directory, you need to sign up with a company that puts pages on the Web; see Chapter 7, "The Host with the Most: Choosing a Web Hosting Provider," for details.) So now you just staple the directory onto the URL and then add another slash on the end, for good measure: http://www.mcfedries.com/creatingawebpage/.

◆ **What**   Almost there. The "what" part is just the name of the file you want to see. For a web page, you use the name of the document that contains the HTML codes and text. The file containing this book's home page is called index.html, so here's the full URL: http://www.mcfedries.com/creatingawebpage/index.html.

Page Pitfalls

I mentioned earlier that you can use uppercase or lowercase letters (the latter are normally used) for the "how" part of the URL. The same is true for the "who" part, but case is often crucial when entering the directory and filename. With most (but not all) websites, if you enter even a single letter of a directory or filename in the wrong case, you may not get to where you want to go. (Technical aside: Web servers that run the Unix operating system are finicky about case, while those that run Windows are not.) That's why I always tell people to use nothing but lowercase letters for directory and filenames; it just keeps things simpler (and saves wear and tear on your typing fingers by not having to stretch over to the Shift key).

Okay Mr. Smartypants writer, lemme ask you this: I visit your website all the time, but to get there, I only have to enter http://www.mcfedries.com/creatingawebpage/. How come I can get away without entering a filename?

Ah, that's because most web servers have something they call a *default filename*. This means that if the user doesn't specify a filename, the server just assumes they want the default file. On most servers, the default file is named index.html, so if you enter this: http://www.mcfedries.com/creatingawebpage/; what you really get is this: http://www.mcfedries.com/creatingawebpage/index.html. When you sign up with a web host, you need to find out what the default filename is and then be sure to use that name for your main page. (Otherwise, your site visitors will just see an ugly list of all the files in your directory or, even worse, an error message.)

Got all that? Yeah, I know—it's as clear as mud. Well, have no fear. If you can keep the "how, who, where, and what" idea in your head, it'll all sink in eventually.

Getting Hyper: Creating Links in HTML

Okay, with that drivel out of the way, it's time to put your newfound know-how to work (assuming, that is, I haven't scarred you for life!). To wit, this section shows you how to use HTML to add links to your web page.

The HTML tags that do the link thing are <A> and </A>. (Why "A"? Well, as you'll find out later on—see the section "Anchors Aweigh: Internal Links"—you can create special links called *anchors* that send your readers to other parts of the same document instead of to a different document.) The <A> tag is a little different from the other tags you've seen (you just knew it would be). Specifically, you don't use it by itself but, instead, you shoehorn the URL of your link into it. Here's how it works:

```
<A HREF="URL">
```

Here, HREF stands for *Hypertext Reference*. Just replace URL with the actual URL of the Web page you want to use for the link (and, yes, you have to enclose the address in quotation marks). Here's an example:

```
<A HREF="http://www.mcfedries.com/creatingawebpage/index.html">
```

Now you can see why I made you suffer through all that URL poppycock earlier: It's crucial for getting the <A> tag to work properly.

You're not done yet, though, not by a long shot (insert groan of disappointment here). What are you missing? Right, you have to give the reader some descriptive link text to click. Happily, that's easier done than said because all you do is insert the text between the <A> and </A> tags, like so:

```
<A HREF="URL">Link text goes here</A>
```

Need an example? You got it (see the file link.htm on the CD in this book):

```
Why not head to this book's
<A HREF="http://www.mcfedries.com/creatingawebpage/index.html">home page</A>?
```

Figure 5.1 shows how it looks in a web browser. Notice how the browser highlights and underlines the link text and when I point my mouse at the link, the URL I specified appears in the browser's status bar.

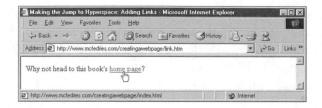

Figure 5.1

How the link appears in Internet Explorer.

Site Organization: Dealing with Directories

You may be aware that a *directory* is a file storage area that's been carved out of a hard disk. If you use Windows or a Mac, you may be more familiar with the term *folder,* which means the same thing. However, the word "directory" is more often used in web page publishing circles, so that's what I use throughout this book. Before continuing with the link lesson, let's take a short side trip to understand how directories work in the web world.

When you sign up with a company that will "host" your web pages, that company will supply you with your very own directory on its server. If you're only putting together a few pages, that directory should be more than adequate. If you're constructing a larger site, however, you should give some thought to how you organize your files. Why? Well, think of your own computer. It's unlikely that you have everything crammed into a single directory. Instead, you probably have separate directories for the different programs you use and other directories for your data files.

There's no reason why you can't cook up a similar scheme in your web home. On my site, to give you a for instance, I have separate directories for many of my books (such as this book's creatingawebpage directory), a directory called ramblings that stores miscellaneous writings, another called toys that has a few online applications, a graphics directory to store all my image files, and so on.

With this type of multidirectory setup, how you reference files in other directories can be a bit tricky. As an example, consider a website that has three directories:

```
/ (this is the main directory)
things/
stuff/
```

Here, "things" and "stuff" are subdirectories of the main directory. There are three scenarios to watch out for:

◆ **Referencing a file in the same directory.** This is the easiest because you don't have to include any directory information. Suppose that the HTML file you're working on is in the writing directory and that you want to reference a page named tirade.html that's also in that directory. In this case, you just use the name of the file, like so:

```
<A HREF="tirade.html">
```

◆ **Referencing a file in a subdirectory from the main directory.** This is a common scenario because your home page (which is almost certainly in the main directory) is likely to have links to files in subdirectories. For example, suppose you want to link to a page named doggerel.html in the things subdirectory from your home page. Then your <A HREF> tag takes the following form:

```
<A HREF="things/doggerel.html">
```

◆ **Referencing a file in a subdirectory from a different subdirectory.** This is the trickiest scenario. For example, suppose you have a page in the things subdirectory and you want to link to a page named duh.html in the stuff subdirectory. Here's the <A HREF> tag:

```
<A HREF="../stuff/duh.html">
```

Weird, eh? The ".." thing represents what's called the *parent* directory (that is, the one that contains the current directory). It essentially says, "From here, go up to the parent directory, and then go down into the stuff subdirectory."

Anchors Aweigh: Internal Links

When a surfer clicks a standard link, the page loads and the browser displays the top part of the page. However, it's possible to set up a special kind of link that will force the browser to initially display some other part of the page, such as a section in the middle of the page. For these special links, I use the term *internal links*, because they take the reader directly to some inner part of the page.

When would you ever use such a link? Most of your HTML pages will probably be short and sweet, and the web surfers who drop by will have no trouble navigating their way around. But if, like me, you suffer from a bad case of terminal verbosity combined with bouts of extreme long windedness, you'll end up with web pages that are lengthy, to say the least. Rather than force your readers to scroll through your tomelike creations, you can set up links to various sections of the document. For example, you could then assemble these links at the top of the page to form a sort of "hypertable of contents."

Internal links actually link to a special version of the <A> tag—called an *anchor*—that you've inserted somewhere in the same page. To understand how anchors work, think of how you might mark a spot in a book you're reading. You might dog-ear the page, attach a note, or place something between the pages, such as a bookmark or your cat's tail.

An anchor performs the same function: It "marks" a particular spot in a web page, and you can then use a regular <A> tag to link to that spot.

I think an example is in order. Suppose I want to create a hypertext version of this chapter. (As a matter of fact, I did! Look for the file named chapter5.htm on this book's CD.) To make it easy to navigate, I want to include a table of contents at the top of the page that includes links to all the section headings. My first chore is to add anchor tags to each heading. Here's the general format for an anchor:

```
<A NAME="Name"></A>
```

As you can see, an anchor tag looks a lot like a regular link tag. The major difference is that the HREF attribute is replaced by NAME="*Name*"; *Name* is the name you want to give the anchor. You can use whatever you like for the name, but most people choose relatively short names to save typing. Notice, too, that you don't need any text between the <A NAME> tag and the </A> end tag.

Where do you put this tag? The best place is immediately before the start of the section you want to link to. For example, this chapter's first section is titled "The URL of Net: A Cyberspace Address Primer." If I want to give this section the uninspired name Section1, I use the following anchor:

```
<A NAME="Section1"></A>
<H2>The URL of Net: A Cyberspace Address Primer</H2>
```

Now, when I set up my table of contents, I can create a link to this section by using a regular <A> tag (with the HREF thing) that points to the section's name. And, just so a web browser doesn't confuse the anchor name with the name of another document, I preface the anchor name with a number sign (#). Here's how it looks:

```
<A HREF="#Section1">The URL of Net: A Cyberspace Address Primer</A>
```

Just so you get the big picture, here's an excerpt from the HTML file for this chapter (Figure 5.2 shows how it looks in a browser):

```
<H3>Hypertable of Contents:</H3>
<DL>
<DD><A HREF="#Section1">The URL of Net: A Cyberspace Address Primer</A>
<DD><A HREF="#Section2">Getting Hyper: Creating Links in HTML</A>
<DL>
<DD><A HREF="#Section2a">Site Organization: Dealing with Directories</A>
<DD><A HREF="#Section2b">Anchors Aweigh: Internal Links</A>
</DL>
<DD><A HREF="#Section3">Creating an E-mail Link</A>
<DD><A HREF="#Section4">The Least You Need to Know</A>
</DL>
<HR>
 [Rambling introduction goes here]
<A NAME="Section1"><H2>The URL of Net: A Cyberspace Address Primer</H2>
</A>
```

Figure 5.2

The hypertext version of this chapter.

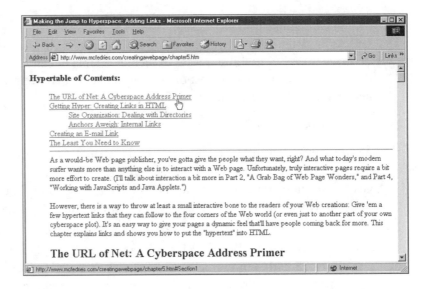

Although you'll mostly use anchors to link to sections of the same web page, there's no law against using them to link to specific sections of other pages. All you do is add the appropriate anchor to the other page and then link to it by adding the anchor's name (preceded, as usual, by #) to the end of the page's filename. For example, suppose you want to put a link in a page and you want that link to whisk the reader immediately to the "Getting Hyper: Creating Links in HTML" section of chapter5.htm. I gave that section the anchor name Section2, so here's a tag that sets up a link to it:

```
<A HREF="chapter5.htm#Section2">How to Create a Link</A>
```

Creating an E-mail Link

As I mentioned earlier, there's no reason a link has to lead to a web page. In fact, all you have to do is alter the "how" part of the URL, and you can connect to most other Internet services, including FTP and Usenet.

Page Pitfalls

Setting up an e-mail link may not work properly if the user has a web-based e-mail service such as Yahoo!. That's because when the user clicks the e-mail link, the browser attempts to launch the user's e-mail software. But that software isn't used for web e-mail, so the browser will have no way of sending the message. Note, however, that recent versions of Outlook Express do allow you to set up a Hotmail account, which is a step in the right direction.

In this section, however, I'll concentrate on the most common type of nonweb link: e-mail. In this case, someone clicking an e-mail link is presented with a window he or she can use to send a message to your e-mail address. Now that's interactive!

This type of link is called a *mailto link* because you include the word *mailto* in the <A> tag. Here's the general form:

```
<A HREF="mailto:YourEmailAddress">The link text goes here</A>
```

Here, *YourEmailAddress* is your Internet e-mail address. For example, suppose I want to include an e-mail link in one of my web pages. The e-mail address for this book is webpages@mcfedries.com, so I'd set up the link as follows:

```
You can write to me at this book's
<A HREF="mailto:webpages@mcfedries.com">e-mail address.</A>
```

Figure 5.3 shows how it looks in Netscape 4. Note that when you point at the link with your mouse, the mailto address appears in the browser's status bar.

Figure 5.3

A web page with an e-mail link.

Webmaster Wisdom

If you want to try your hand at linking to FTP sites or Usenet newsgroups, here's a rundown of the types of URLs to use:

Resource	URL
FTP (directory)	ftp://Who/Where/
FTP (file)	ftp://Who/Where/What
Usenet	news:newsgroup.name

Note that *Who*, *Where*, and *What* are the same as I defined them earlier in this chapter. Also, *newsgroup.name* is just the name of the newsgroup that has articles you want to see.

The Least You Need to Know

◆ Address anatomy. To make URLs easier to figure out, you can break them down into four sections: *How://Who/Where/What*. *How* is the protocol (such as http); *Who* is the host name (such as www.mcfedries.com); *Where* is the directory (such as /creatingawebpage/); and *What* is the filename (such as index.html).

◆ A recipe for links. Here's the basic structure of an HTML link:

```
<A HREF="URL">Link text</A>.
```

◆ The simplest link. If the page you're linking to is in the same directory as the current document, you can get away with specifying only the filename in the link's URL.

◆ Forging an anchor. To create an anchor, use the following variation on the <A> tag theme:

```
<A NAME="Name"></A>.
```

◆ Linking to an anchor. To set up a link to an anchor, use this tag:

```
<A HREF="#Name">Link text</A>.
```

◆ E-mail links. E-mail links use the *mailto* form of the <A> tag:

```
<A HREF="mailto:E-mailAddress">Link Text</A>
```

Chapter 6

A Picture Is Worth a Thousand Clicks: Working with Images

In This Chapter

- ◆ A quick look at some image basics
- ◆ Using the <IMG> tag to insert an image on your web page
- ◆ How to make text and images get along
- ◆ Using an image as the page background
- ◆ Using a "pixel shim" for precise positioning
- ◆ Adding the finishing touches to your web page with icons, bullets, buttons, and other graphical glad rags

You've probably seen those TV ads proclaiming in no uncertain terms (true hipsters are never uncertain about their hipness) that "image is everything." You know they couldn't put it on TV if it wasn't true (!), so you need to think about what kind of image your web page presents to the outside world.

You've seen how tossing a few text tags, a list or two, and a liberal dose of links can do wonders for drab, lifeless pages. But face it: Anybody can do that kind of stuff. If you're looking to make your web abode really stand out from the crowd, you need to go graphical with a few well-chosen images. To that end, this chapter gives you the ins and outs of images, including some background info on the various graphics formats, tags for inserting images, and lots more. (You can even use images as links. I'll show you how it's done in Chapter 9, "Images Can Be Links, Too.")

Images: Some Semi-Important Background Info

Before you get down to brass tacks and start trudging through the HTML tags that plop pictures onto your pages, there are a few things I need to discuss. Not to worry, though; it's nothing that's overly technical. (That, of course, would be contrary to *The Complete Idiot's Guide* bylaw 4.17c: "Thou shalt not cause the eyes of thy readers to glaze over with interminable technical claptrap.") Instead, I just look at a few things that help you choose and work with images, and that should help make all this stuff a bit clearer.

No, images aren't text, but that's okay.

First off, let me answer the main question that's probably running through your mind even now about all this graphics rumpus:

If the innards of a web page are really just text and HTML tags, then how in the name of h-e-double-hockey-sticks am I supposed to get an image in there?

Hey, that's a darn good question. Here's the easy answer: You don't.

Huh?

Yeah. As you see later on (in the section "The Nitty-Gritty at Last: The <IMG> Tag"), all you're really doing is, for each image you want to use, adding a tag to the document that says, in effect, "Yo! Mr. Browser! Insert image here." That tag specifies the name of the graphics file, so the browser just opens the file and displays the image. In other words, you have two files: your HTML file and a separate graphics file. It's the browser's job to combine them into your beautiful web page.

Graphics formats: Can't we all just get along?

Some computer wag once said that the nice thing about standards is that there are so many of them! Graphics files are no exception. It seems that every geek who ever gawked at a graphic has invented his own format for storing them on disk. And talk about alphabet soup! Why, there are images in GIF, JPEG, BMP, PCX, TIFF, DIB, EPS, and TGA formats, and those are just off the top of my head. How's a budding web page architect supposed to make sense of all this acronymic anarchy?

Well, my would-be web welders, I bring tidings of great joy. You can toss most of that graphic traffic into the digital scrap heap because the web has standardized on just two formats—GIF and JPEG—that account for 99 percent of all web imagery. Oh happy day! Here's a quick look at them:

Webmaster Wisdom ___

When you work with graphics files, bear in mind that GIF files use the .gif extension, while JPEG files use the .jpg or .jpeg extensions.

◆ **GIF**   This was the original web graphics format. It's limited to 256 colors, so it's best for simple images: line art, clip art, text, and so on. GIFs are also useful for setting up images with transparent backgrounds (see "Giving a GIF a Transparent Background," later in this chapter) and for creating simple animations (see Chapter 11, "Making Your Web Pages Dance and Sing").

◆ **JPEG**   This format (which gets its name from the Joint Photographic Experts Group that invented it; gee, don't *they* sound like a fun bunch of guys to hang out with?) supports complex images that have many millions of colors. The main advantage of JPEG files is that, given the same image, they're smaller than GIFs, so they take less time to download. This doesn't matter much with simple images, but digitized photographs and other high-quality images tend to be huge, but the JPEG format *compresses* these images so they're easier to manage.

Webmaster Wisdom ___

If you use Windows, then you're probably familiar with the BMP (bitmap) images that you can create with the Paint program. Although Internet Explorer is willing to work with these types of images, Netscape isn't. Therefore, I suggest that you avoid them and use only GIFs and JPEGs. (Even if you know all your users run Internet Explorer, you should still avoid BMPs because they tend to be huge compared to the equivalent GIF or JPEG file.)

How do I get graphics?

The text part of a web page is, at least from a production standpoint, a piece of cake for most folks. After all, even the most pathetic typist can peck out at least a few words a minute. Graphics, on the other hand, are another kettle of digital fish entirely. Creating a snazzy logo or eye-catching illustration requires a modicum of artistic talent, which is a bit harder to come by than basic typing skills.

However, if you have such talent, you're laughing: Just create the image in your favorite graphics program and save it in GIF or JPEG format. (If your program gives you several GIF options, use GIF87 or, even better, GIF89, if possible. If your software doesn't know GIF from a hole in the ground, see the next section, where I show you how to convert the file.)

The nonartists in the crowd have to obtain their graphics goodies from some other source. Fortunately, there's no shortage of images floating around. Here are some ideas:

- Many software packages (including Microsoft Office and most paint and illustration programs) come with clip art libraries. *Clip art* is professional-quality artwork that you can freely incorporate in your own designs. If you don't have a program that comes with its own clip art, most software stores have CDs for sale that are chock-full of clip art images.

- Grab an image from a web page. When your browser displays a web page with an image, the corresponding graphics file is stored temporarily on your computer's hard disk. Most browsers have a command that lets you save that file permanently. (Although see my note about copyright concerns, below.) Here are some examples:

    Internet Explorer: Right-click the graphic and then click **Save Picture As** from the shortcut menu.

    Netscape: Right-click the graphic and click **Save Image As** from the menu that appears.

- Take advantage of the many graphics archives on the Internet. There are sites all over the Net that store dozens, even hundreds, of images. I give you some specifics in Chapter 22, "Some HTML Resources on the Web."

- If you have access to a scanner, you can use it to digitize photos, illustrations, doodles, or whatever.

- If you have a digital camera, you can hook it up to your computer and transfer the photos to your machine.

- Use the images that come with this book. I've included hundreds of GIF and JPEG images on this book's CD that I hope will come in handy.

CAUTION **Page Pitfalls**

Don't forget that many images are the property of the individuals who created them in the first place. Unless you're absolutely sure the picture is in the public domain, you need to get permission from the artist before using it. This is particularly true if your web page has a commercial slant. Note, however, that all the graphics that come on this book's CD are public domain, so you can use them at will.

Converting Graphics to GIF or JPEG

What do you do if you've got the perfect image for your web page, but it's not in GIF or JPEG format? You need to get your hands on a graphics program that's capable of converting images into different formats. Here are three that are commonly used by web graphics gurus:

◆ **Paint Shop Pro.** An excellent all-around graphics program that's great not only for converting graphics, but also for manipulating existing images and for creating new images. Best of all, there's no download required because a trial version of this program is available on this book's CD. See www.jasc.com/.

◆ **GraphX.** This is a neat little program that's happy to convert a whack of graphics formats into GIF or JPEG. A trial version of this one's also available on this book's CD. See www.group42.com.

◆ **ACDSee32.** This is a simple program that works best as a graphics viewer. However, it can also convert many different graphics formats into JPEG (but not GIF, unfortunately). A trial version of this program is available on this book's CD, as well. See www.acdsystems.com.

◆ **LView Pro.** The latest versions can perform lots of image manipulation tricks, but it's still best as a graphics converter. See www.lview.com.

◆ **PolyView.** A good converter with some interesting graphics features (such as the ability to create a web page from a set of images). See www.polybytes.com.

◆ **Graphic Workshop.** This program has a bit of a clunky interface, but it does a good job of converting graphics. See www.mindworkshop.com/alchemy/gwspro.html.

◆ **IrfanView.** This powerful program can not only convert your images to all the major formats, but it's free, too! See www.irfanview.com.

For most of these programs, you use the same steps to convert an image from one format to another:

1. In the program, select the **File, Open** command and use the Open dialog box to open the image file you want to convert.

2. Select the **File, Save As** command. The Save As dialog box drops by.

3. In the **Save as type** list, choose either JPEG or GIF. (In some programs, the latter is called CompuServe Graphics Interchange format.)

4. Click **Save.**

Webmaster Wisdom

Mac users have several graphics conversion programs to play with, including GraphicConverter (see www.lemkesoft.de/index.html) and GIFConverter (see www.kamit.com/gifconverter/).

The Nitty-Gritty at Last: The ‹IMG› Tag

Okay, enough of all that. Let's get the lead out and start squeezing some images onto our web pages. As I mentioned earlier, there's an HTML code that tells a browser to display an image: the <IMG> tag. Here's how it works:

```
<IMG SRC="filename">
```

Here, SRC is short for "source" and *filename* is the name of the graphics file you want to display. For example, suppose you have an image named logo.gif. To add it to your page, you use the following line:

```
<IMG SRC="logo.gif">
```

In effect, this tag says to the browser, "Excuse me? Would you be so kind as to go out and grab the image file named logo.gif and insert it in the page right here where the <IMG> tag is?" Dutifully, the browser loads the image and displays it in the page.

For this simple example to work, bear in mind that your HTML file and your graphics file need to be sitting in the same directory on your computer, assuming you're just testing things at home. (When you put your page online (see the next chapter), you have to send the image file to your web host and make sure it's in the same directory as your HTML file.)

Webmaster Wisdom

Your HTML file and your image file don't *have* to be in the same directory. Many webmasters create a subdirectory just for images, which keeps things neat and tidy. If you plan on doing this, make sure you study my instructions for using directories and subdirectories in Chapter 5.

Let's check out an example. Most folks are constantly tinkering with their website—modifying existing pages, pruning dead wood (I know I do a lot of that!), and adding new stuff. Until the new pages are ready, however, you don't want to subject your visitors to them. Instead, you can just display a generic page (I call it a "Procrastination Page") that tells people the new module isn't quite ready for prime time just yet.

If you'd like something similar for your web pages, here's some HTML code that does the job (look for the file named undercon.htm on this book's CD):

```
<HTML>
<HEAD>
<TITLE>Detour!</TITLE>
</HEAD>
<BODY>
<IMG SRC="constru1.gif">
<FONT SIZE="+2"><B>Web Work In Progress!</B></FONT>
<HR>
```

```
Sorry for all the mess, but I haven't quite got around to
implementing this section yet. I'm hoping to have everything
up and running real soon.
<P>
<A HREF="index.html">Go back to the home page.</A>
</BODY>
</HTML>
```

To emphasize the work-in-progress feel, this page includes a small graphic (constru1.gif) that says "Contents Under Construction" and shows a construction worker in action (see Figure 6.1). Note, too, that the page includes a link that gives the reader an easy way to get back to your home page. (In the <A> tag, make sure you change "index.html" to the appropriate name of your home page. Refer to Chapter 5, "Making the Jump to Hyperspace: Adding Links," if you need a refresher course on this link stuff.)

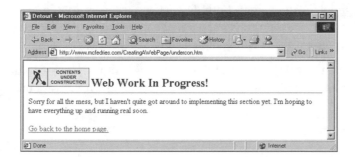

Figure 6.1

A web page to use as a substitute for pages you're still slaving away at.

Help! The #%@*&! browser won't display my images!

After adding your <IMG> tag, you might be dismayed to find that the browser refuses to display the image. Instead, it just shows a little "X" icon where the image should be. Grrrr. Here are some possible solutions to the all too common problem:

- If you're viewing your page on your home machine, the HTML file and the image files might be sitting in separate directories on your computer. Try moving your image file into the directory that holds your HTML file.

- If you're viewing your page on the web, perhaps you didn't send the image file to your server.

- Make sure you have the correct match for uppercase and lowercase letters. If an image is on your server and it's named "image.gif", and your IMG tag refers to "IMAGE.GIF", your image may not show up. In this case, you'd have to edit your IMG tag so that it refers to "image.gif".

- If you're using Netscape to view the page, make sure there are no spaces in the image's filename. Remember, too, that Netscape doesn't understand BMP graphics.

- Make sure you're not missing a quotation mark in the <IMG> tag's SRC attribute.

Specifying Image Height and Width

When surfing websites that contain graphics, have you ever wondered why it sometimes takes quite a while before anything appears on the screen? Well, one of the biggest delays is that most browsers won't display the entire page until they've calculated the height and width of all the images. The ever-intrepid browser programmers realized this, of course, and decided to do something about it. "What if," they asked themselves, "there was some way to tell the browser the size of each image in advance? That way, the browser wouldn't have to worry about it, and things would show up onscreen much faster."

Thus was born two extensions to the <IMG> tag: the HEIGHT and WIDTH attributes:

```
<IMG SRC="filename" WIDTH="x" HEIGHT="y">
```

Here, *filename* is, as usual, the name of the graphics file. For the new attributes, use *x* for the width of the graphic, and *y* for the height. Both dimensions are measured in *pixels* (short for *picture elements*), which are the tiny dots that make up any computer screen image. Any good graphics program tells you the dimensions of an image.

Alternatively, you can express the width and height as percentages of the browser window. For example, the following line displays the image bluebar.gif so its width always takes up 90 percent of the screen:

```
<IMG SRC="bluebar.gif" WIDTH=90%>
```

The advantage here is that, no matter what size screen someone is using, the graphic always takes up the same amount of room across the screen. As proof, check out the next two figures showing the bluebar.gif image with WIDTH set to 90 percent. As you can see in Figures 6.2 and 6.3, the image always usurps 90 percent of the available width, no matter how big the Internet Explorer window. (Note, too, that because I didn't specify the HEIGHT, Internet Explorer adjusts the height in proportion to the increase or decrease of the width.)

Figure 6.2

The bluebar.gif image in a relatively narrow window.

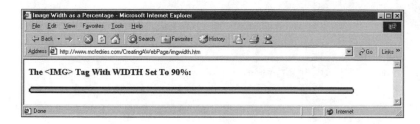

Figure 6.3

The same image in a wider window.

Aligning Text and Images

As you saw earlier in the Work-In-Progress example, you can display images and text on the same line. You set this up by inserting the <IMG> tag inside the page text.

This is all very reasonable, but you might run into problems with tall images, because the bottom of the image is aligned with the bottom of the line of text. If you prefer your text to appear at the top or the middle of the image, or if you want text to wrap around the image, the <IMG> tag has an extra ALIGN attribute that you can use. Here's how it works:

```
<IMG SRC="filename" ALIGN="VALUE">
```

Here, the *value* can be any one of the following:

- ◆ **Top.** Text is aligned with the top of the image.
- ◆ **Middle.** Text is aligned with the middle of the image.
- ◆ **Bottom.** Text is aligned with the bottom of the image.
- ◆ **Left.** The image appears on the left side of the browser window, and text wraps around the image on the right.
- ◆ **Right.** The image appears on the right side of the browser window, and text wraps around the image on the left.

The following HTML listing (align.htm) gives you a demo (Figure 6.4 shows the results):

```
<HTML>
<HEAD>
<TITLE>Aligning Text and Images</TITLE>
</HEAD>
<BODY>
<IMG SRC="constru1.gif" ALIGN="TOP"> This text appears at the top of the image.
<P>
<IMG SRC="constru1.gif" ALIGN="MIDDLE"> This text appears in the middle of the
image.
</P><P>
```

```
<IMG SRC="constru1.gif" ALIGN="BOTTOM"> This text appears at the bottom of the
image.
</P><P>
<IMG SRC="constru1.gif" ALIGN="LEFT">
As you saw earlier in the Work-In-Progress example, you can display images and
text on the same line. You set this up by inserting the &lt;IMG&gt; tag inside
the page text.
<IMG SRC="constru1.gif" ALIGN="RIGHT">
This is all very reasonable, but you might run into problems with tall images,
because the bottom of the image is aligned with the bottom of the line. If you
prefer your text to appear at the top or the middle of the image, or if you
want text to wrap around the image, the &lt;IMG&gt; tag has an extra ALIGN
attribute that you can use.
</P>
</BODY>
</HTML>
```

Figure 6.4

The <IMG> tag's ALIGN options.

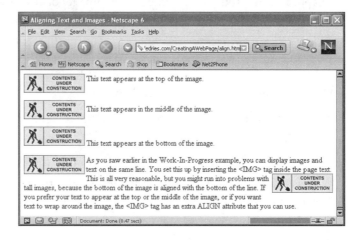

Webmaster Wisdom

What happens if you're using ALIGN="LEFT" or ALIGN="RIGHT" to wrap text around an image, but then you want to start a new line or a new paragraph *after* the image? The solution here is to toss in a
 (line break) tag that uses the CLEAR attribute. There are three different CLEAR values you can use:

```
<BR CLEAR="LEFT">
<BR CLEAR="RIGHT">
<BR CLEAR="ALL">
```

Use CLEAR="LEFT" to start the next line when the left margin is clear; use CLEAR="RIGHT" to start the next line when the right margin is clear; use CLEAR="ALL" to start the next line when both margins are clear.

Handling Graphically Challenged Text Browsers

Most browsers come with a feature that enables you to turn off the display of images. This feature is a favorite among people with slow Internet connections because it means that most web pages load considerably faster. In this case, the user sees only an icon where the image would normally appear.

If you want to help out these users, you can provide a description of each of your images. To do this, the <IMG> tag offers an extra ALT attribute you can throw in to provide alternative text that appears in place of the image. Here's the general format:

```
<IMG SRC="filename" ALT="alternative text">
```

Here, *alternative text* is whatever text you want to use instead of the graphic. For example, if you have a picture of your hometown in your page, you can display the words *A lovely pic of my hometown* with the following line:

```
<IMG SRC="hometown.gif" ALT="A lovely pic of my hometown">
```

Webmaster Wisdom

Another excellent reason to include the ALT attribute in all your <IMG> tags is that it helps visually impaired surfers to navigate your page because they depend upon the ALT text to "see" what an image is all about.

Note, too, that even if a surfer does have graphics turned on, using ALT is still a good idea because many modern browsers (particularly Internet Explorer) display the ALT text in a banner when users hover their mouse pointers over the image.

Separating Text and Images

If you surround your images with text, you'll find that the text often bumps up against the image borders. To create a margin between the image and the surrounding text, add the HSPACE and VSPACE attributes to the <IMG> tag:

```
<IMG SRC="filename" HSPACE="h" VSPACE="v">
```

HSPACE creates a margin between the image and the text to its left and right (where *h* is the size of the margin, in pixels). VSPACE creates a margin between the image and the text above and below (where *v* is the size of the margin, in pixels).

Good Uses for Images on Your Web Page

Images are endlessly useful, and they're an easy way to give your page a professional look and feel. Although I'm sure you can think of all kinds of ways to put pictures to work, here are a few suggestions:

- A company logo on a business-related page
- Graphics from an ad
- Drawings done by the kids in a paint program
- Charts and graphs
- Fancy-schmancy fonts
- Your signature
- Using a graphic line in place of the <HR> tag
- Using graphic bullets to create a better bulleted list

> **Words from the Web**
>
> A **Jpig** is a web page that takes forever to load because it's either jammed to the hilt with graphics, or because it contains one or two really large images. Also, a **vanity plate** is an annoyingly large image that serves no useful purpose.

> **Page Pitfalls**
>
> Although graphics have a thousand-and-one uses, that doesn't mean you should include a thousand-and-one images in each page. Bear in mind that many of your readers are accessing your site from a slow modem link, so graphics take forever to load. If you have too many images, most folks give up and head somewhere else.

You might be wondering how to do that last item. Well, there are a number of ways to go about it, but the one I use for short lists is to create a definition list (see Chapter 4, "The Gist of a List: Adding Lists to Your Page") and precede each item in the list with a graphic bullet. For example, the following code uses a file called redball.gif:

```
<DL>
<DD><IMG SRC="redball.gif">First item</DD>
<DD><IMG SRC="redball.gif">Second item</DD>
<DD><IMG SRC="redball.gif">Third item</DD>
</DL>
```

If the text in one or more of the bullets is quite long, a better approach is to create a table. I show you how to do this in Chapter 10, "Table Talk: Adding Tables to Your Page."

Changing the Page Background

Depending on the browser you use, web page text and graphics often float in a sea of dull, drab gray, or plain white. It's about as exciting as a yawning festival. To give things a little pep, you can change the background color your page appears on to whatever suits your style. You can also specify an image to appear as the background.

Using a Color as the Background

The guts of your page appears within the body, so it makes sense that you change the background by tweaking the <BODY> tag. The simplest method is specifying a new background color:

```
<BODY BGCOLOR="#rrggbb">
```

Yes, you're right: The *rrggbb* part is the same color code that I talked about back in Chapter 3, "From Buck-Naked to Beautiful: Dressing Up Your Page." Figure 6.5 shows an example page that uses a black background (see blakback.htm on this book's CD). Note, too, that I had to use white for the page text so the surfer can read the page (which is kind of important).

CAUTION

Page Pitfalls

If the user tries to print your page, note most browsers don't include the background color (that is, they print using a white background). So white or light text (such as the text shown in Figure 6.5) won't show up in the printout.

Figure 6.5

A page that uses a black background and white text.

Using an Image as the Background

Instead of a color, you can specify an image to use as the background (similar to the way Windows and the Mac let you cover the desktop with wallpaper). This doesn't have to be (nor should it be) a large image. The browser takes smaller graphics and *tiles* them so they fill up the entire window. The secret to background images is the <BODY> tag's BACKGROUND attribute:

```
<BODY BACKGROUND="filename">
```

Here, *filename* is the name of the graphics file you want to use.

Webmaster Wisdom

One of the most popular styles of web page backgrounds these days is the margined background which features a colored strip down the left (and sometimes also the right) side of the page. I show you how to create this attractive background style in Chapter 10.

In general, I recommend sticking with just a different background color. Tiled background images take longer to load, and they can make text devilishly difficult to read. If you really want to use a background image, then I suggest you also use the BGCOLOR attribute and set it equal to a color that more or less approximates the background color of the image. This will make your page look a bit nicer while it's loading.

A Special Image: The Pixel Shim (spacer.gif)

One of the biggest problems faced by web designers is positioning text and images with precision. Regular HTML just doesn't have any way of manipulating the position of any object.

You can get around this limitation by using something called a *pixel shim*. A pixel shim is a transparent GIF that's 1 pixel wide and 1 pixel tall. Because it's transparent, it doesn't show up on the page. However, by manipulating the <IMG> tag's HEIGHT and WIDTH attributes, you can create any amount of blank space that you need, which is great for precise positioning of text and images (I'll show you an example in Chapter 10).

I've put a pixel shim on this book's CD. Look for the file named spacer.gif.

Giving a GIF a Transparent Background

I talked about the page background earlier, but there's another type of background that you have to worry about, as well: the background of a specific image. For example, if you have an image of a house that's surrounded by black, the black is said to be the image's background color.

One of the features you get with a GIF image is the ability to set the background color to be "transparent." This just means that the browser doesn't show the background when it displays the file. This can make an image look much neater. For example, compare the two images shown in Figure 6.6. See how the one on the right doesn't show the black background?

Figure 6.6

GIF files can have transparent backgrounds.

Here's how you give a GIF file a transparent background in Paint Shop Pro:

1. Load your image into the program.
2. Select the **Colors, Set Palette Transparency** command.
3. If Paint Shop Pro mumbles something about reducing the number of layers and colors, click **Yes** and then click **OK** in the Decrease Color Depth dialog box.
4. In the Set Palette Transparency dialog box, activate the **Set the transparency value to palette entry** option.
5. Move the mouse pointer into the image and then click the color that you want to be transparent.
6. Click **OK.**
7. Activate the **Colors, View Palette Transparency** command. This will show the background color as a checkerboard pattern, which is what Paint Shop Pro uses to indicate transparency.
8. Select **File, Save As** to open the Save As dialog box.
9. In the **Save as type** list, choose **CompuServe Graphics Interchange (*.gif).**
10. Click **Options,** activate the **Version 89a** option, and click **OK.**
11. Click **Save.**

CAUTION

Page Pitfalls

For this transparency stuff to work, your image must have a solid color background. If you try to use an image that has a shaded or multi-colored background, you won't get a proper transparent effect.

It's also possible to make a transparent background in Paint Shop Pro when you start an image from scratch. In the New Image dialog box, select **Transparent** in the **Background color** list box. Then select **Colors, Set Palette Transparency.** In the dialog box, activate **Set the transparency value to the current background color** and then click **OK.**

The Least You Need to Know

♦ Graphics formats knocked down to size. There are billions and billions of graphics formats floating around, but only two are used extensively on the web: GIF and JPEG.

♦ Where to get images. Other than your own artistic endeavors, graphics are available from clip art libraries, other web pages, Internet archives, via scanner or fax, and on the CD that accompanies this book.

♦ Converting graphics to web-friendly formats. If you have a graphic that isn't GIF or JPEG, convert it using Paint Shop Pro or one of the other graphics programs that comes on the CD in this book.

♦ The <IMG> tag. To add an image to your web page, include the <IMG SRC= "*filename*"> tag, where *filename* is the name of the graphics file.

♦ Page background makeovers. To change the page background, use the <BODY> tag's BGCOLOR attribute to change the color and/or the BACKGROUND attribute to use an image as the background.

♦ Pixel perfect positioning. The pixel shim (spacer.gif) is a 1 × 1 transparent image. You use it to precisely position text and other graphics by putting spacer.gif in an <IMG> tag and then manipulating the HEIGHT and WIDTH attributes as needed.

Chapter 7

The Host with the Most: Choosing a Web Hosting Provider

In This Chapter

- ◆ Understanding web hosting providers
- ◆ A rundown of the various choices for hosting your page
- ◆ A guide to choosing the host that's right for you
- ◆ A review of some companies that will put your pages on the web
- ◆ Everything you need to know about this web hosting hoo-ha

I've covered a lot of ground in the past few chapters, and no doubt you've worked your fingers to the bone applying the electronic equivalent of spit and polish to buff your web page to an impressive sheen. However, there are still a couple of related tasks you need to perform before you can cross "Make Web Page" off your to-do list:

- ◆ You have to find a web home for your home page.
- ◆ You have to move your files into that new home.

This chapter takes care of the first task by showing you how to look for and choose a spot on the web where friends, family, and even total strangers from far-flung corners of the world can eyeball your creation. Once you've done that, Chapter 8, "Publish or Perish: Putting Your Page on the Web," gives you the details of getting your files from here to there.

What in the name of Sam Hill is a web hosting provider?

The third most common question posed by web page publishing neophytes is "Where the heck do I put my page when I'm done?" (The most common question, in case you're wondering, is "How do I get started?" The second most common question is "Why is Jerry Lewis so popular in France?") If you've asked that question yourself, then you're doing okay, because it means you're clued into something crucial: Just because you've created a web page and you have an Internet connection doesn't mean your page is automatically a part of the web.

The reasons for this are mind-numbingly technical, but the basic idea is that people on the Net have no way of "getting to" your computer and, even if they did, your computer isn't set up to hand out documents (such as web pages) to visitors who ask for them.

Computers that can do this are called *servers* (because they "serve" stuff out to the Net), and computers that specialize in distributing web pages are called *web servers*. So, to get to the point at long last, your web page isn't on the web until you store it on a web server. Because this computer is, in effect, playing "host" to your pages, such machines are also called *web hosts*. Companies that run these web hosts are called *web hosting providers*.

Okay, that's all more or less reasonable. Now, just how does one go about finding one of these web server thingamajigs? Well, the answer to that depends on a bunch of factors, including the type of page you have, how you got connected to the Internet in the first place, and how much money you're willing to shell out for the privilege. In the end, you have three choices:

- Use your existing Internet provider.
- Try to find a free hosting provider.
- Sign up with a commercial hosting provider.

Use your existing Internet provider.

If you access the Internet via a corporate or educational network, your institution might have its own web server that you can use. If you get your Net jollies through an Internet service provider (ISP), ask it if it has a web server available. Many providers provide space so that their customers can put up personal pages free of charge. (This is particularly true of the big online service providers such as AOL.)

Try to find a free hosting provider.

If cash is in short supply, or if you just have a naturally thrifty nature, there are a few hosting providers that will bring your web pages in from the cold out of the goodness of their hearts. In some cases these services are open only to specific groups, such as students, artists, nonprofit organizations, less fortunate members of the Partridge Family, and so on. However, there are plenty of providers that put up personal home pages free of charge. What's the catch? Well, there are almost always restrictions both on how much data you can store and on the type of data you can store (no ads, no dirty pictures, and so on). You'll probably also be required to display on your pages some kind of "banner" advertisement for the hosting provider.

Later in this chapter, I supply you with a collection of sites that offer lists of free web hosts. See the section titled "Lists of Free Web Hosts."

Sign up with a commercial hosting provider.

For personal and business-related web pages, many web artisans end up renting a chunk of a web server from a commercial hosting provider. You normally fork over a setup fee to get your account going, and then you're looking at a monthly fee. Why fork out all those shekels when there are so many free sites lying around? Because, as with most things in life, you get what you pay for. By paying for your host, you generally get more features, better service, and fewer annoyances (such as the ads that most free sites have to display).

Again, later in this chapter I take you through a bunch of sites that provide lists of commercial web hosts. See the section titled "Lists of Commercial Web Hosts."

A Buyer's Guide to Web Hosting

Unfortunately, choosing a web host isn't as straightforward as you might like it to be. For one thing, there are hundreds of hosts out there clamoring for your business; for another, the pitches and come-ons employed by your average web host are strewn with jargon and technical terms. I can't help reduce the number of web hosts, but I can help you to understand what the heck those hosts are yammering on about. Here's a list of the terms that you're most likely to come across when researching web hosts:

Page Pitfalls

If you exceed your bandwidth limit, users will still be able to get to your pages. However, almost all web hosts charge you an extra fee for exceeding your bandwidth, so check this out before signing up. The usual penalty is a set fee per megabyte or gigabyte that you exceed your cap.

Page Pitfalls

If you decide to get your own domain name, make sure that *you* own the domain, not the web host. Also, make sure that your name is listed as the domain's "administrative" contact and that the web host is listed only as the "technical" contact.

◆ **Storage space**   This refers to the amount of room allotted to you on the host's web server to store your files. The amount of acreage you get determines the amount of data you can store. For example, if you get a 1MB (one megabyte) limit, you can't store more than 1MB worth of files on the server. HTML files don't take up much real estate, but large graphics sure do, so you need to watch your limit. Generally speaking, the more you pay for a host, the more storage space you get.

◆ **Bandwidth**   This is a measure of how much of your data the server serves. For example, suppose the HTML file for your page is 1KB (one kilo-byte) and the graphics associated with the page consume 9KB. If someone accesses your page, the server ships out a total of 10KB; if 10 people access the page (either at the same time or over a period of time), the total bandwidth is 100KB. Most hosts give you a bandwidth limit (or "cap"), which is most often a certain number of mega-bytes or gigabytes per month. (A gigabyte is equal to 1,000 megabytes.) Again, the more you pay the greater the bandwidth you get.

◆ **Domain name**   A domain name is a general Internet address such as mcfedries. com or whitehouse.gov. They tend to be easier to remember than the long-winded addresses that most web hosts supply you by default, so they're a popular feature. There are two types of domain names available:

A regular domain name (yourdomain.com or yourdomain.org)   To get one of these domains, you either need to contact Network Solutions (www. networksolutions.com) directly, or you can use one of the many other registration services (such as register.com). A more convenient route is to choose a web hosting provider that will do this for you. Either way, it will usually cost you US$35 per year. (Although some hosts offer cheap domains as a "loss leader" and recoup their costs with hosting fees.) If you go the direct route, you have to find a web host who is willing to host your domain.

A subdomain name (yourdomain.webhostdomain.com)   In this case, "webhostdomain.com" is the domain name of the web hosting company, and they simply tack on whatever name you want to the beginning. There are many web hosts who will provide you with this type of domain, often for free.

- **E-mail mailboxes**   Most hosts offer you an e-mail mailbox along with your web space. The more you pay, the more mailboxes you get.

- **E-mail forwarding**   This service enables you to have messages that are sent to your web host address rerouted to some other e-mail address.

- **Shared server**   If the host offers this type of server (it's also called a *virtual server*), it means that you'll be sharing the server with other websites (there could be dozens or even hundreds of them). The web host takes care of all the highly technical server management chores, so all you have to do is maintain your site. This is by far the best (and cheapest) choice for individuals or small business types.

- **Dedicated server**   This type of server means that you get your very own server computer on the host. That may sound like a good thing, but it's usually up to you to manage the server, which can be a dauntingly technical task. Also, dedicated servers are hideously expensive (they usually start at a few hundred dollars a month).

- **Operating system**   This refers to the operating system on the web server. You usually have two choices: Unix (or Linux) and Windows (NT or 2000). Unix systems have the reputation of being very reliable and fast, even under heavy traffic loads, so they're usually the best choice for a shared server. Windows systems are a better choice for dedicated servers because they're easier to administer than their Unix brethren. Note, too, that Unix servers are case sensitive in terms of file and directory names, but Windows servers are not.

- **Ad requirements**   Almost all free web hosts require you to display some type of advertising on your pages. This could be a banner ad across the top of the page, a "pop-up" ad that appears each time a person accesses your pages, or a "watermark" ad, usually a semitransparent logo that "hovers" over your page. Escaping these annoying ads is the number one reason, by far, that webmasters switch to a commercial host.

- **Uptime**   This refers to the percentage of time that the host's server is up and serving. There's no such thing as 100 percent uptime because all servers require maintenance and upgrades at some point. However, the best hosts will have uptime numbers over 99 percent. (If a host doesn't advertise its uptime, it's probably because it's very low. Be sure to ask before committing yourself.)

- **Tech support**   If you have problems setting up or accessing your site, you want to know that help is just around the corner. Therefore, the best hosts offer "24/7" tech

Webmaster Wisdom

People often ask me if I can supply them with a script or some other means to disable or hide the ads displayed by their free web host. My answer is always an emphatic "No!" because those ads are how the host makes its money. If enough people circumvent the ads, the host will eventually lose money and will no longer be able to offer free hosting.

support, which means that you can contact the company—either by phone or e-mail—24 hours a day, seven days a week.

- **cgi-bin**   This is a special directory that is meant to store CGI "scripts" that perform behind-the-scenes tasks. The most common use for these scripts is to process form data, as described in Chapter 12, "Need Feedback? Create a Form!" If you want to use any of the prefab scripts available on the web, or if you want to create your own, then you'll need a cgi-bin directory in which to store them. You should also check to see if the cgi-bin is shared with other sites or if you have your own. In general, the host will place greater restrictions on a shared cgi-bin than on a personal one.

- **Scripts**   Speaking of scripts, most good hosts will also offer you a selection of ready-to-run scripts for things such as guest books and e-mailing form data.

- **FTP access**   As you'll see in Chapter 8, you'll usually use the Internet's FTP service to transfer your files from your computer to the web host. If a host offers FTP access (some hosts have their own method for transferring files), make sure that you can use it any time you like and that there are no restrictions on the amount of data you can transfer at one time.

- **Anonymous FTP**   This variation on the FTP theme enables you to set up your own FTP server where other people can log in and download files from or upload files to your site. The more you pay for your site, the more likely you are to get this feature.

- **FrontPage support**   This means that you can use a program called Microsoft FrontPage to manage your website from the comfort of your computer.

- **Website statistics**   These stats tell you things such as how many people have visited your site, which pages are the most popular, how much bandwidth you're consuming, which browsers and browser versions surfers are using, and more. Most decent hosts will offer a ready-made stats package, but the best ones will also give you access to the "raw" log files so that you can play with the data yourself.

- **E-commerce**   Some hosts offer a service that lets you set up a web "store" so that you can sell stuff on your site. That service usually includes a "shopping script" script, access to credit card authorization and other payment systems, and the ability to set up a secure connection. You usually get this only in the more expensive hosting packages, and you'll most often have to pay a setup fee to get your store built.

- **Scalability**   This buzzword means that the host is able to modify your site's features as required. For example, if your site becomes very popular, you might need to increase your bandwidth limit. If the host is scalable, then it can easily change your limit (or any other feature of your site).

A List of Lists: Sites That Offer Lists of Web Hosts

Now that you understand some of the lingo and concepts that surround this web hosting business, you're ready to start researching the hosts to find one that suits your web style. As I mentioned earlier, there are hundreds of hosts, so how is a body supposed to whittle them down to some kind of short list? Here are a few pointers:

- ◆ **Ask your friends and colleagues.** The best way to find a good host is that old standby, word of mouth. If someone you trust says a host is good, chances are you won't be disappointed. (This is assuming that you and your pal have similar hosting needs. If you want a full-blown e-commerce site, don't solicit recommendations from someone who has only a humble homepage.)

- ◆ **Solicit host reviews from experts.** Ask existing webmasters and other people "in the know" about which hosts they recommend or have heard good things about. Sites such as Epinions.com are also good sources of host reviews.

- ◆ **Contact web host customers.** Visit sites that use a particular web host and send an e-mail message to the webmaster asking what she thinks of the host's service.

- ◆ **Peruse the lists of web hosts.** There are a number of sites out there that track and compare web hosts, so they're an easy way to get in a lot of research.

The next couple of sections provide you with capsule reviews and addresses of these host lists.

Lists of Free Web Hosts

During the height of the dot-com frenzy, free web hosts seemed to sprout with a weed-like intensity. When the alleged "new economy" became old news and the dot-commers went down in flames, a lot of the free hosts went sneakers up, as well. Of the survivors, many converted themselves into commercial hosts to survive. There are still lots of free hosts left, however, and you can find most of them via the following sites that review or compare these hosts.

- ◆ **www.100best-free-web-space.com.** This top-quality site gives you a summary of the features of each free host, ranks the host on a scale of one to five, and offers a short review of the host.

- ◆ **www.fwpreview.com.** Max Lee maintains this excellent resource. Not only do you get

> **Webmaster Wisdom**
>
> For your shopping convenience, I've gathered the links shown here and in the next section and dropped them into a web page. It's called hostlist.htm, and you'll find it on this book's CD. To check out a list, open the page in your favorite browser, click the link, and you're there!

links to sites that offer free web hosting, but Max also tells you how much disk space you get, whether or not the service provides an HTML editor, and more.

♦ **www.freewebsiteproviders.com.** This comprehensive site lists hundreds of free hosts divided into various categories, including Personal, Business, Nonprofit, and Special Interest. The site provides you with a chart showing the features offered by each host and there are also reviews of some hosts.

♦ **www.freeindex.com.** This site contains not only a decent list of free web hosts, but also info on free e-mail, counters, CGI hosting, graphics, guest books, chat rooms, and more.

♦ **www.freewebspace.net.** One of the nice features about this site is that it includes a large number of user reviews for various free web hosts. There are also discussion areas, news stories about hosts, and much more.

♦ **dir.yahoo.com/Business_and_Economy/Business_to_Business/ Communications_and_Networking/Internet_and_World_Wide_Web/Network _Service_Providers/Hosting/Web_Site_Hosting/Free_Web_Pages.** As usual, Yahoo! is one of the best places to go for information. In this case, it offers an extensive index of free web hosting providers. And, as usual, the URL is finger-numbingly long.

Lists of Commercial Web Hosts

The world's capitalists—efficient free-market types that they are—smelled plenty of money to be had after the explosive growth of the web became apparent. This means there's certainly no shortage of commercial web hosting providers available. In fact, there are hundreds of the darn things. Once again, here are some sites that can supply you with lists of such providers.

♦ **www.cnet.com/internet.** This excellent site divides hosts into various categories and it also offers a "Most Popular" list so you can see who's using who.

♦ **www.findahost.com.** This site lets you search for a web host by selecting the features you need.

♦ **www.hostfinders.com.** As the name implies, this site also offers a search feature for finding a web host that has what you want.

♦ **www.hostindex.com.** This site offers a large index of web hosts. However, its best feature is a monthly ranking of web hosts based on user feedback, features, pricing, and more.

♦ **www.thelist.internet.com.** This is *the* site for listings of Internet Service Providers. For our purposes, it also tells you whether or not the providers host web pages.

- **www.tophosts.com.** This impressively comprehensive site lists hosts in various categories, offers a "HostMatch" service to help you find a host that's right for you, has news articles and information related to hosting, and much more.

- **www.webhostdir.com.** Make sure you have plenty of time to spare when you visit this site. It not only lists hosts in a wide range of categories, but it also offers a quotation service, a search service, news and how-to articles, discussion forums, host awards, and more.

- **dir.yahoo.com/Business_and_Economy/Business_to_Business/ Communications_and_Networking/Internet_and_World_Wide_Web/ Network_Service_Providers/Hosting/Web_Site_Hosting/Directories.** Yahoo! maintains a list of web hosting directories at this address.

The Least You Need to Know

- Web hosting provider. This is a company that runs a web server and supplies you with a chunk of hard disk real estate on that server so that other people can enjoy your pages.

- The thrifty route. If you don't want to spend any money to host your site, either ask your ISP if it does web hosting, or try out one of the free web hosts.

- Much ado about data. The two most important things to bear in mind when shopping for a web host are storage—how much room you have on the server to store your files—and bandwidth—how much of your data can be served up to surfers.

- The domain name game. If you want to get yourself your very own domain name, either you can ask your web host to register one for you or you can find a host who'll create a subdomain.

- Finding a good host. To help you choose from the hundreds of hosts out there, ask people you know to recommend a host, look for expert reviews, contact a web host's customers, and use the hosts lists that I provided in this chapter.

Chapter 8

Publish or Perish: Putting Your Page on the Web

In This Chapter

- A look inside your new web home
- How to get your web pages to the provider
- Getting your site on the search engines
- A blow-by-blow description of the whole web page publishing thing

In the same way that (some say) a tree falling in the forest makes no sound if no one is around to hear it, a web page makes no impact if no one else can see it. In philosophical circles, this conundrum is known as the Use-It-Or-Lose-It Paradox. What it really means is that all your efforts of the past few chapters will have been wasted if you don't take that final step, your biggest and boldest one yet: publishing your pages to the web.

This chapter shows you how to help your web pages emigrate from their native land (your hard disk) to the New World (the web). I show you how to best prepare them for the journey, how to select a mode of transportation, and how to settle your pages when they've arrived.

What does your web home look like?

After you sign up with a web hosting provider and your account is established, the web administrator creates two things for you: a directory on the server computer that you can use to store your web page files, and your very own web address. (This is also true if you're using a web server associated with your corporate or school network.)

The directory usually takes one of the following forms:

```
/yourname/
/usr/yourname/
/usr/yourname/www-docs/
```

In each case, *yourname* is the login name (or user name) that the provider assigns to you, or it may be your domain name (minus the .com part). Remember, this is a slice of the host's web server and this slice is yours to monkey around with as you see fit. This usually means you can do all or most of the following:

◆ Add files to the directory

◆ Add subdirectories to the directory

◆ Move or copy files from one directory to another

◆ Rename files or directories

◆ Delete files from the directory

Your web address will normally take one of the following shapes:

> http://provider/yourname/
>
> http://yourname.provider/
>
> http://www.yourname/

Here, *provider* is the host name of your provider (for example, www.angelfire.com or just angelfire.com) and *login* is your login name or domain name. Here are some examples:

> http://www.geocities.com/paulmcfedries/
>
> http://mcfedries.150m.com/
>
> http://www.mcfedries.com/

The Relationship Between Your Directory and Your Web Address

There's a direct and important relationship between your server directory and your address. That is, your address actually "points to" your directory and it enables other people to view the files that you store in that directory. For example, suppose I decide to store a file named thingamajig.html in my directory and that my main address is http://mcfedries.150m.com/. This means that someone else can view that file by typing the following URL into his browser:

> http://mcfedries.150m.com/thingamajig.html

Similarly, suppose I create a subdirectory named CreatingAWebPage and I use it to store a file named index.html. This means that a surfer can view that file by convincing her browser to head for the following URL:

> http://mcfedries.150m.com/
> creatingawebpage/index.html

In other words, folks can surf to your files and directories just by strategically tacking on the appropriate filenames and directory names after your main web address.

> **Words from the Web**
> Moving a file from your computer to a remote location (such as your web host's server) is known in the file transfer trade as **uploading**.

Making Your Hard Disk and Your Web Home Mirror Images of Each Other

For largish sites, I mentioned back in Chapter 5, "Making the Jump to Hyperspace: Adding Links," that you should divide your stuff into separate subdirectories to keep things organized. (If you have a small site and are planning to keep all your files in a single directory, feel free to leap right over this section without penalty or embarrassment.) If you're going to go this route, then you can make your uploading duties immeasurably easier if you set up your own computer to have the same directory setup as the one you plan to use at your website. You can go about this in a number of ways, but here's the simplest:

◆ Create a folder on your computer that acts as the "home base" for all your HTML files. This is the equivalent of your main directory at your web hosting provider. Note that you can name this folder whatever you like (for example, HTML Stuff or My Web Weavings).

◆ Create your subfolders under this home base folder. In this case, the subfolders you create must have the same names as the ones you want to use on your website.

> **Webmaster Wisdom**
> To help reduce the confusion, in this chapter when I use the word **folder**, I'm referring to a directory on your computer; when I use the term **directory**, I'm referring to a directory on your web host's server.

To see why this is so useful, suppose you set up a subfolder on your computer named graphics that you use to store your image files. To insert into your page a file named mydog.jpg from that folder, you'd use the following tag:

```
<IMG SRC="graphics/mydog.jpg">
```

When you send your HTML file to the server and you then display the file in a browser, it will look for mydog.jpg in the graphics subdirectory. If you don't have such a subdirectory—either you didn't create it or you used a different name, such as images—the browser won't find mydog.jpg and your image won't show. In other words, if you match the subdirectories on your web server with the subfolders on your computer, your page will work properly without modifications both at home and on the web.

CAUTION: Page Pitfalls

One common faux pas that beginning HTMLers make is to include the drive and all the folder names when referencing a file. Here's an example:

```
<IMG SRC="C:\My Documents\HTML Stuff\graphics\mydog.jpg">
```

This image will show up just fine when it's viewed from your computer, but it will fail miserably when you upload it to the server and view it on the web. That's because the "C:\My Documents\HTML Stuff\" part exists only on your computer.

Figure 8.1 shows a folder structure that I'll use as an example in this chapter. The main folder is called HTML Stuff, there's a subfolder called graphics for image files, and there are four subfolders that store related HTML files: books (which has its own subfolders), links, tirades, and wordplay.

Figure 8.1

The folder structure I'll use as an example.

A Pre-Trip Checklist

After you decide on a hosting provider and a directory structure, you're just about ready to transfer your files to your directory on your hosting provider's server. Before you do that, however, you need to do the look-before-you-leap thing. That is, you need to give

your files the once-over to make sure everything's on the up-and-up. Here's a short check-
list to run through:

- HTML isn't hard, but it's fussy, persnick-
  ety stuff. If you miss even the smallest
  part of a single tag, your entire page could
  look like a real dog's breakfast (or not show
  up at all). To avoid this, recheck your tags to
  make sure they look right. In particular,
  make sure that each tag's opening angle
  bracket (<) has a corresponding closing angle
  bracket (>). Also, make sure that links and
  <IMG> tags have both opening and closing
  quotation marks ("), and that tags such as
  <B>, <I>, <U>, <H1>, <OL>, <DL>, and
  <A>—have their appropriate closing tags
  (</B>, </I>, and so on).

- URLs are easy to mistype, so double-
  check all your links. The best way to do
  this is to load the page into a browser and
  then try clicking the links.

- Different browsers have different ways of
  interpreting your HTML codes. To make
  sure your web page looks good to a large
  percentage of your readers, load the page
  into as many different browsers as you can.
  Note that Netscape Navigator and Internet
  Explorer together control about 98 percent
  of the browser market, so you should always
  run your page through some version of these
  two programs.

Webmaster Wisdom

The Big Two browsers—
Internet Explorer and
Netscape Navigator—have
come out with various versions over the years, and
they render HTML in subtly different ways. So, if possible, you
should check your page with as
many different versions as you
can. At the very least, you should
try out Internet Explorer 5.x and
Netscape Navigator 4.x.

Webmaster Wisdom

If you want to give your
page a thorough HTML
check, there are resources
on the web that do the
dirty work for you. These
so-called HTML "analyzers"
check your page for improper
tags, mismatched brackets, missing quotation marks, and more.
I tell you about a few of these
in Chapter 22, "Some HTML
Resources on the Web."

- Pages can also look radically different depending on the screen resolution. If your
  video card supports them, make sure you view your page using the following resolutions: 640 × 480, 800 × 600, and 1024 × 768. (To change the resolution in Windows,
  right-click the desktop, click **Properties,** and then select the **Settings** tab. For the
  Mac, pull down the Apple menu and then select **Control Panels, Monitors.**)

- One of the advantages of using a word processor to create HTML files is that you
  usually have access to a spell checker. If so, make sure you use it to look for spelling
  gaffes in your page. You might want to add all the HTML tags to your custom

dictionary so they don't constantly trip up the spell checker. In any case, you should always reread your text to make sure things make sense and are at least semigrammatical.

♦ Make backup copies of all your files before beginning the transfer. If anything untoward should happen while you're sending your files, you'll be able to recover gracefully.

Okay, ship it!

Now, at long last, you're ready to get your page on the web. If the web server is on your company's or school's network, you send the files over the network to the directory set up by your system administrator. Otherwise, you send the files to the directory created for you on the hosting provider's web server.

In the latter case, you probably need to use the Internet's FTP (File Transfer Protocol) service. (Note, however, that AOL and some web hosts offer their own file upload services.) For this portion of the show, you have a number of ways to proceed:

♦ Use the demo version of CuteFTP that comes on the CD with this book. This is a Windows FTP program that makes it easy to send files from your computer to the web server. The next couple of sections show how to configure and use CuteFTP to get the job done.

♦ If you're an America Online user, you can use AOL's FTP service to ship your files to your "My Place" home directory.

♦ Mac users have a number of FTP programs to try out, including the most popular one, which is called Fetch. You can get them via TUCOWS (www.tucows.com/). Click the Macintosh link.

Adding Your Web Host's FTP Site

Before you can send anything to the web server, you have to tell CuteFTP how to find it and how to log on. Thankfully, you have to do this only once, and you're set for life (or at least until you move to another web host). Before you begin, you need three pieces of data, which your web host should have given to you when you signed up:

♦ The address of the host's FTP site. (This most often takes the form ftp.myhost.com, but in many cases you use the address of the web host, such as www.myhost.com.)

♦ Your FTP user name (which is usually the same as your website user name).

♦ Your FTP password (which, again, is usually the same as your website password)

With that info in hand, here's how it's done:

1. Start CuteFTP. The Site Manager dialog box appears.

2. Click the **New site** button. CuteFTP then prompts you to enter the settings for the new site.

3. In the **Label for site** text box, enter a name for this site (something like "My Web Home" or the name of the web host is just fine).

4. In the **FTP Host Address** text box, enter the address of the host's FTP site.

5. Enter your FTP user name in the **FTP site User Name** text box.

6. Enter your FTP password in the **FTP site Password** text box. (Note that, for security reasons, the password appears as asterisks.)

7. Click the **Edit** button to come face to face with the Site Properties dialog box.

8. Use the **Default Local Directory** text box to enter the drive and folder on your computer that contains your web page files. (If you're not sure, click the folder icon to the right of this box to pick out the folder using a dialog box.)

9. Click **OK** to the Site Settings dialog box. Figure 8.2 shows this dialog box with the settings completed for a GeoCities account.

10. Click **Exit** to store your settings.

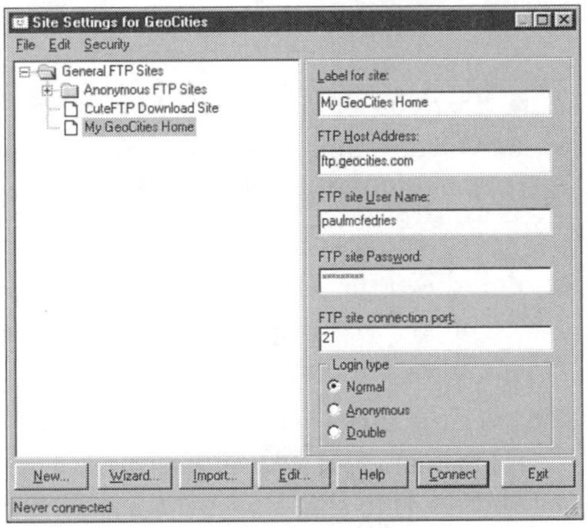

Figure 8.2

An example of a completed FTP Site Edit dialog box.

Sending the Files via FTP

With CuteFTP ready for action, you can get down to it. Here are the basic steps to follow to send your files to the web server via FTP:

1. If you haven't done so already, establish a connection with your regular Internet Service Provider.

2. Select **File, Site Manager** (or press **F4**) to get reacquainted with the Site Manager.

3. Make sure the site you just added is highlighted and then click the **Connect** button. After you're logged in to the server, CuteFTP might display a Login Messages dialog box.

4. If so, click **OK.** You're now at the main CuteFTP window. As you can see in Figure 8.3, this window shows your computer's files on the left and your web server files on the right. (The latter, not surprisingly, will be empty right now since you haven't sent anything to the server yet.)

Figure 8.3

CuteFTP shows your computer's files on the left and your web server files on the right.

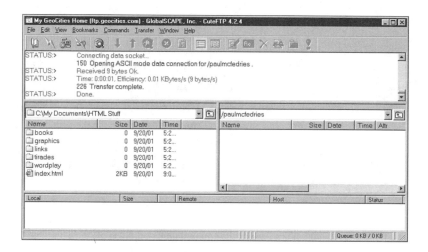

5. Select all the files on your computer that you want to send. The easiest way to do this is to hold down the **Ctrl** key, move your mouse into the left box, and then click each file that you're sending. When you finish selecting the files, release the **Ctrl** key.

Webmaster Wisdom

A quick way to send files to the server is to use your mouse to drag the highlighted files from the left pane and drop them on the right pane. When CuteFTP asks you to confirm, click **Yes.**

---

6. Pull down the **Transfer** menu and select **Upload** (or press **Ctrl+Page Up**). CuteFTP sends the files one by one to the web server.

7. After the files have arrived safely, pull down the **FTP** menu and select **Disconnect** (or press **Shift+F4**) to shut down the connection.

To make sure everything's working okay, plug your web address into your browser and give your page a test surf. If all goes well, then congratulations are in order, because you've officially earned your webmeister stripes!

Page Pitfalls

I mentioned back in Chapter 5 that the Unix computers that play host to the vast majority of web servers are downright finicky when it comes to the uppercase and lowercase letters used in file and directory names.

Therefore, it's crucial that you check your <A> tags and <IMG> tags to make sure that the file and directory names you use match the combination of uppercase and lowercase letters used on your server. For example, suppose you have a graphics file on your server that's named vacation.gif. If your <IMG> tag points to, say, VACATION.GIF, the image won't appear. To help prevent problems, you can tell CuteFTP to force all your filenames to lowercase letters. In the Site Manager, highlight your FTP site, click **Edit**, and then display the **Advanced** tab. In the **Filenames** group, activate the **Force Lowercase** option and then click **OK**.

Creating a New Directory

If you need to create separate subdirectories for your graphics or HTML files, CuteFTP makes it easy. You have two choices:

◆ If you already have the corresponding subfolder on your computer, upload the entire folder to the server. (That is, you highlight the folder in CuteFTP's left file pane and then select **Transfer, Upload.**

◆ To create a new subdirectory on the server, first open the server directory you want to work (or just click anywhere inside the right file pane to activate it). Then select the **Commands, Directory, Make new directory** command (or press **Ctrl+M**). In the dialog box that appears, enter the name of the new directory and then click **OK.**

Again, remember that your goal is to end up with exactly the same directory structure on both your own computer and on the server. Figure 8.4 shows an example.

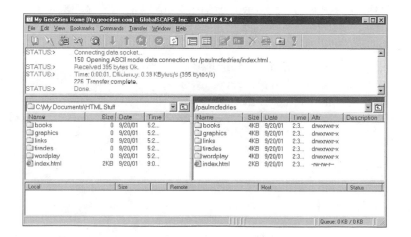

Figure 8.4

When you're finished, the list of files and directories on the web server (right) should be identical to the list of files and folders on your computer (left).

Making Changes to Your Web Files

What happens if you send an HTML file to your web provider and then realize you've made a typing gaffe? Or what if you have more information to add to one of your web pages? How do you make changes to the files that you've already sent?

> **CAUTION**
>
> **Page Pitfalls**
>
> Make sure you send the updated file to the correct directory on the server. Otherwise, you may overwrite a file that happens to have the same name in some other directory.

Well, here's the short answer: You don't. That's right, after you've sent your files, you never have to bother with them again. That doesn't mean you can never update your site, however. Instead, you make your changes to the HTML files that reside on your computer and then send these revised files to your web provider. These files replace the old files, and your site is updated with no questions asked.

"Hey, I'm over here!" Getting Your Site on the Search Engines

If you build it, they will come, right? Unfortunately, the answer to that is, "not necessarily." The web is a massive place that boasts billions (yes, I said *billions*) of pages. So even though your magnificent and hard-won work is on the web, all you've really done at this point is add your own needle to the web's digital haystack.

How are people supposed to know that your new cyberhome is up and running and ready for visitors? Well, people won't beat a path to your door unless you tell them how to get there. For starters, you can spread the news via word of mouth, e-mail notes to friends and colleagues, and by handing out your shiny, new business cards that have your home page address plastered all over them. Also, it's worth checking to see if your hosting provider has a section devoted to announcing new customer pages. And don't forget that I've set up a page that contains nothing but links to my readers' web pages. Here's the address: www.mcfedries.com/CreatingAWebPage/links.html.

However, if you want to count your visitors in the hundreds or even the thousands, you need to cast a wider net. That is, you need to get your site listed in the web's major search engines so that other people can find you when they search for sites that have content similar to yours. The rest of this chapter takes you through the fine art of getting on the search engines and getting good rankings once you're there.

Submitting Your Site

The most straightforward way to get your site listed on a search engine is to stick the search engine's nose in it, so to speak. All search engines have a page that you can use to submit the particulars of your site. Here are the addresses of the submission pages for a dozen of the top search engines (see engines.htm on this book's CD):

AllTheWeb: www.alltheweb.com/add_url.php

AltaVista: www.altavista.com/sites/search/addurl

AOL Search: search.aol.com/add.adp

Excite: www.excite.com/info/add_url

Google: www.google.com/intl/en_extra/addurl.html

HotBot: hotbot.lycos.com/addurl.asp

InfoSpace: www.infospace.com/submit.html

Lycos: home.lycos.com/addasite.html

MSN: submit.looksmart.com/info.jhtml?synd=zdd&chan=zddhome

Northern Light: www.northernlight.com/docs/regurl_help.html

Webcrawler: www.webcrawler.com/info/add_url/

Yahoo!: docs.yahoo.com/info/suggest/

Bear in mind, however, that your page won't necessarily show up on a search engine immediately after you make your submission. Some search engines are remarkably fast at updating their databases, but others can take weeks or even *months*, so patience is the key.

Webmaster Wisdom

Rather than submitting your site to the search engines by hand, there are services out there that will perform this drudgery for you. Although some will charge you a fee, there are many free services available, although most of the freebies will submit your site to only a limited number of search engines. Here are some of the more popular ones:

Submit It: www.submit-it.com/

Add Me: addme.com/

!Register-It!: register-it.netscape.com/

See also the Yahoo! Promotion index: yahoo.com/Business_and_Economy/Business_to_Business/Marketing_and_Advertising/Internet/Promotion/.

Also, don't submit *all* of your pages to the search engine, just your main page. The search engine's crawler will visit your main page and then follow your links to get to your other pages.

Using the ‹META› Tag to Make Search Engines Notice Your Site

The big search engines such as Google and AltaVista scour the web for new and updated sites. If you haven't submitted your site by hand, chances are they'll stumble upon your humble home one of these days and add your pages to their massive databases. Either way, is it possible to ensure that your pages will come out near the top if someone runs a search for topics related to your site? Well, no, there isn't any way to guarantee a good placement. However, you can help things along tremendously by adding a couple of special <META> tags that you insert between the <HEAD> and </HEAD> tags.

The first of these tags defines a description of your site:

```
<META NAME="Description" CONTENT="Your description goes here">
```

Most search engines use this description when they display your page in the results of a web search.

The second <META> tag defines one or more keywords that correspond to the key topics in the page. The search engines use these keywords to match your page with keywords entered by users when they perform a web search. Here's the syntax:

```
<META NAME="Keywords" CONTENT="keyword1, keyword2, etc.">
```

Here's an example:

```
<HTML>
<HEAD>
<TITLE>Tickle Me Elmomentum</TITLE>
<META NAME="Description"
CONTENT="This page examines the Tickle Me Elmo
phenomenon and attempts to understand its social ramifications.">
<META NAME="Keywords" CONTENT="tickle me elmo, toy, doll, giggle,
frenzy, fad, parental pressure">
</HEAD>
<BODY>
etc.
```

Tips for Composing Search Engine-Friendly ‹META› Tags

The mere fact that you're conscientious enough to add <META> tags to your pages is no guarantee that you'll get excellent positions within search results. Instead, you need to take a bit of extra time to craft your <META> tags for maximum effect. Here are some pointers:

- **Watch the length of your <META> content.** Most search engines have a limit on the length of the <META> tag CONTENT values. For the Description tag, don't go longer than about 200 characters; for the Keywords tag, a maximum of 1,000 characters will keep you in good stead.

- **Use lowercase keywords.** To ensure compatibility with most search engines, you should put all of your keywords in lowercase.

- **Spread your keywords around.** Search engines rank sites based not only on the words in the Keywords <META> tag, but also on those found in the <TITLE> and in the page text, especially the first few lines.

- **Don't go keyword crazy.** You might think you could conjure yourself up a better search result placement by repeating some of your keywords a large number of times. Don't do it! Search engines *hate* this and they'll usually disqualify your site if they think you're trying to pull the web wool over their eyes. Use a word a maximum of six or seven times.

- **You can't fool them.** Over the years, webmasters have tried all kinds of tricks to fool search engine rankings. For example, they've included important keywords numerous times in the body of the page, but changed the text color to match the background so the user doesn't see the repeated words. Search engines are hip to this and other tricks.

> **Words from the Web**
>
> Including a keyword an excessive number of times is called **spamdexing**.

- **Okay, you can fool them a little ....** One way to get around the keyword limitation is to include the keyword in appropriate phrases, like so:

```
<META NAME="Keywords" CONTENT="rutabaga, rutabaga recipes, rutabaga
biology, rutabaga quotations, rutabaga philosophy, rutabaga
worship, rutabaga news, rutabaga heroes">
```

- **Include keyword variations.** Include different parts of speech for important keywords (for example, play, plays, and playing). Also, you might want to allow for the different spelling used by American and Canadian or British users (for example, color and colour).

- **Crucial keywords go first.** Search engines tend to prioritize keywords in the order they appear. Therefore, if you have one or more important keywords, put them at the beginning of the <META> tag.

Perhaps the best advice I can give you is to try and get your head inside the searcher. If it was *you* who was searching for data similar to what's on your page, what keywords and phrases would you use?

The Least You Need to Know

◆ Your directory and your address are related. Your main web address points to your main directory on the host's web server. This means that any files or subdirectories you add can be viewed by adding the appropriate file and directory names to the address.

◆ Mirroring your HTML stuff. Make sure that the folder structure you use on your computer is identical to the directory structure you set up on the host.

◆ Check your pages. Before sending your page to the host, check for things such as missing angle brackets, quotations marks, and end tags, and mistyped link addresses. Also, be sure to check your page in different browsers and at different screen resolutions.

◆ Submit your site to search engines. Use the pages provided by most search engines to tell them about your new site.

◆ <META> tags are a must. For search engines to properly index your site, and for surfers to find it, include both a Description and a Keywords <META> tag on all of your pages.

Part 2

A Grab Bag of Web Page Wonders

The HTML hoops I made you jump through in Part 1 will stand you in good stead for the majority of your web page projects. In fact, you now have enough HTML trivia crammed into your brain to keep you going strong for the rest of your career as a web author. But that doesn't mean you should rip out the rest of this book and turn it into confetti. Heck no. You still have quite a few nuggets of HTML gold to mine, and that's just what you do here in Part 2. Think of the next few chapters as page-bound piñatas, stuffed full of various HTML candies and toys. You only have to whack each one with a stick (metaphorically speaking, of course) to spill out things like using images as links (Chapter 9), adding sounds (Chapter 11), creating tables (Chapter 10), forms (Chapter 12), and frames (Chapter 13).

Images Can Be Links, Too

In This Chapter

- ◆ How to set up an image as a hypertext link
- ◆ Some handy ideas for using image links
- ◆ A few image pitfalls to watch out for
- ◆ How to create your own image maps—without programming!
- ◆ Lots of nifty techniques for turning image *lead* into link *gold*

You might think that web page images are all show and no go, but I assure you they can "go" with the best of them. Specifically, I mean you can use them as links, just like regular text. The reader just clicks the image, and then goes off to whatever corner of the web you specify. This chapter shows you not only how to set up an image as a link but also how to create *image maps*—graphics that contain multiple links.

Turning an Image into a Link

Recall from Chapter 5, "Making the Jump to Hyperspace: Adding Links," that you use the <A> tag to build a link into a web page:

```
<A HREF="URL">The link text goes here</A>
```

The *URL* part is the Internet address of the web page (or whatever) to which you want to link.

Designating an image as a link is not a whole lot different from using text. You use the same <A> tag, but you insert an <IMG> tag between the <A> and </A> tags, like this:

```
<A HREF="URL"><IMG SRC="filename"></A>
```

Again, *URL* is the address of the linked page, and *filename* is the name of the graphics file that you want to appear in the page and that you want the surfer to click.

Page Pitfalls _____

Always keep the <IMG> tag and the </A> end tag on the same line in your HTML file. In other words, don't do this:

```
<A HREF="URL"><IMG SRC="filename">
</A>
```

If you do, you'll see a tiny (yet very annoying) line protruding from the bottom right corner of your image.

For example, it's often a good idea to include a link from all your other web pages back to your home page. This makes it easy for your readers to start over again. Here's a document (backhome.htm on this book's CD) that sets up an image of a house as the link back to the home page:

```
<HTML>
<HEAD>
<TITLE>Images Can Be Links, Too</TITLE>
</HEAD>
<BODY>
Click this house <A HREF="index.htm"><IMG SRC="house.gif"></A>
to return to my home page.
</BODY>
</HTML>
```

Figure 9.1 shows how it looks. Notice how the browser displays a border around the image to identify it as a link.

Figure 9.1

An image masquerading as a link.

Webmaster Wisdom _____

The link border that appears around an image link isn't usually very flattering to the image. To keep your images looking good, get rid of the border by adding BORDER="0" to your <IMG> tag:`<IMG SRC="house.gif" BORDER="0">`

Why should I use an image as a link?

That's a good question, and I can answer it with two simple words: eye candy. You already know that adding images is a great way to liven up a dull-as-dishwater web page. So if it's your goal to encourage people to surf your site and see what you have to offer, it's just more tempting for would-be surfers to click interesting-looking images.

That's not to say you have to turn every last one of your links into an image (or vice versa). As always, prudence is the order of the day, and a page with just a few image links is more effective than a page that's covered in them. So, for example, you might want to add links to get people back to your home page, to enable visitors to send you an e-mail message, or for important areas of your site. The next two sections also take you through three common uses for image links: toolbars, navigation buttons, and thumbnails.

Example 1: A Web Page Toolbar

Most modern programs have toolbars with various buttons that give you one-click access to the program's most-used commands and features. You can use image links to provide similar convenience to the folks who trudge through your site.

The basic process for setting this up involves three steps:

1. Use your favorite graphics program to create buttonlike images that represent important sections of your website (your home page, your guest book, your list of links to *Animaniacs* sites, and so on).

2. Create <IMG> tags to set up these buttons as image links that point to the appropriate pages.

Webmaster Wisdom _____

Every good graphics program has some kind of "Text" tool that enables you to add text to an image.

3. Insert these <IMG> tags consecutively (that is, on a *single* line) at the top and/or bottom of each page. The consecutive <IMG> tags cause the images to appear side by side. Presto: instant web toolbar!

The design of your buttons is entirely up to you, but most web toolbars use some combination of image and text. Personally, I don't have an artistic bone in my body, so I prefer to use "text-only" images, as shown in Figure 9.2. This toolbar is just six linked images displayed on a single line. Here's the HTML code that I used to create this toolbar:

```
<HTML>
<HEAD>
<TITLE>A Web Page Toolbar</TITLE>
</HEAD>
<BODY>
<A HREF="/Books/index.html">
➥<IMG SRC="books.gif" BORDER=0></A>
➥<A HREF="/Ramblings/index.html">
➥<IMG SRC="ramblings.gif" BORDER=0></A>
➥<A HREF="/Toys/index.html">
➥<IMG SRC="toys.gif" BORDER=0></A>
➥<A HREF="/guestbook.html">
➥<IMG SRC="guestbk.gif" BORDER=0></A>
➥<A HREF="/search.html">
➥<IMG SRC="search.gif" BORDER=0></A>
➥<A HREF="/index.html">
➥<IMG SRC="homepage.gif" BORDER=0></A>
</BODY>
</HTML>
```

To make sure the buttons are smushed together, be sure to type out all the <A> tags and <IMG> tags on a single line.

Figure 9.2

Cram consecutive image links together for a handy web page toolbar.

Example 2: Navigation Buttons

Some websites contain material that could (or should) be read serially. That is, you read one page and then the next page, and so on. In these situations, it's convenient to give the reader an easy method for navigating back and forth through these pages. The solution that many sites use is to set up VCR-style buttons on the page. These are usually arrows that point forward or backward, as well as a "rewind" button that takes the reader to the first page in the series.

For example, Figure 9.3 shows a page from my website. This page is part of a primer on Internet e-mail and the buttons near the top of each page enable you to navigate to the next installment (the Next button), the previous installment (the Prev button), the first installment (the Top button), or to the home page for this section of my site (the Index button).

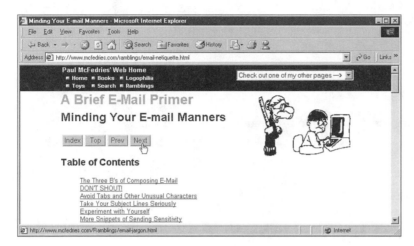

Figure 9.3

An example of a web page that uses image links as navigation buttons.

Example 3: Creating Image Thumbnails

Painters, photographers, and other artistic types often turn their websites into online galleries to show off their work. Unfortunately, the image files associated with this kind of work are often huge, so putting even a couple of them on a single page can lead surfers to seek their highbrow entertainment elsewhere.

A better approach is to create a smaller version—called a *thumbnail*, in the trade—of each large image and display those scaled-down copies on your "gallery" page or pages. You then set up each thumbnail to link directly to the larger version of the image.

To create a thumbnail you first load the full-size image into your favorite graphics program. You then use the program's "Resize" command to chop the image down to size. Here's how you do this with Paint Shop Pro:

1. Select the **Image, Resize** command. The Resize dialog box checks in.

2. Make sure the **Maintain aspect ration of** check box is activated.

Webmaster Wisdom

If you have a lot of images, you might want to avoid the drudgery of converting them all to thumbnails. Here are three programs that can automate the thumbnail process:

Easy Thumbnails: www.fookes.com/ezthumbs

irfanview: www.irfanview.com

allThumbs: slideshow-refinery.com.

3. Use either the **Width** or the **Height** text box to enter the thumbnail's width or height. (Note that you need to adjust only one of these values because Paint Shop Pro will adjust the other value automatically to compensate.)

4. Click **OK.**

5. Select the **File, Save As** command, give the thumbnail a name that's different from the original file, and then click **Save.**

That last step is important because you don't want to change anything about the original file, so you save your changes to a new file.

With the thumbnail created, you then do the linking part. For example, suppose your original image is named photo.jpg and your thumbnail is named photo-thumb.jpg. Here's the code you'd use:

```
<A HREF="photo.jpg"><IMG SRC="photo-thumb.jpg"></A>
```

The Ins and Outs of Image Links

If you plan on using images and links on your web pages, here are a few tidbits to bear in mind when designing these links:

- **Don't use massive images for your links.** It's frustrating enough waiting for a humungous image to load if you have a slow Internet connection. However, it's doubly frustrating if that image is an important part of the site's navigation system. In this case, most folks simply take their surfing business elsewhere. As a general rule, it shouldn't take more than a few seconds for surfers with slow connections to download your image.

> **Webmaster Wisdom**
>
> Remember that most modern browsers display the <IMG> tag's ALT text as a banner when the user hovers the mouse over an image. With an image link, you can use the ALT text to tell the surfer where the link takes him or her.

- **Try to use images that have at least some connection to the link.** For example, suppose you want to set up a link back to your home page. You might have some kind of personal logo or symbol that might seem appropriate, but how many of your surfers will know what this means? A simple icon of a house would probably be more effective.

- **Unless your image is ridiculously obvious, you should always accompany the graphic with explanatory text.** A simple line such as "Click the mailbox icon to send me a message" does wonders for making your site easier to figure out.

- **Consider turning the explanatory text itself into a link that points to the same page as the image.** That way, if the surfer is using a text-only browser or a graphical browser with images turned off, he or she can still navigate your site. Figure 9.4 shows an example where I've augmented the toolbar with the equivalent text links.

Figure 9.4

It's often useful to supplement your image links with the equivalent text links.

Images can be maps, too.

An *image map* is a web page graphic with several defined "clickable" areas. (These areas are also called *hot spots*.) Click one area and a particular web page loads; click a different area and a different page loads. In other words, each of these areas is just a special kind of link. Image maps give you much more flexibility than simple image links because you have more freedom to arrange the links and you can use more elaborate graphics (but not *too* elaborate; remember those poor surfers with slow modem connections).

Originally, setting up an image map was a complicated affair in which you actually had to write a program that would decipher clicks on the image and tell the web server which page to load. Although gluttons for punishment can still take that road, the rest of us now have an easier method. The tall-forehead types call this method *client-side image maps*, but a better name would probably be *browser-based image maps*. In other words, in contrast to the old method that required the intervention of a program and a web server, this new method has everything built right into the browser. You also get the following extra benefits:

◆ Browser-based image maps are faster because the web server doesn't have to process any image map info.

◆ The browser shows the actual URL of each image map link. With server-based image maps, all you get are the coordinates of the map.

◆ You can test out your map on your own computer before you load everything onto the web.

For your image map to work correctly, you have to perform three steps:

1. Decide which distinct image regions you want to use and then determine the coordinates of each region.

2. Use the <MAP> and <AREA> tags to assign a link to each of these regions.

3. Add a special version of the <IMG> tag to your web page.

The next few sections take you through each of these steps to show you how to create your own browser-based image maps.

Step 1: Determine the Map Coordinates

All the information that you see on your computer screen is divided into tiny little points of light called *pixels*. Suppose you went insane one day and decided you wanted to invent a way to specify any particular pixel on the screen. Well, because a typical screen arranges these pixels in 800 columns by 600 rows, you might do this:

- Number the columns from left to right starting with 0 as the first column (remember, you're insane) and 799 as the last column.
- Number the rows from top to bottom starting with 0 as the first row and 599 as the last row.

So far, so good(!). Now you can pinpoint any pixel just by giving its column number followed by its row number. For example, pixel 10,15 is the teensy bit of light in the 11th column and 16th row. And, because your insanity has math-geek overtones, you call the column value "X" and the row value "Y."

This "coordinate system" that you've so cleverly developed is exactly what you use to divide an image map, where the top-left corner of the image is 0,0. For example, check out the image displayed in Figure 9.5. This image is 600 pixels wide and 100 pixels high, and it's divided into three areas, each of which is 200 pixels wide and 100 pixels high:

- **Area A**   This area is defined by coordinate 0,0 in the upper-left corner and coordinate 199,99 in the lower-right corner.
- **Area B**   This area is defined by coordinate 199,0 in the upper-left corner and coordinate 399,99 in the lower-right corner.
- **Area C**   This area is defined by coordinate 399,0 in the upper-left corner and coordinate 599,99 in the lower-right corner.

Figure 9.5

Use a coordinate system to divide your image.

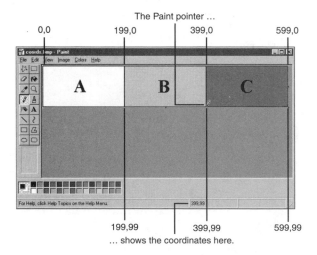

Why bother with all this coordinate malarkey? Well, it's how you let the browser know what to do when the user clicks the image. For example, suppose you want to load a page named a.htm when the surfer clicks inside area A in the preceding image. Then you'd tell the browser (this is explained in the next section) that if the mouse pointer is within the rectangle bounded by the coordinates 0,0 and 199,99, load a.htm.

That's all well and good, but how the heck are you supposed to figure out these coordinates? One way would be to load the image into a graphics program. Paint, for example, shows the current coordinates in the status bar when you slide the mouse around inside the image (as shown in Figure 9.5).

If you don't have a graphics program that does this, there's a method you can use to display the coordinates within the browser. (Note, however, that this works only in Windows; Mac browsers aren't hip to this trick.) What you have to do is set up an HTML file with a link that uses the following format:

```
<A HREF="whatever"><IMG SRC="YourImageMap" ISMAP></A>
```

Here, replace *YourImageMap* with the name of the image file you want to use for your map. The ISMAP attribute fools the browser into thinking this is a server-based image map. So what? So this: Now load this HTML file into a browser, move your mouse pointer over the image and—voilà!—the image coordinates of the current mouse position appear in the status bar! As shown in Figure 9.6, you just point at the corners that define the image areas and record the coordinates that appear.

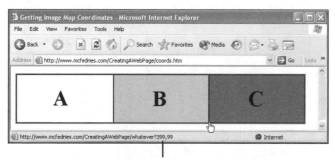

Jot down the coordinates for each image area.

Figure 9.6

To determine coordinates, set up your image as a link with the ISMAP attribute, and Netscape does all the hard work for you.

Step 2: Use <MAP> to Define the Image Map

With your image coordinates now scribbled on a piece of paper, you can set about defining the image map. To do this, you start with the <MAP> tag, which uses the following general form:

```
<MAP NAME="MapName">
</MAP>
```

The *MapName* part is a name that you assign to this map definition. Next, you have to specify the clickable areas on the image. You do this by using the <AREA> tag:

```
<AREA SHAPE="Shape" COORDS="Coords" HREF="URL">
```

Looks pretty ugly, doesn't it? Well, it's not too bad. The SHAPE attribute determines the shape of the area, the COORDS attribute defines the area's coordinates, and the HREF attribute specifies the web page that loads when the user clicks this area.

The COORDS attribute depends on what value you use for the SHAPE attribute. Most image map areas are rectangles, so you specify RECT as the SHAPE and set the COORDS attribute equal to the coordinates of the area's upper-left corner and lower-right corner. For example, here's an <AREA> tag for area A in the example we've been using:

```
<AREA SHAPE="RECT" COORDS="0, 0, 199, 99" HREF="a.htm">
```

You then stuff all your <AREA> tags between the <MAP> and </MAP> tags, like so:

```
<MAP NAME="TestMap">
<AREA SHAPE="RECT" COORDS="0, 0, 199, 99" HREF="a.htm">
<AREA SHAPE="RECT" COORDS="199, 0, 399, 99" HREF="b.htm">
<AREA SHAPE="RECT" COORDS="399, 0, 599, 99" HREF="c.htm">
</MAP>
```

> **Webmaster Wisdom**
>
> The <AREA> tag's SHAPE attribute also accepts the values CIRCLE (for, duh, a circle) and POLY (for a polygon).
>
> For a circle, the COORDS attribute takes three values: the x coordinate of the circle's center point, the y coordinate of the center point, and the radius of the circle.
>
> For a polygon, the COORDS attribute takes three or more sets of coordinates. The browser determines the area by joining a line from one coordinate to the other.

Step 3: Add the Image Map to Your Web Page

Okay, it's all over but the shouting, as they say. To put all that coordinate stuff to good use, you just toss a special version of the <IMG> tag into your web page:

```
<IMG SRC="YourImageMap" USEMAP="#MapName">
```

As before, you replace *YourImageMap* with the name of the image map file. The key, though, is the USEMAP attribute. By setting this attribute equal to the name of the map you just created (with an extra # tacked on the front), the browser treats the graphic as an image map. For example, here's an <IMG> tag that sets up an image map for the example we've been using:

```
<IMG SRC="coords.gif" USEMAP="#TestMap">
```

Figure 9.7 shows you that this stuff actually works. Notice that when I point to area A, the name of the linked page (a.htm, in this case) appears in the status bar.

> **Webmaster Wisdom**
>
> There are also programs available that can automate most of this image map malarkey (now I tell you!). See Appendix B, "Frequently Asked Questions About HTML," for the addresses of some image map software.

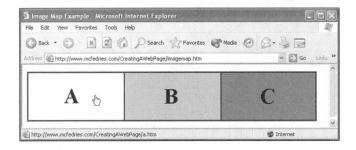

Figure 9.7

The image map is now ready for prime time.

The Least You Need to Know

◆ **Images as links.** To set up an image as a link, shoehorn the appropriate <IMG> tag between <A> and </A>:

```
<A HREF="URL"><IMG SRC="filename"></A>
```

◆ **Image link pointers.** Use small images that have some connection with the link, and add explanatory text so that people know exactly what they're clicking.

◆ **Image maps, step 1.** Determine the coordinates of the various clickable areas on your map. A graphics program is the best way to do this, but you can also use the ISMAP trick:

```
<A HREF="whatever"><IMG SRC="YourImageMap" ISMAP></A>
```

◆ **Image maps, step 2.** Use the <MAP> tag to name the map (for example, <MAP NAME="MyMap"> and then use the <AREA> tag to define the clickable areas of the image map:

```
<AREA SHAPE="Shape" COORDS="Coords" HREF="URL">
```

◆ **Image maps, step 3.** Tell the browser about the image map by adding the USEMAP attribute to the <IMG> tag:

```
<IMG SRC="YourImageMap" USEMAP="#MapName">
```

Chapter 10

Table Talk: Adding Tables to Your Page

In This Chapter

◆ What are tables, and why are they useful?

◆ Creating simple tables

◆ Ever-so-slightly advanced tables

◆ Using tables to create a page with a margin

◆ Tons of table tips and techniques

In this chapter, you learn a bit of computer carpentry as I show you how to build and work with *tables*. Don't worry if you can't tell a hammer from a hacksaw; the tables you'll be dealing with are purely electronic. An HTML table is a rectangular grid of rows and columns on a web page, into which you can enter all kinds of info, including text, numbers, links, and even images. This chapter tells you everything you need to know to build your own table specimens.

What is a table?

Despite the name, HTML tables aren't really analogous to the big wooden thing you eat on every night. Instead, as I've said, a table is a rectangular arrangement of rows and columns on your screen. Figure 10.1 shows an example table.

Figure 10.1

An HTML table in a web document.

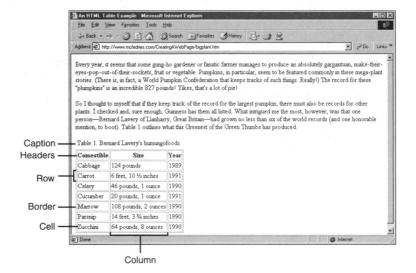

To make sure you understand what's going on (that *is* my job, after all), let's check out a bit of table lingo:

- ◆ **Row**   A single "line" of data that runs across the table. In the example table shown in Figure 10.1, there are eight rows in all.

- ◆ **Column**   A single vertical section of data. In the Figure 10.1 table, there are three columns.

- ◆ **Cell**   The intersection of a row and column. The cells are where you enter the data that appears in the table.

- ◆ **Caption**   This is text that appears (usually) above the table and is used to describe the contents of the table.

- ◆ **Headers**   The first row of the table. The headers are optional, but many people use them to label each column.

- ◆ **Borders**   These are the lines that surround the table and each cell.

Nothing too rocket science-y there.

Wait a minute. Way back in Chapter 3, "From Buck-Naked to Beautiful: Dressing Up Your Page," you showed me how to use the <PRE> tag to make text line up all nice and neat. So why use a table when <PRE> can do a similar job?

Good question. Here are just a few advantages that tables bring to the, uh, table:

◆ Getting text to line up using <PRE> is frustrating at best, and a hair-pulling, head-pounding, curse-the-very-existence-of-the-@#$%&!-World-Wide-Web chore at worst. With tables, though, you can get your text to line up like boot camp recruits with very little effort (and without having to yell orders at the top of your lungs).

◆ Each table cell is self-contained. You can edit and format the contents of a cell without disturbing the arrangement of the other table elements.

◆ The text "wraps" inside each cell, making it a snap to create multiple-line entries.

◆ Tables can include not only text, but images and links as well (even other tables!).

◆ Most text tags (such as <B>, <I>, <H1>, and so on) are fair game inside a table, so you can format the table to suit your needs (with some cautions, as you'll see a bit later).

Web Woodworking: How to Build a Table

Okay, it's time to put the table pedal to the HTML metal and start cranking out some of these table things. The next few sections take you through the basic steps. As an example, I'll show you how I created the table in Figure 10.1.

The Simplest Case: A One-Row Table

Tables always use the following basic container:

```
<TABLE>
</TABLE>
```

All the other table tags fit between these two tags. There are two things you need to know about the <TABLE> tag:

◆ If you want your table to show a border, use the <TABLE BORDER="*n*"> tag instead of <TABLE>, where *n* is the border width you want.

◆ If you don't want a border, use just <TABLE>.

Webmaster Wisdom

I can't tell you how many table troubles I've solved just by turning on the border to get a good look at the table structure. Therefore, I highly recommend that you use a border while constructing your table. You can always get rid of it after you're done.

After you do that, most of your remaining table chores involve the following four-step process:

1. Add a row.
2. Divide the row into the number of columns you want.
3. Insert data into each cell.
4. Repeat Steps 1 through 3 until done.

To add a row, you toss a <TR> (table row) tag and a </TR> tag (its corresponding end tag) between <TABLE> and </TABLE>:

```
<TABLE BORDER="1">
<TR>
</TR>
</TABLE>
```

Now you divide that row into columns by placing the <TD> (table data) and </TD> tags between <TR> and </TR>. Each <TD></TD> combination represents one column (or, more specifically, an individual cell in the row), so if you want a three-column table (with a border), you do this:

```
<TABLE BORDER="1">
<TR>
<TD></TD>
<TD></TD>
<TD></TD>
</TR>
</TABLE>
```

Now you enter the row's cell data by typing text between each <TD> tag and its </TD> end tag:

```
<TABLE BORDER="1">
<TR>
<TD>Cabbage</TD>
<TD>124 pounds</TD>
<TD>1989</TD>
</TR>
</TABLE>
```

Remember that you can put any of the following within the <TD> and </TD> tags:

- Text
- HTML text-formatting tags (such as <B> and <I>)
- Links
- Lists
- Images

Adding More Rows

When your first row is firmly in place, you repeat the procedure for the other rows in the table. For our example table, here's the HTML that includes the data for all the rows:

```
<TABLE BORDER="1">
<TR>
<TD>Cabbage</TD><TD>124
pounds</TD><TD>1989</TD>
</TR>
<TR>
<TD>Carrot</TD><TD>6 feet, 10 &#189; inches</TD><TD>1991</TD>
</TR>
<TR>
<TD>Celery</TD><TD>46 pounds, 1 ounce</TD><TD>1990</TD>
</TR>
<TR>
<TD>Cucumber</TD><TD>20 pounds, 1 ounce</TD><TD>1991</TD>
</TR>
<TR>
<TD>Marrow</TD><TD>108 pounds, 2 ounces</TD><TD>1990</TD>
</TR>
<TR>
<TD>Parsnip</TD><TD>14 feet, 3 &#190; inches</TD><TD>1990</TD>
</TR>
<TR>
<TD>Zucchini</TD><TD>64 pounds, 8 ounces</TD><TD>1990</TD>
</TR>
</TABLE>
```

Page Pitfalls

Text formatting tags will work within only a *single* cell at a time. For example, you can't surround a table with the <FONT> and </FONT> tags in an effort to format, say, the font color for all the text in the table.

Creating a Row of Headers

If your table displays stats, data, or other info, you can make your readers' lives easier by including at the top of each column labels that define what's in the column. (You don't need a long-winded explanation; in most cases, a word or two should do the job.) To define a header, use the <TH> and </TH> tags within a row, like so:

```
<TR>
<TH>First Column Header</TH>
<TH>Second Column Header</TH>
<TH>And So On, Ad Nauseum</TH>
</TR>
```

As you can see, the <TH> tag is a lot like the <TD> tag. The difference is that the browser displays text that appears between the <TH> and </TH> tags as bold and centered within the cell. This helps the reader differentiate the header from the rest of the table data. Remember, though, that headers are optional; you can bypass them if your table doesn't need them.

Here's how I added the headers for the example you saw at the beginning of the chapter:

```
<TABLE BORDER="1">
<TR>
<TH>Comestible</TH><TH>Size</TH><TH>Year</TH>
</TR>
etc.
</TABLE>
```

Including a Caption

The last basic table element is the caption. A *caption* is a short description (a sentence or two) that tells the reader the purpose of the table. You define the caption with the <CAPTION> tag:

```
<CAPTION ALIGN="where">Caption text goes here.</CAPTION>
```

Here, *where* is either TOP or BOTTOM; if you use TOP, the caption appears above the table; if you use BOTTOM, the caption appears—you guessed it—below the table. Here's the <CAPTION> tag from the example (for the complete document, look for bigplant.htm on this book's CD):

```
<TABLE BORDER>
<CAPTION ALIGN="TOP">Table 1. Bernard Lavery's humungofoods.</CAPTION>
etc.
</TABLE>
```

Table Refinishing—More Table Tidbits

The tags we've eyeballed so far are enough to enable you to build tables that are sturdy, if not altogether flashy. If that's all you need, you can safely ignore the rest of the flapdoodle in this chapter. However, if you'd like a tad more control over the layout of your tables, the next few sections take you through a few refinements that can give your tables that certain *je ne sais quoi*.

Aligning Text Within Cells

The standard-issue alignment for table cells is left aligned for data (<TD>) cells and centered for header (<TH>) cells. Not good enough? No sweat. Just shoehorn an ALIGN attribute inside the <TD> or <TH> tag and you can specify the text to be left aligned, centered, or right aligned. Here's how it works:

```
<TD ALIGN="alignment">
<TH ALIGN="alignment">
```

In both cases, *alignment* can be LEFT, CENTER, or RIGHT. That's not bad, but there's even more alignment fun to be had. You can also align your text vertically within a cell. This comes in handy if one cell is quite large (because it contains either a truckload of text or a relatively large image), and you'd like to adjust the vertical position of the other cells in the same row. In this case, you use the VALIGN (vertical alignment) attribute with <TD> or <TH>:

```
<TD VALIGN="vertical">
<TH VALIGN="vertical">
```

Here, *vertical* can be TOP, MIDDLE (the default alignment), or BOTTOM. Here's an example document (tblalign.htm on this book's CD) that demonstrates each of these alignment options:

```
<HTML>
<HEAD>
<TITLE>Table Alignment</TITLE>
</HEAD>
<BODY>
<TABLE BORDER>
<CAPTION>Aligning Text Within Cells:</CAPTION>
<TR>
<TD></TD>
<TD ALIGN=LEFT>Left</TD>
<TD ALIGN=CENTER>Center</TD>
<TD ALIGN=RIGHT>Right</TD>
</TR>
<TR>
<TD><IMG SRC="constru1.gif">
<TD VALIGN=TOP>Top o' the cell</TD>
<TD VALIGN=MIDDLE>Middle o' the cell</TD>
<TD VALIGN=BOTTOM>Bottom o' the cell</TD>
</TR>
</TABLE>
</BODY>
</HTML>
```

Figure 10.2 shows how the table looks in the browser.

Figure 10.2

The various and sundry cell alignment options.

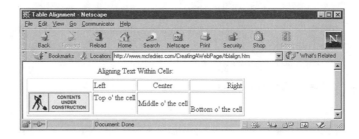

Webmaster Wisdom

In Figure 10.2, did you notice that the cell in the top-left corner of the table is empty? I did this just by placing a <TD> tag and </TD> tag side by side, with nothing in between. Note that, in the browser, the cell appears "filled in." If you want a truly empty cell, insert a nonbreaking space, like so: <TD> </TD>.

Spanning Text Across Multiple Rows or Columns

The data we've entered into our table cells so far has been decidedly monogamous. That is, each hunk of data has shacked up with only one cell. But it's possible (and perfectly legal) for data to be bigamous (take up two cells) or even polygamous (take up three or more cells). Such cells are said to *span* multiple rows or columns, which can come in quite handy for headers and graphics.

Let's start with spanning multiple columns. To do this, you need to interpose the COLSPAN (column span) attribute into the <TD> or <TH> tag:

```
<TD COLSPAN="cols">
<TH COLSPAN="cols">
```

In this case, *cols* is the number of columns you want the cell to span. Here's a simple example (tblspan1.htm on this book's CD) that shows a cell spanning two columns:

```
<HTML>
<HEAD>
<TITLE>Spanning Text Across Multiple Columns</TITLE>
</HEAD>
<BODY>
<TABLE BORDER="1">
<CAPTION>The Spanning Thing -- Example #1 (COLSPAN)</CAPTION>
```

```
<TR>
<TD COLSPAN="2">This item spans two columns</TD>
<TD>This one doesn't</TD>
</TR>

<TR>
<TD>The 1st Column</TD>
<TD>The 2nd Column</TD>
<TD>The 3rd Column</TD>
</TR>

</TABLE>
</BODY>
</HTML>
```

Figure 10.3 shows how the table looks in Internet Explorer.

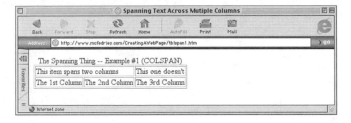

Figure 10.3

A cell that spans two columns.

Spanning multiple rows is similar, except that you substitute ROWSPAN for COLSPAN in <TD> or <TH>:

```
<TD ROWSPAN="rows">
<TH ROWSPAN="rows">
```

The *rows* value is the number of rows you want the cell to span. Here's an example (tblspan2.htm on this book's CD) that shows a cell spanning two rows:

```
<HTML>
<HEAD>
<TITLE>Spanning Text Across Multiple Rows</TITLE>
</HEAD>
<BODY>
<TABLE BORDER="1">
<CAPTION>The Spanning Thing -- Example #2 (ROWSPAN)</CAPTION>

<TR>
<TD ROWSPAN="2">This here item spans two whole rows</TD>
<TD>The 1st Row</TD>
</TR>
```

```
<TR>
<TD>The 2nd Row</TD>
</TR>

<TR>
<TD>This one doesn't</TD>
<TD>The 3rd Row</TD>
</TR>

</TABLE>
</BODY>
</HTML>
```

Figure 10.4 shows the result.

Figure 10.4

A cell that spans two rows.

A Whack of Table Attributes

For our next table trick, we pull a few more table attributes out of our HTML hat. There are all kinds of wild extras, but the following are the most useful ones:

- **The background color.** You learned in Chapter 6, "A Picture Is Worth a Thousand Clicks: Working with Images," that you can adjust the background color of your entire web page. However, you can also assign a custom color to just the background of a table or even an individual cell. To do this, you add the BGCOLOR="#rrggbb" attribute to the <TABLE> tag or the <TD> tag, where *rrggbb* is a value that specifies the color you want (see Chapter 3). For example, the following tag gives your table a light gray background:

  ```
  <TABLE BGCOLOR="#CCCCCC">
  ```

- **A background image.** Another thing you can do is set a background image instead of just a background color for a table or cell. This is just like setting a background image for a web page. In this case, you toss the BACKGROUND attribute inside the <TABLE> or <TD> tag and set the attribute equal to the name of the image file you want to use, as in this example:

  ```
  <TABLE BACKGROUND="tablebg.gif">
  ```

♦ **The border size.** To change the thickness of the table border, you can assign a value to the <TABLE> tag's BORDER attribute. (Note that this applies only to the part of the border that surrounds the outside of the table; the inner borders aren't affected.) For example, to display your table with a border that's five units thick, you use the following:

```
<TABLE BORDER="5">
```

♦ **The width of the table.** The browser usually does a pretty good job of adjusting the width of a table to accommodate the current window size. If you need your table to be a particular width, however, use the WIDTH attribute for the <TABLE> tag. You can either specify a value in pixels or, more likely, a percentage of the available window width. For example, to make sure your table always usurps 75 percent of the window width, you use this version of the <TABLE> tag:

Webmaster Wisdom

You can also use the HEIGHT attribute to set the overall height of the table, although this is rarely done. The most common use is to set HEIGHT to 100 percent so that the table always spans the height of the browser window.

```
<TABLE WIDTH="75%">
```

♦ **The width of a cell.** You can also specify the width of an individual cell by adding the WIDTH attribute to a <TD> or <TH> tag. Again, you can either specify a value in pixels or a percentage of the entire table. (Note that all the cells in the column will adopt the same width.) In this example, the cell takes up 50 percent of the table's width:

```
<TD WIDTH="50%">
```

♦ **The amount of space between cells.** By default, browsers allow just two pixels of space between each cell (vertically and horizontally). To bump that up, use the CELLSPACING attribute for the <TABLE> tag. Here's an example that increases the cell spacing to 10:

```
<TABLE CELLSPACING="10">
```

♦ **The amount of space between a cell's contents and its border.** Browsers like to cram data into a cell as tightly as possible. To that end, they leave a mere one pixel of space between the contents of the cell and the cell border. (This space is called the *cell padding.*) To give your table data more room to breathe, use the <TABLE> tag's CELLPADDING attribute. For example, the following line tells the browser to reserve a full 10 pixels of padding above, below, left, and right of the content in each cell:

```
<TABLE CELLPADDING="10">
```

Here's a web page that shows you a for-instance for most of these attributes (see tblattr.htm on this book's CD):

```
<HTML>
<HEAD>
<TITLE>Some Table Extensions</TITLE>
</HEAD>
<BODY>

<B>&lt;TABLE BGCOLOR="#CCCCCC"&gt;</B>
<TABLE BORDER="1" BGCOLOR="#CCCCCC">
<TR>
<TD>Dumb</TD>
<TD>Dumber</TD>
<TD>Dumbest</TD>
</TR>
</TABLE>

<P>
<B>&lt;TABLE BORDER="5"&gt;</B>
<TABLE BORDER="5">
<TR>
<TD>One</TD>
<TD>Two</TD>
<TD>Buckle my shoe</TD>
</TR>
</TABLE>

<P>
<B>&lt;TABLE WIDTH="75%"&gt;</B>
<TABLE BORDER WIDTH="75%">
<TR>
<TD>Three</TD>
<TD>Four</TD>
<TD>Shut the door</TD>
</TR>
</TABLE>

<P>
<B>&lt;TD WIDTH="50%"&gt;</B>
<TABLE BORDER>
<TR>
<TD WIDTH="50%">WIDTH="50%"</TD>
<TD>Normal width</TD>
<TD>Normal width</TD>
</TR>
</TABLE>
```

```
<P>
<B>&lt;TABLE CELLSPACING="10"&gt;</B>
<TABLE BORDER CELLSPACING="10">
<TR>
<TD>Eeny</TD>
<TD>Meeny</TD>
<TD>Miney</TD>
<TD>Mo</TD>
</TR>
</TABLE>

<P>
<B>&lt;TABLE CELLPADDING="10"&gt;</B>
<TABLE BORDER CELLPADDING="10">
<TR>
<TD>Veni</TD>
<TD>Vidi</TD>
<TD>Vici</TD>
</TR>
</TABLE>

</BODY>
</HTML>
```

When you load this file into Internet Explorer, you see the tables shown in Figure 10.5.

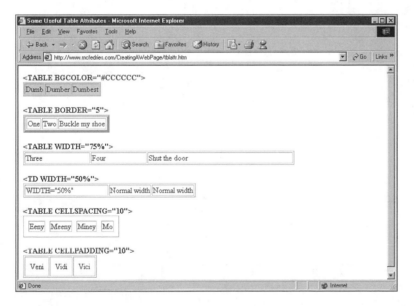

Figure 10.5

Examples of some useful table attributes.

Using a Table to Set Up a Page with a Margin

Many websites set up their pages with a "margin" down the left side. This margin can be an image or, more likely, a color that's different from the page background color. These margins can be either purely decorative or they can contain links and other info.

The good news is that it's easy to create such a margin by using a table that has the following characteristics:

- Set the table's height to 100 percent using the <TABLE> tag's HEIGHT attribute.
- The first column is the margin. Use the BACKGROUND or BGCOLOR attribute to define the image or color you want to use as the margin pattern. Also, set the WIDTH attribute equal to the width of the margin you want. (Note, too, that you need *something* inside the column or Netscape won't display the margin. I use a non-breaking space: .)
- The second column is where you put all your regular web page text and graphics.

Here's the basic layout for the web page (see margin1.htm on this book's CD):

```
<HTML>
<HEAD>
<TITLE>A Page with a Left-Hand Margin</TITLE>
</HEAD>
<BODY LEFTMARGIN="0" TOPMARGIN="0" MARGINWIDTH="0" MARGINHEIGHT="0">

<TABLE HEIGHT="100%">
<TR>

<TD BACKGROUND="grn2.gif" WIDTH="100"> </TD>

<TD VALIGN="TOP">
The rest of your Web page stuff goes here.
</TD>

</TR>
</TABLE>

</BODY>
</HTML>
```

Webmaster Wisdom

Notice how the <BODY> tag includes four new attributes: LEFTMARGIN, TOPMARGIN, MARGINWIDTH, and MARGINHEIGHT. Setting all of these to 0 ensures that you don't end up with extra space above and to the left of the main table.

Figure 10.6 shows the page in the browser. As you can see, the left side of the page (that is, the left column of the table) displays an image that serves as the page margin.

Figure 10.6

This page features a margin down the side.

Web designers commonly use the margin to insert text, links, images, and other stuff. Here's some sample code that does this (see margin2.htm on this book's CD):

```
<HTML>
<HEAD>
<TITLE>Populating the Margin with Text and Links</TITLE>
</HEAD>
<BODY LEFTMARGIN="0" TOPMARGIN="0" MARGINWIDTH="0" MARGINHEIGHT="0">

<TABLE HEIGHT="100%">
<TR>

<TD BGCOLOR="#FFFF00" WIDTH="200" VALIGN="TOP">
<B>The Complete Idiot's Guide to Creating a Web Page</B>
<P>
Here are some links for your surfing pleasure:
</P>
<A HREF="index.html">Home</A><BR>
<A HREF="about.html">About the Book</A><BR>
<A HREF="links.html">Links to Reader Pages</A><BR>
<A HREF="faq.html">Frequently Asked Questions</A><BR>
<A HREF="mailing-list.html">The CIGHTML Mailing List</A>
</TD>

<TD VALIGN="TOP">
The rest of your Web page stuff goes here.
</TD>

</TR>
</TABLE>

</BODY>
</HTML>
```

Figure 10.7 shows what it looks like.

Figure 10.7

This page crams some text and links inside the margin.

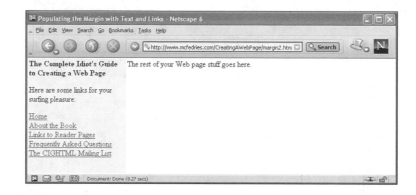

The Least You Need to Know

◆ The <TABLE> tag. This tag defines the table as a whole. Use the WIDTH and HEIGHT attributes to define the size of the table; use the BORDER attribute to define the size of the table border; use the BACKGROUND or BGCOLOR attributes to set a background image or color.

◆ The <TR> tag. This tag defines a row inside the table.

◆ The <TD> tag. This tag defines a column in the table (or, more precisely, it defines a cell inside the current row). Use the ALIGN attribute to align the cell data horizontally; use the VALIGN attribute to align the cell data vertically.

◆ Creating a page with a margin. Set up a table with two columns: the left column is the margin (a background image or color) and the right column contains the regular page data.

Making Your Web Pages Dance and Sing

In This Chapter

- ◆ Combining multiple images into a single, animated GIF
- ◆ Animating text with the <MARQUEE> tag
- ◆ Adding beeps, boops, burps, and other sounds to your web page
- ◆ How to turn a web page into a full-fledged entertainment center

Web pages are no longer restricted to static displays of text and graphics, but instead they're dynamic, kinetic, and truly interactive environments. Instead of mere documents to read and look at, pages have become programs that you can manipulate and play with. We've moved away from the simple type-it-and-send-it world of forms to a world in which pages have started performing the web equivalent of singing and dancing.

This chapter shows you a few techniques for enhancing your own pages with this kind of HTML technology. You learn how to turn your website into a multimedia marvel that includes sounds, animated GIF images, moving text, and more.

Sound Advice: Adding Sounds to Your Page

The web is alive with the sounds of, well, you name it! There's music, poetry, special effects, and sound snippets of every stripe. So now that you've labored long and hard to make your web page pleasing to the eye, perhaps you'd like to add a few extras to appeal to your viewers' ears, as well. It's actually pretty easy to do, and you hear all about it in this section.

First, Some Mumbo Jumbo About Sound Formats

If you read Chapter 6, "A Picture Is Worth a Thousand Clicks: Working with Images," you were no doubt traumatized by all those graphic formats and their incomprehensible TLAs (three-letter acronyms). The bad news is that the world's audio geeks (yes, these are the same guys who were the audio/visual nerds back in high school) also derive great pleasure in creating a constant stream of new sound formats. However, like graphic formats, the good news is that there are just a few audio formats that the web has ordained as standards:

- **AU**   This is a common format in the web soundscape. It's supported by both Netscape Navigator and Internet Explorer.

- **WAV**   This is the standard format used with Windows, which means it's becoming the standard format on the web. It's supported by all versions of Internet Explorer and by Netscape Navigator 3.0 and up.

- **MP3**   This is an incredibly popular format for digital music. The latest versions of Internet Explorer and Netscape use the Windows Media Player as the helper application for playing MP3 files. You can also get MP3 players from the MP3.com site (www.mp3.com/).

- **RA**   This is the RealAudio format, which is used to "stream" large audio files. This means that you don't wait for the entire file to download. Instead, the browser grabs the first part of the file and starts playing it while the rest of the file downloads in the background.

- **MIDI**   This is the Musical Instrument Digital Interface format, and it's used to represent electronic music created with a MIDI synthesizer. This format is supported by Internet Explorer and Netscape Navigator 4.0 (for Navigator 3.0, you need the appropriate helper application set up).

I provide a list of some sites that serve sound files in Chapter 22, "Some HTML Resources on the Web."

Sounding Off with Sound Links

After you have your mitts on a sound file, adding the sound to your web page is a no-brainer. All you have to do is copy the file to your website and then set up a link that points to that file, like so:

```
<A HREF="burp.wav">Click here for a special greeting!</A>
```

Assuming the viewer's browser is set up to handle the sound format you're using, the sound file downloads and then plays without further fuss.

Embedding Sound Files

If you want to add MIDI music or other sounds files to your pages, one way to go is the <EMBED> tag, which is supported by both Netscape Navigator and Internet Explorer. At its simplest, you use the SRC attribute to specify the name of the sound file, like so:

```
<EMBED SRC="playme.mid">
```

Here's an example page (see midi.htm on this book's CD), and Figure 11.1 shows the Internet Explorer interpretation.

```
<HTML>
<HEAD>
<TITLE>A MIDI Example</TITLE>
</HEAD>
<BODY>

Click the Play button to hear some cool jazz music:<BR>
<EMBED SRC="jazz.mid">

</BODY>
</HTML>
```

Webmaster Wisdom

If you load midi.htm into Netscape, the program might tell you that it needs a "plug-in" in order to play the MIDI file. You should see a window with a "Get the Plug-In" link. If you don't see that link, use the following address: home.netscape.com/plugins/index.html. Since this might happen to some of your visitors, as well, consider putting in a link to this address on the same page as your embedded sound file.

Figure 11.1

The <EMBED> tag adds a "player" to the web page.

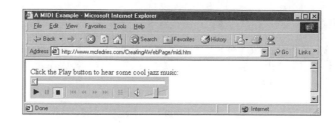

The <EMBED> tag also supports the following extras:

- ◆ **AUTOSTART="FALSE"** If you add this attribute, the browser doesn't play the sound file automatically when the user surfs to your page.

- ◆ **LOOP="*Value*"** The LOOP attribute tells the browser how many times to play the sound. If you set *Value* to 2, for example, the browser runs through the sound twice. If you really want to drive your visitors away, set *Value* to INFINITE to tell the browser to play the sound indefinitely.

- ◆ **HIDDEN="TRUE"** If you add this attribute, the browser hides the controls. (If you use this, don't use AUTOSTART="FALSE" or the user will have no way of launching the sound file.)

Another Way to Add a Background Sound

With Internet Explorer, the <EMBED> tag isn't the only way to wire your site for sound. Specifically, Internet Explorer supports the <BGSOUND> tag that enables you to specify a sound that plays automatically when someone surfs to your site. (Much like the <EMBED> tag's AUTOSTART=TRUE attribute.) Here's the generic format:

```
<BGSOUND SRC="Filename" LOOP="Times">
```

The *Filename* part is the name of the sound file that you want to play (you can use AU, WAV, or MIDI files). The *Times* part tells the browser how many times to play the sound. You can either enter some positive number or use LOOP="INFINITE" to play the sound until the surfer puts their fist through the screen. (Note that you can put this tag anywhere you like in the page.) Here's an example:

```
<BGSOUND SRC="newagetouchyfeely.mid" LOOP="1">
```

Do-It-Yourself Disney: Animated GIF Images

In Chapter 6, I talked about how you can spruce up an otherwise drab web page by adding an image or two. However, if you *really* want to catch the eye of a busy web surfer, why not go one step further and add an animation to your page?

Sound impossible? It's actually a lot easier than you might think thanks to an interesting variation on the GIF file theme: an *animated GIF*. This format actually incorporates several GIF images into a single package. By using a special program, you can specify that these images be displayed sequentially, thus creating an animation! And the really great news is that the program you need—it's called GIF Animator—resides right on this book's CD, so you don't have to bother hunting it down and suffering through an endless download. (Please note that GIF Animator is shareware. If you plan on using it regularly, be sure to fork over the measly US$44.95 it costs to register the program.)

Webmaster Wisdom

Mac users can also get in on the GIF animation fun. Just check out a nifty (and free!) program called GIFBuilder, which is available in Download.com's Mac Animation section: download.cnet.com/downloads/0,10151,0-10215-106-0-1-0,00.html. To use it, you create a series of images in a separate graphics program, import the images into GIFBuilder, and then set up the animation (the time between each image, the number of loops, and so on).

To get started, first use Paint, Paint Shop Pro, or some other drawing program to create the individual image files that will comprise your animation. (It doesn't matter which format you use to save the files; GIF Animator can use most graphic formats, including the BMP files created by Paint. There is one caveat, though: To ensure a smooth animation, make each image the same size.) Figure 11.2 shows the images I'm using as an example. (These images are on this book's CD as well. They're named aninew1.gif through aninew5.gif. The resulting animated GIF is called aninew.gif.) As you can see, all I've done is change the coloring of the letters from image to image. For your own animations, you can change colors, shapes, text, or whatever else you need to create the effect you're looking for.

Figure 11.2

These images can be combined into a single animated GIF.

Launch GIF Animator and you eventually see the Startup Wizard dialog box. Now follow these steps:

1. In the Startup Wizard dialog box, click the **Animation Wizard** button to launch the Animation Wizard. (If you closed the Startup Wizard, select the **File, Animation Wizard** command, instead.)

2. Enter the **Width** and **Height** of the animation. This should be the same as the width and height of the GIF files you'll be incorporating into the animation. In my example, the width is 75 and the height is 47. Click **Next.**

3. Click **Add Image** to get to the Open dialog box, and then open the folder that contains the image or images you want to use.

4. You now have two ways to proceed:

    ◆ If all the image files you need for the animation are in the folder, hold down the **Ctrl** key and click each file name. Click **Open** when you're done.

    ◆ If you need only a single image from the folder, click it to highlight it and then click **Open.** You need to repeat steps 4 and 5 until you've selected all the image files for the animation.

5. Drag the files up and down to put them in the proper order, and then click **Next.** The wizard now asks for the amount of time to display each image (this is called the *delay*).

6. To set the delay, use the **Delay time** spinner to enter a value in 100ths of a second. (You might need to experiment with this value to get your animation just right. A value of 25 is a good place to start.) Alternatively, use the **Specify by frame rate** spin box to set the number of images you want displayed per second. Click **Next.**

7. In the final wizard dialog box, click **Finish.**

8. Select the **File** menu's **Save** command, enter a name for the new GIF file, and then click **Save.**

9. To check out your animation, click the **Preview** tab, or select **View, Play Animation.**

That's it! Your animated GIF is ready for action. Now you can add it to a web page by setting up a regular <IMG> tag where the SRC attribute points to the GIF file that you just created.

Page Pitfalls

GIF Animator makes it a breeze to create your own animations. There's also no shortage of ready-to-roll animated GIFs on the web (see Chapter 21, "The Elements of Web Page Style"), and I've even included a few on this book's CD. So this is probably as good a place as any to caution you against using too many animated images on your pages. One or two animations can add a nice touch to a page, but any more than that is distracting at best, and downright annoying at worst.

Creating a Marquee

Internet Explorer offers webmeisters an easy way to insert a chunk of animated text on a page. Specifically, you can display a word or phrase that enters the browser screen on the right, scrolls all the way across the screen, and then exits on the left. You can repeat this any number of times and even change the direction of the text. Because this is somewhat reminiscent of text on a theater marquee, the tag you use to control is called the <MARQUEE> tag. In its basic, no-frills guise, this tag has the following structure:

```
<MARQUEE>Put your scrolling text
here.</MARQUEE>
```

The text you cram between the <MARQUEE> and </MARQUEE> tags is what scrolls across the screen. To gain a little more control over the scrolling, the <MARQUEE> tag supports quite a few attributes. Here are a the most useful ones:

> **Webmaster Wisdom**
>
> The <MARQUEE> tag is supported only by Internet Explorer, so it doesn't work in Netscape or any other browser. If you want scrolling text that works in most browsers, you can use JavaScript, as described in Chapter 17, "The Programmable Page: Adding JavaScripts to Your Pages."

- ◆ **ALIGN=**"*Alignment*"   Determines how the surrounding text is aligned vertically with the marquee. For *Alignment*, use either TOP or BOTTOM.

- ◆ **BEHAVIOR=**"*Type*"   Determines how the text behaves within the marquee. For *Type*, use SCROLL to get the standard scroll-across movement; use SLIDE to make the text scroll in and then stop when it reaches the opposite side; use ALTERNATE to make the text "bounce" back and forth within the marquee.

- ◆ **BGCOLOR=**"*Color*"   Sets the color of the marquee background.

- ◆ **DIRECTION=**"*WhichWay*"   This attribute tells the browser which way to scroll the text. *WhichWay* can be either LEFT or RIGHT.

- ◆ **LOOP=**"*Times*"   This attribute specifies the number of times you want the text to scroll. If you set *Times* to INFINITE or –1, the text will scroll until kingdom come.

- ◆ **SCROLLDELAY=**"*Time*"   This attribute sets the delay in milliseconds between each loop.

- ◆ **SCROLLAMOUNT=**"*Pixels*"   This attribute determines how many pixels the text jumps with each iteration. The higher the value for *Pixels*, the faster the text scrolls.

- ◆ **HEIGHT=**"*Value*"   Specifies the marquee height either in pixels or as a percentage of the screen.

- ◆ **WIDTH=**"*Value*"   Specifies the marquee width either in pixels or as a percentage of the screen.

Here's an HTML file (look for marquee.htm on this book's CD) that uses several of these attributes. Figure 11.3 shows how it looks in Internet Explorer. (When Netscape users view this page, they see all of the text between <MARQUEE> and </MARQUEE> at once.)

```
<HTML>
<HEAD>
<TITLE>Marquee Malarkey</TITLE>
</HEAD>
<BODY>
Welcome Web<MARQUEE ALIGN="BOTTOM" BGCOLOR="SILVER" WIDTH="50"
SCROLLAMOUNT="4">
maker.........master..........meister..........
spinner..........weaver..........welder..........
</MARQUEE>!
</BODY>
</HTML>
```

Figure 11.3

Only Internet Explorer supports the <MARQUEE> tag.

Redirecting Browsers with Client Pull

If you move your site—or if you rename a page—it's best (when possible) to create a page in the old location that includes a link to the new site or page. Surfers can then click the link to get where you want them to go.

Words from the Web

A page that serves only to redirect surfers to a newer location is called a **Century-21 page.**

However, you can also use a nifty feature called *client pull* to send visitors to your new page automatically. To see an example, dial the following address into your browser: www.mcfedries.com/books/cightml/index.html.

This is the old address of this book's home page. When you go there, the page loads and—magic!—two seconds later you're whisked automatically to the book's current home page. Here's the header for the page you loaded:

```
<HTML>
<HEAD>
<TITLE>This page has moved!</TITLE>

<META
   NAME="REFRESH"
   CONTENT="2; URL=http://www.mcfedries.com/CreatingAWebPage/">

</HEAD>
```

The secret is the extra <META> tag in the header. The guts of the tag is the CONTENT attribute, which uses the following format:

```
CONTENT="seconds; URL=NewPage"
```

Here, *seconds* is the number of seconds the browser waits before loading the page specified with the URL value.

The Least You Need to Know

- ◆ Sound formats. There are four standard sound formats on the web: AU, WAV, MP3, and MIDI.
- ◆ The simplest of sounds. The easiest way to add sound to your site is to set up the sound file as a link using the <A HREF> tag:

  ```
  <A HREF="burp.wav">Click here for a special greeting!</A>
  ```

- ◆ Embedding sounds. To place the sound file right in the page, use the <EMBED> tag, instead:

  ```
  <EMBED SRC="playme.mid">
  ```

- ◆ <BGSOUND> and <MARQUEE> are IE-only. Remember that the <BGSOUND> and <MARQUEE> tags only work with Internet Explorer.
- ◆ Yanking the browser. To automatically redirect a browser to another page, use this form of the <META> tag:

  ```
  <META
      NAME="REFRESH"
      CONTENT="seconds; URL=NewPage">
  ```

Need Feedback?
Create a Form!

In This Chapter

- ◆ An introduction to forms
- ◆ Populating your form with buttons, boxes, and other bangles
- ◆ Where to find the programs that make your form run
- ◆ Almost everything you need to know to create great forms

Back in Chapter 5, "Making the Jump to Hyperspace: Adding Links," and Chapter 9, "Images Can Be Links, Too," I showed you how to use hypertext links to add a semblance of interactivity to your pages. However, beyond this basic level of interaction lies a whole genre of web pages called *forms*. This chapter tells you what forms are all about and takes you step-by-step through the creation of a basic form. I even point out a few resources that you can turn to for processing forms (including a special resource designed just for readers of this book).

What is a form, anyway?

Most modern programs toss a dialog box in your face if they need to extract some information from you. For example, selecting a program's Print command most likely results in some kind of Print dialog box showing up. The purpose of this dialog box is to pester you for information, such as the number of copies you want, the pages you want to print, and so on.

A form is essentially the web-page equivalent of a dialog box. It's a page populated with text boxes, drop-down lists, and command buttons to get information from the user. For example, Figure 12.1 shows a form from my website. This is a search form that people can use to search the archives of my Word Spy site. As you can see, it's possible to create forms that look just like dialog boxes.

Figure 12.1

A form used for searching.

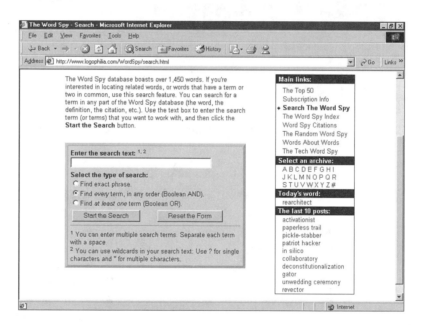

Of course, there are lots of possible uses for forms. If you put out a newsletter or magazine, you can use forms to gather information from subscribers. If your website includes pages with restricted access, you can use a form to get a person's user name and password for verification. If you have information in a database, you can use a form to have people specify what type of information they want to access.

Creating a Form

You create forms using special HTML tags, and it's pretty easy to set up a form. To get started, enter the <FORM> and </FORM> tags. These tags can be inserted anywhere inside the body of the page. You place all the other form-related tags (which I show you in the rest of this chapter) between <FORM> and </FORM>.

The <FORM> tag always includes a couple of extra goodies that tell the web server how to process the form. Here's the general format:

```
<FORM ACTION="url" METHOD="METHOD">
</FORM>
```

Here, the ACTION attribute tells the browser where to send the form's data. This is almost always a program (or *script*, as they're often called) that processes the data and then performs some kind of action (hence the name). The *url* is the address of the script file that contains the program.

Page Pitfalls

Creating a form is fairly easy, but getting your mitts on the information that the reader types into the form is another matter. The problem is that this requires some programming, so it's well beyond the scope of a humble book such as this. So what's a poor, programming-challenged web wizard to do? Check out the section titled "Oh say, can you CGI?" later in this chapter.

The METHOD attribute tells the browser how to send the form's data to the URL specified with ACTION. You have two choices here for *METHOD:* POST and GET. The method you use depends on the script, but POST is the most common method.

Let's bring all this gobbledygook down to earth with a concrete example. You can test your forms by using a special script that I host on my server. Here's how to use it:

```
<FORM ACTION="http://www.mcfedries.com/scripts/formtest.asp" METHOD="POST">
```

What this script does is return a page that shows you the data that you entered into the form. You can try this out after you build a working form. Speaking of which, the next few sections take you through the basic form elements.

Making It Go: The Submit Button

Most dialog boxes, as you probably know from hard-won experience, have an OK command button. Clicking this button says, in effect, "All right, I've made my choices. Now go put everything into effect." Forms also have command buttons, and they come in two flavors: submit buttons and reset buttons.

A *submit button* (I talk about the reset button in the next section) is the form equivalent of an OK dialog box button. When the reader clicks the submit button, the form data is shipped out to the program specified by the <FORM> tag's ACTION attribute. Here's the simplest format for the submit button:

```
<INPUT TYPE="SUBMIT">
```

As you'll see, most form elements use some variation on the <INPUT> tag and, as I said before, you place all these tags between <FORM> and </FORM>. In this case, the TYPE="SUBMIT" attribute tells the browser to display a command button labeled Submit Query (or, on some browsers, Submit or Send). Note that each form can have just one submit button.

If the standard Submit Query label is a bit too stuffy for your needs, you can make up your own label, as follows:

```
<INPUT TYPE="SUBMIT" VALUE="Label">
```

Here, *Label* is the label that appears on the button. In the following example (submit.htm on this book's CD), I've inserted a submit button with the label Make It So!, and Figure 12.2 shows how it looks in a browser.

```
<HTML>
<HEAD>
<TITLE>Submit Button Custom Label Example</TITLE>
</HEAD>
<BODY>
<H3>An example of a custom label for a submit button:</H3>

<FORM ACTION="http://www.mcfedries.com/scripts/formtest.asp" METHOD="POST">
<INPUT TYPE="SUBMIT" VALUE="Make It So!">
</FORM>

</BODY>
</HTML>
```

Figure 12.2

A submit button with a custom label.

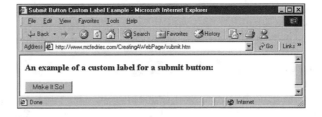

Webmaster Wisdom

Rather than using a boring command button to submit a form, you might prefer to have the user click an image. That's no sweat. What you need to do is add TYPE="IMAGE" to the <INPUT> tag, and add a SRC attribute that specifies the name of the graphics file (much like you do with the <IMG> tag). Here's an example:

```
<INPUT TYPE="IMAGE" SRC="go.gif">
```

You should know, too, that when you use an image as a submit button, the test script returns two extra values named "x" and "y". These give you the coordinates of the spot on the image that the user clicked. They can be safely ignored.

Starting Over: The Reset Button

If you plan on creating fairly large forms, you can do your readers a big favor by including a reset button somewhere on the form. A reset button clears all the data from the form's fields and reenters any default values that you specified in the fields. (I explain how to set up default values for each type of field as we go along.) Here's the tag you use to include a reset button:

```
<INPUT TYPE="RESET">
```

This creates a command button labeled Reset. Yes, you can create a custom label by tossing the VALUE attribute into the <INPUT> tag, as in the following example:

```
<INPUT TYPE="RESET" VALUE="Start From Scratch">
```

Using Text Boxes for Single-Line Text

For simple text entries, such as a person's name or his favorite Beatle, use text boxes. These are just rectangles within which the reader can type whatever he likes. Here's the basic format for a text box:

```
<INPUT TYPE="TEXT" NAME="Field Name">
```

In this case, *Field Name* is a name you assign to the field that's unique among the other fields in the form. For example, to create a text box the reader can use to enter his first name (let's call it First), you'd enter the following:

```
<INPUT TYPE="TEXT" NAME="First">
```

CAUTION

Page Pitfalls

It's crucial to remember that every form control (button, text box, and so on) must have a unique name. The only exception to this is that a group of related radio buttons (discussed a bit later) must have the same name.

For clarity, you also want to precede each text box with a label that tells the reader what kind of information to type in. For example, the following line precedes a text box with First Name: so the reader knows to type in his first name:

```
First Name: <INPUT TYPE="TEXT" NAME="First">
```

Here's some HTML code (textbox.htm on this book's CD) that utilizes a few text boxes to gather some information from the reader:

```
<HTML>
<HEAD>
<TITLE>Text Box Example</TITLE>
</HEAD>
<BODY>
<H3>Please tell me about yourself:</H3>

<FORM ACTION="http://www.mcfedries.com/scripts/formtest.asp" METHOD="POST">
First Name: <INPUT TYPE="TEXT" NAME="First">
<P>
Last Name: <INPUT TYPE="TEXT" NAME="Last">
<P>
Nickname: <INPUT TYPE="TEXT" NAME="Nick">
<P>
<INPUT TYPE="SUBMIT" VALUE="Just Do It!">
<INPUT TYPE="RESET" VALUE="Just Reset It!">
</FORM>

</BODY>
</HTML>
```

Figure 12.3 shows how it looks in Internet Explorer.

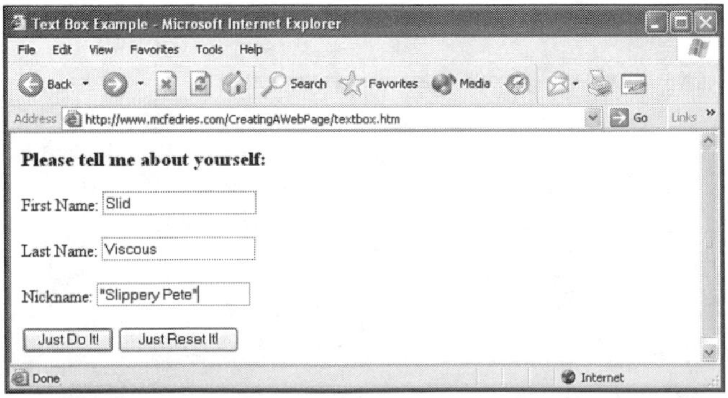

Figure 12.3

A form with a few text boxes.

If you run this form (that is, if you click the Just Do It! button), the data is sent to my test script. Why? Because I included the following line:

```
<FORM ACTION="http://www.mcfedries.com/scripts/formtest.asp" METHOD="POST">
```

You'd normally replace this ACTION attribute with one that points to a script that does something useful to the data. You don't have such a script right now, so it's safe just to use my script for testing purposes. Remember that this script doesn't do much of anything except send your data back to you. If everything comes back okay (that is, there are no error messages), then you know your form is working properly. Just so you know what to expect, Figure 12.4 shows an example of the page that gets returned to the browser. Notice how the page shows the names of the fields followed by the value the user entered.

Figure 12.4

An example of the page that's returned when you send the form data to my text script.

Text boxes also come with the following bells and whistles:

◆ **Setting the default value.** If you'd like to put some prefab text into the field, include the VALUE attribute in the <INPUT> tag. For example, suppose you want to know the address of the user's home page. To include *http://* in the field (because most addresses begin with this), you'd use the following tag:

```
<INPUT TYPE=TEXT NAME="URL" VALUE="http://">
```

◆ **Setting the size of the box.** To determine the length of the text box, use the SIZE attribute. (Note that this attribute affects only the size of the box and not the length of the entry; for the latter, see the MAXLENGTH attribute in the following paragraph.) For example, the following tag displays a text box that's 40 characters long:

```
<INPUT TYPE=TEXT NAME="Address" SIZE="40">
```

◆ **Limiting the length of the text.** In a standard text box, the reader can type away until her fingers are numb. If you'd prefer to restrict the length of the entry, use the MAXLENGTH attribute. For example, the following text box is used to enter a person's age and sensibly restricts the length of the entry to three characters:

```
<INPUT TYPE=TEXT NAME="Age" MAXLENGTH="3">
```

Using Text Areas for Multiline Text

If you want to give your readers lots of room to type their hearts out, or if you need multiline entries (such as an address), you're better off using a *text area* than a text box. A text area is also a rectangle that accepts text input, but text areas can display two or more lines at once. Here's how they work:

```
<TEXTAREA NAME="Field Name" ROWS="Total Rows" COLS="Total Columns" WRAP>
</TEXTAREA>
```

Here, *Field Name* is a unique name for the field, *Total Rows* specifies the total number of lines displayed, and *Total Columns* specifies the total number of columns displayed. The optional WRAP attribute tells the browser to wrap the text onto the next line whenever the user's typing hits the right edge of the text area.

Note, too, that the <TEXTAREA> tag requires the </TEXTAREA> end tag. If you want to include default values in the text area, just enter them—on separate lines, if necessary—between <TEXTAREA> and </TEXTAREA>.

The following HTML tags (textarea.htm on this book's CD) show a text area in action, and Figure 12.5 shows how it looks in a browser.

```
<HTML>
<HEAD>
<TITLE>Text Area Example</TITLE>
</HEAD>
<BODY>
<H3>Today's Burning Question</H3>

<FORM ACTION="http://www.mcfedries.com/scritps/formtest.asp" METHOD="POST">
First Name: <INPUT TYPE="TEXT" NAME="First">
<P>
Last Name: <INPUT TYPE="TEXT" NAME="Last">
<P>
Today's <I>Burning Question</I>: <B>How did the fool and his money get
together in the first place?</B>
<P>
Please enter your answer in the text area below:
<BR>
<TEXTAREA NAME="Answer" ROWS="10" COLS="60" WRAP>
</TEXTAREA>
<P>
<INPUT TYPE="SUBMIT" VALUE="I Know!">
<INPUT TYPE="RESET">
</FORM>

</BODY>
</HTML>
```

Figure 12.5

An example of a text area.

Toggling an Option On and Off with Check Boxes

If you want to elicit yes/no or true/false information from your readers, use check boxes because it's a lot easier to check a box than it is to type in the required data. Here's the general format for an HTML check box:

```
<INPUT TYPE="CHECKBOX" NAME="Field Name">
```

As usual, *Field Name* is a unique name for the field. You can also add the CHECKED attribute to the <INPUT> tag, which tells the browser to display the check box "prechecked." Here's an example:

```
<INPUT TYPE="CHECKBOX" NAME="Species" CHECKED>Human
```

Notice in the preceding example that I placed some text beside the <INPUT> tag. This text is used as a label that tells the reader what the check box represents. Here's a longer example (checkbox.htm on this book's CD) that uses a whole mess of check boxes. Figure 12.6 shows how it looks (I've checked a few of the boxes so you can see how they appear):

```
<HTML>
<HEAD>
<TITLE>Check Box Example</TITLE>
</HEAD>
<BODY>
<H3>Welcome to Hooked On Phobics!</H3>
<HR>
```

```
<FORM ACTION="http://www.mcfedries.com/scripts/formtest.asp" METHOD="POST">
What's <I>your</I> phobia? (Please check all that apply):
<P>
<INPUT TYPE="CHECKBOX" NAME="Ants">Myrmecophobia (Fear of ants)<BR>
<INPUT TYPE="CHECKBOX" NAME="Bald">Peladophobia (Fear of becoming bald)<BR>
<INPUT TYPE="CHECKBOX" NAME="Beards" CHECKED>Pogonophobia (Fear of beards)<BR>
<INPUT TYPE="CHECKBOX" NAME="Bed">Clinophobia (Fear of going to bed)<BR>
<INPUT TYPE="CHECKBOX" NAME="Chins" CHECKED>Geniophobia (Fear of chins)<BR>
<INPUT TYPE="CHECKBOX" NAME="Flowers">Anthophobia (Fear of flowers)<BR>
<INPUT TYPE="CHECKBOX" NAME="Flying">Aviatophobia (Fear of flying)<BR>
<INPUT TYPE="CHECKBOX" NAME="Purple">Porphyrophobia (Fear of purple)<BR>
<INPUT TYPE="CHECKBOX" NAME="Teeth" CHECKED>Odontophobia (Fear of teeth)<BR>
<INPUT TYPE="CHECKBOX" NAME="Thinking">Phronemophobia (Fear of thinking)<BR>
<INPUT TYPE="CHECKBOX" NAME="Vegetables">Lachanophobia (Fear of vegetables)<BR>
<INPUT TYPE="CHECKBOX" NAME="Fear" CHECKED>Phobophobia (Fear of fear)<BR>
<INPUT TYPE="CHECKBOX" NAME="Everything">Pantophobia (Fear of everything)<BR>
<P>
<INPUT TYPE="SUBMIT" VALUE="Submit">
<INPUT TYPE="RESET">

</FORM>
</BODY>
</HTML>
```

Figure 12.6

Some check box examples.

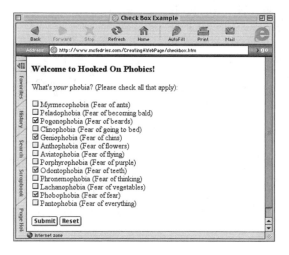

> **Webmaster Wisdom**
>
> When you submit a form with a check box, the data returned by the test script is a bit different from the data returned by the other controls. For one thing, the script returns only the values for check boxes that were activated; for another, the value returned for these checked check boxes is "on". For example, in the checkbox.htm file, if the check box named "Beards" is activated when the form is submitted, the following line will appear in the results:
>
>   Beards = on

Multiple Choice Options: Radio Buttons

Instead of yes/no choices, you might want your readers to have a choice between three or four options. In this case, radio buttons are your best bet. With radio buttons, the user gets two or more options, but they can pick only one at a time.

Here's the general format:

```
<INPUT TYPE="RADIO" NAME="Field Name" VALUE="Value">
```

Field Name is the usual field name, except in this case you supply the same name to *all* the radio buttons that you want grouped together. (More on this in a sec.) *Value* is a unique text string that specifies the value of the option when it's selected. In addition, you can also add CHECKED to one of the buttons to have the browser activate the option by default. The following HTML document (radiobtn.htm on this book's CD) puts a few radio buttons through their paces.

> **Webmaster Wisdom**
>
> In a rare burst of nerd whimsy, the HTML powers-that-be named *radio buttons* after the old car radio buttons that you had to push to select a station.

```
<HTML>
<HEAD>
<TITLE>Radio Button Example</TITLE>
</HEAD>
<BODY>
<H3>Survey</H3>
```

```
<FORM ACTION="http://www.mcfedries.com/scripts/formtest.asp" METHOD="POST">
Which of the following best describes your current salary level:
<DL><DD>
<INPUT TYPE="RADIO" NAME="Salary" VALUE="Poverty" CHECKED>Below the poverty
line<BR>
<INPUT TYPE="RADIO" NAME="Salary" VALUE="Living">Living wage<BR>
<INPUT TYPE="RADIO" NAME="Salary" VALUE="Comfy">Comfy<BR>
<INPUT TYPE="RADIO" NAME="Salary" VALUE="DINK">DINK (Double Income, No
Kids)<BR>
```

```
<INPUT TYPE="RADIO" NAME="Salary" VALUE="Rockefellerish">Rockefellerish<BR>
</DD></DL>
Which of the following best describes your political leanings:
<DL><DD>
<INPUT TYPE="RADIO" NAME="Politics" VALUE="Way Left" CHECKED>So far left, I'm
right<BR>
<INPUT TYPE="RADIO" NAME="Politics" VALUE="Yellow Dog">Yellow Dog Democrat<BR>
<INPUT TYPE="RADIO" NAME="Politics" VALUE="Middle">Right down the middle<BR>
<INPUT TYPE="RADIO" NAME="Politics" VALUE="Republican">Country Club
Republican<BR>
<INPUT TYPE="RADIO" NAME="Politics" VALUE="Way Right">So far right, I'm
left<BR>
</DD></DL>
<P>
<INPUT TYPE="SUBMIT" VALUE="Submit">
<INPUT TYPE="RESET">
</FORM>

</BODY>
</HTML>
```

Notice that the first five radio buttons all use the name "Salary" and the next five all use the name "Politics." This tells the browser that it's dealing with two separate groups of buttons. This way, the user can select one (and only one) button in the "Salary" group and one (and only one) button in the "Politics" groups, as shown in Figure 12.7.

Figure 12.7

A form that uses radio buttons for multiple-choice input.

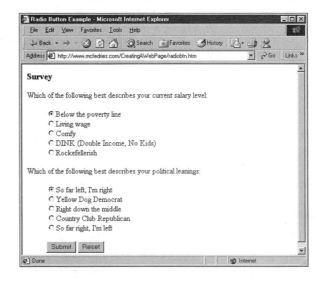

Selecting from Lists

Radio buttons are a great way to give your readers multiple choices, but they get unwieldy if you have more than about five or six options. For longer sets of options, you're better off using lists, or *selection lists* as they're called in the HTML world. Selection lists are a wee bit more complex than the other form tags we've looked at, but not by much. Here's the general format:

Webmaster Wisdom

To select multiple list items in Windows, hold down the Ctrl key and click each item. To do this on a Mac, hold down the ⌘ key and click each item.

```
<SELECT NAME="Field Name" SIZE="Items">
<OPTION>First item text</OPTION>
<OPTION>Second item text</OPTION>
<OPTION>And so on...</OPTION>
</SELECT>
```

As I'm sure you've guessed by now, *Field Name* is the unique name for the list. For the SIZE attribute, *Items* is the number of items you want the browser to display. If you omit SIZE, the list becomes a drop-down list. If SIZE is two or more, the list becomes a rectangle with scroll bars for navigating the choices. Also, you can insert the MULTIPLE attribute into the <SELECT> tag. This tells the browser to enable the user to select multiple items from the list.

Between the <SELECT> and </SELECT> tags are the <OPTION></OPTION> tags; these define the list items. If you add the SELECTED attribute to one of the items, the browser selects that item by default.

To get some examples on the table, the following document (lists.htm on this book's CD) defines no less than three selection lists. Figure 12.8 shows what the Netscape 6 browser does with them.

```
<HTML>
<HEAD>
<TITLE>Selection List Example</TITLE>
</HEAD>
<BODY>
<H3>Putting On Hairs: Reader Survey</H3>

<FORM ACTION="http://www.mcfedries.com/scripts/formtest.asp" METHOD="POST">
Select your hair color:<BR>
<SELECT NAME="Color">
<OPTION>Black</OPTION>
<OPTION>Blonde</OPTION>
<OPTION SELECTED>Brunette</OPTION>
```

```
<OPTION>Red</OPTION>
<OPTION>Something neon</OPTION>
<OPTION>None</OPTION>
</SELECT>
<P>
Select your hair style:<BR>
<SELECT NAME="Style" SIZE="4">
<OPTION>Bouffant</OPTION>
<OPTION>Mohawk</OPTION>
<OPTION>Page Boy</OPTION>
<OPTION>Permed</OPTION>
<OPTION>Shag</OPTION>
<OPTION SELECTED>Straight</OPTION>
<OPTION>Style? What style?</OPTION>
</SELECT>
<P>
Hair products used in the last year:<BR>
<SELECT NAME="Products" SIZE="5" MULTIPLE>
<OPTION>Gel</OPTION>
<OPTION>Grecian Formula</OPTION>
<OPTION>Mousse</OPTION>
<OPTION>Peroxide</OPTION>
<OPTION>Shoe black</OPTION>
</SELECT>
<P>
<INPUT TYPE="SUBMIT" VALUE="Hair Mail It!">
<INPUT TYPE="RESET">
</FORM>

</BODY>
</HTML>
```

Figure 12.8

A form with a few selection list examples.

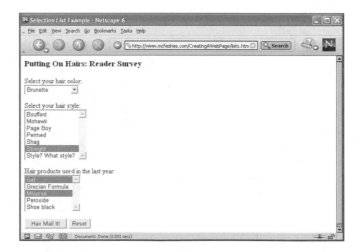

Oh say, can you CGI?

All this form folderol is fine, but what good is a form if it doesn't really do much of anything? That is, why bother building a fancy form if you have no way to get the data? Unfortunately, as I mentioned earlier, grabbing form data and manipulating it is a programmer's job. Specifically, you have to use something called the *Common Gateway Interface*, or CGI for short. CGI is a method of transferring form data in a manner that makes it relatively easy to incorporate into a program and then massage it all you need. Easy, that is, if you have the requisite nerd skills.

Well, I might not have room to teach you how to program forms, and you might not have the inclination in any case, but that doesn't mean you're totally stuck. The next few sections give you some ideas for getting your forms to do something useful.

A Service Exclusively for Readers

The easy solution to this CGI stuff is to have a helpful author write a program that you can use for submitting your form data. And that's exactly what I've done. I've created a program called MailForm that takes form data and e-mails it to an address you specify.

To use MailForm, you have to register on my website. Here's the place to go: www.mcfedries.com/mailform/register.asp. After you register, you'll receive instructions that tell you how to set up your form to take advantage of what MailForm has to offer.

Ask your provider.

Many people want to add simple guest books and feedback mechanisms to their sites, but they don't want to have to bother with the programming aspect. So, in response to their customers' needs, most web hosting providers make some simple CGI scripts (programs) available to their customers. For example, one common type of script grabs form data, extracts the field names and values, and sends them to an e-mail address you specify (like my MailForm program). Check with the provider's administrator or webmaster to see if it has any CGI scripts that you can use. And if you haven't settled on a provider yet, you should ask in advance if it has CGI programs available.

The CGI-Joe Route

A more expensive alternative is to hire the services of a CGI wizard (also known as a *CGI-Joe* in web programming circles) to create a custom program for you. Most web hosting providers are only too happy to put together a nice little program tailored to your needs. There's also no shortage of hired guns on the web who create programs to your specifications. As a starting point, check out some of the resources mentioned in the next section.

Check out the web's CGI resources.

If your service provider or web hosting provider doesn't have ready-to-run CGI programs that you can use, there's no shortage of sites on the Net that are willing and able to either teach you CGI or supply you with programs. This section runs through a list of some of these sites (see cgisites.htm on this book's CD):

Webmaster Wisdom

Note that if you grab a program or two to use, you need to contact your service provider's administrator to get the full lowdown on how to set up the program. In most cases, the administrator will want to examine the program code to make sure it's up to snuff. If it passes muster, it is put in a special directory (usually called a cgi-bin), and then you can refer to the program in your form.

- ◆ **Bravenet.** This site offers lots of free scripts and other webmaster goodies. See www.bravenet.com.

- ◆ **CGI 101.** As its name implies, this site offers beginner-level training and tutorials for CGI wanna-be programmers. It also offers CGI hosting, links to other CGI sites, and much more. See www.cgi101.com.

- ◆ **The CGI Collection.** This is a nice site with lots of links to scripts, tutorials, mailing lists, books, and much more. See www.itm.com/cgicollection.

- ◆ **The CGI Directory.** This site is bursting at the seams with great CGI info. There are tutorials, book reviews, an FAQ, links to other CGI sites, and hundreds of scripts. See www.cgidir.com.

- ◆ **CGI For Me.** This site offers what's known in the trade as remote CGI hosting. This means that the scripts run on the CGI For Me server and you link to them from your own page. You don't have to worry about script installation or configuration, and it's perfect if your web host doesn't allow CGI scripts. See www. cgiforme.com.

- ◆ **The CGI Resource Index.** If there's a good CGI resource on the web, this site knows about it. It has thousands of links to scripts, tutorials, articles, programmers for hire, and much more. See www.cgi-resources.com.

- ◆ **Extropia.** This site is the brainchild of Selena Sol and Gunther Birznieks, and it's one of the best CGI resources on the web. See www.extropia.com/applications. html.

- ◆ **Matt's Script Archive.** Matt Wright has written tons of CGI scripts and graciously offers them gratis to the web community. He has scripts for a guest book, random link generator, animation, and lots more. It's a great site and a must for would-be CGI mavens. See www.worldwidemart.com/scripts.

- **NCSA—The Common Gateway Interface.** This is *the* place on the web for CGI info. NCSA (the same folks who made the original Mosaic browser) has put together a great collection of tutorials, tips, and sample programs. See hoohoo.ncsa. uiuc.edu/cgi.

- **ScriptSearch.** This site bills itself as "The World's Largest CGI Library," and with thousands of scripts in dozens of categories, I can believe it. See www. scriptsearch.com.

- **comp.infosystems.www.authoring.cgi.** This newsgroup is a useful spot for CGI tips and tricks, and it's just a good place to hang around with fellow web programmers.

- **Yahoo's CGI Index.** This is a long list of CGI-related resources. Many of the links have either CGI how-to info or actual programs you can use. See dir.yahoo.com/ Computers_and_Internet/Software/Internet/World_Wide_Web_Servers/Server_ Side_Scripting/Common_Gateway_Interface__CGI.

The Least You Need to Know

- Submit button. <INPUT TYPE="SUBMIT" VALUE="*Label*">

- Reset button. <INPUT TYPE="RESET" VALUE="*Label*">

- Text box. <INPUT TYPE="TEXT" NAME="*Field Name*">

- Text area. <TEXTAREA NAME="*Field Name*" ROWS="*Total Rows*" COLS="*Total Columns*" WRAP></TEXTAREA>

- Check box. <INPUT TYPE="CHECKBOX" NAME="*Field Name*">

- Radio button. <INPUT TYPE="RADIO" NAME="*Field Name*" VALUE="*Value*"> (make sure all related radio buttons use the same name)

- Selection list. <SELECT NAME="*Field Name*" SIZE="*Items*"></SELECT> and <OPTION>Item text</OPTION>

- Testing, testing .... To make sure your forms are doing what you want them to do, use my FormTest script:

```
<FORM ACTION="http://www.mcfedries.com/scripts/formtest.asp"
METHOD="POST">
```

- Getting form data. Readers of this book can use my MailForm script to get form data e-mailed to them. Begin by registering at www.mcfedries.com/mailform/ registration.asp:

Chapter 13

Fooling Around with Frames

In This Chapter

- ◆ What frames are all about
- ◆ How to get a basic frame layout up and running
- ◆ Tweaking frames to get them just so
- ◆ How to handle browsers that don't understand frames
- ◆ A step-by-step approach with the aim to tame the frame game

Like most guys, I enjoy technology and take every opportunity to ring the bells and blow the whistles on whatever new techtoy comes my way. Take picture-in-picture (PIP) for instance. I think the engineering genius who came up with PIP should be awarded some kind of Nobel Geeks Prize. For my money, it's just insanely great to be able to leave one channel in view while you surf around to see what else is happening.

Whether you're a PIP fan or foe, you'll be interested to know that you can apply the PIP concept to your web pages. That is, you can set up your site so that one page remains in view in part of the browser screen and your visitors can use the rest of the screen to trip the link fantastic. The secret to this seemingly miraculous feat is a concept called *frames*, and you learn all about it in this chapter.

What's with all the frame fuss?

The competent web forger always includes a section on each page that enables the user to navigate the important landmarks in her site. This could be a collection of links, a web page "toolbar" (like the ones I showed you how to whip up back in Chapter 9, "Images Can Be Links, Too"), or an image map (again, see Chapter 9). The problem with these navigation sections, though, is that they end up scrolling off the screen whenever the reader moves down the page. (This is assuming the navigation stuff is sitting at the top of the page.) For example, Figure 13.1 shows a page from my site, and Figure 13.2 shows what happens if you scroll down to read more of the text.

Figure 13.1

A page from my site showing my navigation aids at the top.

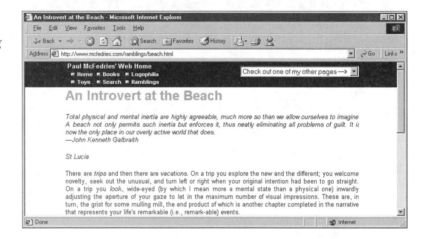

Figure 13.2

Where oh where have my links gone?

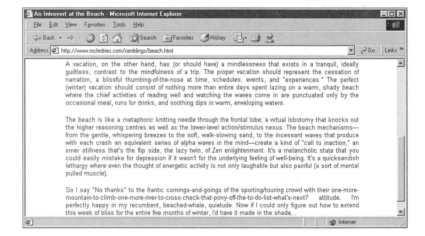

Figure 13.1 shows the various navigation aids that I've plopped onto the top of all the pages on my site. As you can see in the second figure, however, after I scroll down a bit, those navigation doodads are gone like wild geese in winter.

Now have a gander (no pun intended; no, *really*) at Figure 13.3. See how I've scrolled down to the same spot, but the navigation section remains conveniently in view. Weird, huh? The window seems to be divided into two sections: The top section holds the navigation knickknacks, and the bottom section shows the regular page text and graphics. What the heck is happening here?

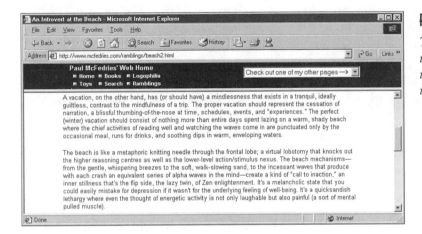

Figure 13.3

This version of the page mysteriously displays the navigation stuff in its own section at the top of the page.

To perform this magic trick, I had to do three things:

♦ I grabbed the HTML tags and text that make up my navigation section, and I put it all into a separate file called header.html.

♦ I grabbed the rest of the page text and put it into another file called beach-f.html.

♦ I created a third page called beach2.html that has a few special tags that serve to divide the browser window into two *frames*. I included in this page the instructions to load the header.html file into the top frame, and the beach-f.html file into the bottom frame.

The big deal is that with this view, surfers can scroll through beach-f.html in the bottom frame until they're blue in the face, and the navigation section remains steadfastly in place. It's even possible to arrange things so that if you click any link, the new page appears in the bottom frame. In other words, the top frame is really the web equivalent of picture-in-picture!

Okay, now that you know what frames are and why you might want to bother with them, let's see how you go about constructing them.

Forging a Frameset Page

The good news about frames is that you can build them using just a few not-too-hard-to-master HTML tags. Unfortunately, most frame neophytes get thrown for a loop right off the bat because the first thing you have to create is a web page that doesn't display anything! *Huh?*

Let me explain. After you enter the frames world, you're faced with not one, but *two* species of web page:

◆ **Content pages**   A content page is just a regular HTML page like the ones you've dealt with throughout this book. That is, they display text, graphics, and whatever other goodies the author packs into the page.

◆ **Frameset pages**   A frameset page has only one mission in life: to divide the browser window into a set of frames, define the size of each frame, and specify which content pages are displayed in each frame. Note that (as you'll soon see) frameset pages have no body section, so you shouldn't populate a frameset page with anything that would normally appear in the body, including regular text and HTML tags such as <B> and <IMG>. If you try, the browser simply ignores your efforts completely and concentrates solely on the frame information.

In other words, the frameset page is really just an empty shell like, say, an ice cube tray. An ice cube tray doesn't do much of anything by itself, and it becomes useful only after you fill in the compartments with water. It's the same with a frameset page: It just divvies up the browser screen into two or more frames, and you have to fill these compartments with separate content pages.

The Basic Frame Tags

Building a frameset page requires two tag types: <FRAMESET> and <FRAME>. The idea is that you begin with <FRAMESET> and between this tag and its corresponding </FRAMESET> end tag, you add one <FRAME> tag for each frame you want to work with. So, to divide the browser window into two frames, you start like this:

```
<HTML>
<HEAD>
<TITLE></TITLE>
</HEAD>

<FRAMESET>
<FRAME>
<FRAME>
</FRAMESET>

</HTML>
```

Notice two things about the structure of this basic frameset page:

◆ You still use the <HTML> and </HTML> tags, and the head section (the part between <HEAD> and </HEAD>) is exactly the same as in a regular page.

◆ There's no body section (that is, no <BODY> tag).

Now you have to tell the browser whether you want the frames to divide the screen horizontally or vertically.

Dividing the Screen Horizontally

If you want the frame divider to run horizontally so that the screen is cleaved into a top part and a bottom part, you toss the ROWS attribute inside the <FRAMESET> tag:

```
<FRAMESET ROWS="Size1,Size2,...">
```

Here, *Size1* and *Size2* are numbers that tell the browser how much screen real estate to give to each frame. There are two types of numbers you can use:

Page Pitfalls

One of most common mistakes that frame rookies make is to include a <BODY> tag somewhere in the frameset page, which usually causes the frames not to work. If you're having trouble seeing your frames, check for a <BODY> tag and delete it if you find one.

◆ **Percentages.** Use percentages to assign a portion of the browser window to each frame. You need to include a percentage value for each frame, and the percentages should add up to 100.

◆ **Pixels.** Use pixels if you know exactly how tall you want a frame to be.

For example, suppose you have two frames and you want the top frame to usurp 25 percent of the screen and the bottom to take the remaining 75 percent. Here's a frameset page (see frame1.htm on this book's CD) that does the job:

```
<HTML>
<HEAD>
<TITLE>Horizontal Frames</TITLE>
</HEAD>

<FRAMESET ROWS="25%,75%">
<FRAME>
<FRAME>
</FRAMESET>

</HTML>
```

If you load this sucker into a browser, you see the rather uninspiring screen shown in Figure 13.4. Now you see what I meant earlier when I said that the frame page is just an empty shell!

Figure 13.4

A frame page that divides the browser screen horizontally.

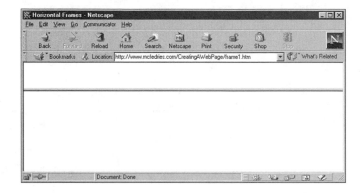

Webmaster Wisdom _____

It's a common frame scenario to want to give one frame a certain size and to want the second frame to take up whatever room is left in the window. To do the latter, enter an asterisk (*) as the "size" of the second frame. For example, if you want the top frame's height to be 100 pixels and the bottom frame to take up whatever's left, you'd use this tag:
`<FRAMESET ROWS="100,*">`

Dividing the Screen Vertically

If you'd prefer that the frame divider run vertically to cut the screen into left and right sections, you populate the <FRAMESET> tag with the COLS (columns) attribute and some numbers:

```
<FRAMESET COLS="Size1,Size2,...">
```

Again, *Size1* and *Size2* tell the browser how much of the window to parcel out to each frame. Here's another HTML file (frame2.htm on this book's CD) that divides the browser screen into three sections that take up 20 percent, 60 percent, and 20 percent of the screen. Figure 13.5 shows the frames loaded into Internet Explorer.

```
<HTML>
<HEAD>
<TITLE>Vertical Frames</TITLE>
</HEAD>
```

```
<FRAMESET COLS="20%,60%,20%">
<FRAME>
<FRAME>
<FRAME>
</FRAMESET>

</HTML>
```

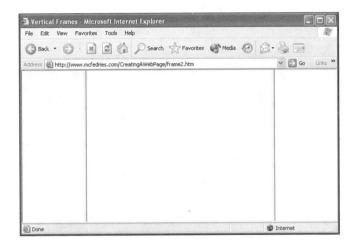

Figure 13.5

This frame page sunders the browser screen into three vertical sections.

Filling the Frames with Content Pages

The nearly naked frame pages you've seen so far aren't too exciting. What happens if you add some regular text or even an <IMG> tag or two? That's an easy one: not a gosh-darned thing! Feel free to type away until your fingers fall off, but you won't get the browser to show anything but the empty frames.

So how do you fill in the frames? You have to specify a separate content page to show in each frame. You do that by adding the SRC attribute into each of the <FRAME> tags. Here's the general format:

```
<FRAME SRC="URL">
```

As you might expect, the *URL* part is the address of the web page you want to display in the frame. Here's an example (frame3.htm on this book's CD):

```
<HTML>
<HEAD>
<TITLE>Horizontal Frames with Content</TITLE>
</HEAD>
```

```
<FRAMESET ROWS="25%,75%">
<FRAME SRC="1.htm">
<FRAME SRC="2.htm">
</FRAMESET>

</HTML>
```

Here, 1.htm and 2.htm are just regular HTML web pages. Figure 13.6 shows how things look in the browser. Notice that 1.htm gets displayed in the top frame and 2.htm gets displayed in the bottom frame.

Figure 13.6

To get the frame page to show something useful, specify a separate content page for each frame.

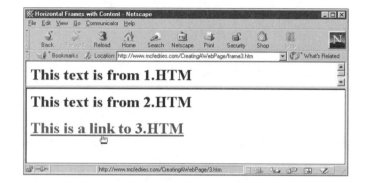

Teaching Frames and Links to Get Along

What happens if one of your framed content pages contains a link? Well, clicking the link loads the page as usual, but you can't be sure *where* the page appears. In some browsers, the new page takes over the entire window and your carefully laid out frames are toast. In other browsers, the new page appears in a separate window.

To avoid this random behavior, you need to control exactly where the linked pages show up. The trick is that you first have to assign a name to each frame. After that's done, it becomes an easy matter of modifying your link tags to specify the name of the frame in which you want the page to load.

To assign a name to a frame, you drop the NAME attribute inside the <FRAME> tag, like so:

```
<FRAME SRC="something.htm" NAME="Whatever">
```

For example, here's an updated frame page (frame4.htm on this book's CD) that includes names for the upper and lower frame:

```
<HTML>
<HEAD>
<TITLE>Named Horizontal Frames</TITLE>
</HEAD>

<FRAMESET ROWS="25%,75%">
<FRAME SRC="1.htm" NAME="upper">
<FRAME SRC="2.htm" NAME="lower">
</FRAMESET>

</HTML>
```

With your frames named, you can make any link load inside a particular frame by adding a TARGET attribute to the <A HREF> tag. For example, here's the <A HREF> tag from 2.HTM:

```
<A HREF="3.htm" TARGET="lower">This is a link to 3.HTM</A>
```

As you can see, the TARGET attribute is set to Lower, which is the name of the bottom frame. Clicking this link, therefore, loads the new page in this frame, as shown in Figure 13.7.

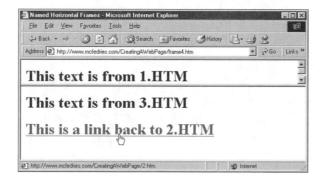

Figure 13.7

Adding TARGET to a link tag forces the new page to load inside the specified frame.

Page Pitfalls

You'll notice in the previous figure that even though I clicked a link to load 2.htm into the bottom frame, Internet Explorer's Address box still shows the same address (that is, the address of the frameset page). That's one of the downsides to frames: The displayed address doesn't change as your readers click from link to link, so the viewers never really know where they are within your site.

Ready-Made Names for Frames

HTML also has three prefab frame names that you can specify with the TARGET attribute:

_self	Loads the new page into the same frame that contains the link.
_top	Loads the new page into the entire window.
_blank	Loads the new page into a new browser window.

Webmaster Wisdom

In frame circles, proper etiquette dictates that links to external sites should either take over the entire screen (TARGET="_top") or be displayed in a separate browser window (TARGET="_blank"). Unfortunately, many framesters don't follow this etiquette and, instead, greedily display *every* link within their frames. Besides cursing their ancestry, what can you do to make sure that *your* page doesn't get jailed within someone else's frames? Include a link on your page that points to the same page, but uses the TARGET="_top" attribute. For example, if your page is named index.html, add a link like this one:

```
<A HREF="index.html" TARGET="_top">Deframe this page</A>
```

Specifying a Default Target

What do you do if you have a frame that contains tons of links? Do you really have to go through the drudgery of adding the TARGET tag to all those <A> tags? Happily, no, you don't. It's possible to specify a default target, and the browser will send every linked page to whatever frame you specify.

To set the default target, add the following tag to the head section (that is, between the <HEAD> and </HEAD> tags) of the page that contains all the links:

```
<BASE TARGET="Whatever">
```

For example, to load every link into a frame named "content," you'd use the following:

```
<BASE TARGET="content">
```

Frame Frills and Frippery

The frames we've seen so far are serviceable beasts. However, the <FRAME> tag comes with a few extra options that you might need to use. Here's a quick summary of these attributes:

♦ **NORESIZE**   Stick this attribute inside a <FRAME> tag to prevent surfers from changing the size of the frame. (Otherwise, the frame can be resized by dragging the frame border with the mouse.)

♦ **SCROLLING**   This attribute determines whether or not a scroll bar appears with a frame. If you set this to YES (that is, SCROLLING="YES") and the content page is too big to fit entirely inside the frame, a scroll bar appears on the right side of the frame. Use SCROLLING="NO" to prevent the scroll bar from appearing.

♦ **BORDER**   Set this attribute to 0 to tell the browser not to display the border between frames. For now, this works only in Netscape version 3.0 and up. For Internet Explorer, also use FRAMEBORDER="0".

Handling Frame-Feeble Browsers

I mentioned earlier that you can't add regular text or HTML tags to a frame page. (Actually, you could if you put in a <BODY> tag. However, this would nullify the <FRAMESET> tag, so it would defeat the purpose.) So what happens when a browser that doesn't understand frames comes across your frame page? You guessed it, it doesn't display anything!

This isn't a great way to welcome these surfers to your site, to say the least. However, there is a way to handle these nonframe browsers and at least give them something to chew on. It's called the <NOFRAMES> tag. Any text or HTML tags you insert between this tag and its </NOFRAMES> end tag shows up in a frameless browser. For example, here's the HTML for a page (frame5.htm on this book's CD) that includes the <NOFRAMES> tag, and you can see the result in Figure 13.8:

```
<HTML>
<HEAD>
<TITLE>Handling Lame Frame Browsers</TITLE>
</HEAD>

<FRAMESET ROWS="25%,75%">
<FRAME SRC="1.htm" NAME="upper">
<FRAME SRC="2.htm" NAME="lower">

<NOFRAMES>
<H3>Doh! Looks like you have a browser that is frames-challenged.
<P>
Here's a <A HREF="2.htm">frame-free page</A> that should be more to your
browser's liking.</H3>
</NOFRAMES>

</FRAMESET>
</HTML>
```

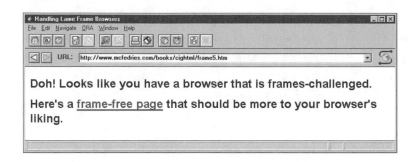

Now wait just a cotton-picking minute! If a browser can't handle frames, how can it know about the <NOFRAMES> tag?

Good question! The answer is that it doesn't. These older browsers are really just bypassing the <FRAMESET> and <FRAME> tags (since they don't understand them) and displaying whatever other text is in the file. The <NOFRAMES> tag actually serves to prevent frame-capable browsers from displaying the text.

Oh.

Fancier Frames

To finish this frames tutorial, let's kick things up a notch and look at a technique that enables you to create some pretty fancy frame effects.

So far, you've learned only how to divide the browser window into horizontal regions or vertical regions. What do you do if you want to combine these types? For example, suppose you define an upper frame and a lower frame and you then want to divide the lower frame into two vertical sections? Well, it turns out that you can use as many <FRAMESET> tags as you like in a single frame page. So you can get your desired layout by defining one <FRAMESET> tag to divide the screen in two horizontally and then insert a second <FRAMESET> tag that divides the lower region vertically. Here's the code for an HTML page (frame6.htm on the CD) that does this:

```
<HTML>
<HEAD>
<TITLE>Nested Frames</TITLE>
</HEAD>

<FRAMESET ROWS="25%,75%">
<FRAME SRC="1.htm" NAME="Upper">
   <FRAMESET COLS="50%,50%">
   <FRAME SRC="2.htm" NAME="Lower">
   <FRAME SRC="3.htm" NAME="Right">
```

```
        </FRAMESET>
</FRAMESET>

</HTML>
```

This technique is called *nesting* frames, and you can use it to create whatever layout suits your needs. Figure 13.9 shows how the example looks in the browser.

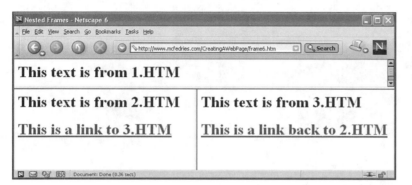

Figure 13.9

You can nest frames to achieve some interesting layouts.

The Least You Need to Know

◆ Frames: an out of <BODY> experience. In your frameset page, you use <FRAMESET> and </FRAMESET> instead of <BODY> and </BODY>.

◆ Horizontal or vertical frames. In the <FRAMESET> tag, use the ROWS attribute to divide the browser into horizontal frames, or use the COLS attribute to divide the browser into vertical frames.

◆ Use <FRAME> to fill in the frames. Add the SRC attribute to each <FRAME> tag and set it equal to the address of the regular page that you want loaded into the frame.

◆ The frame name game. If you want a link to display a page in a specific frame, first name all your frames by adding the NAME attribute to each <FRAME> tag. Then plop the TARGET attribute inside the <A HREF> tag and set it equal to the name of the frame in which you want the page to show up.

◆ Ready-to-roll names. For the TARGET value, use _self for the current frame (that is, the one containing the link), _top for the entire browser window, and _blank for a new browser window.

Part 3

High HTML Style: Working with Style Sheets

After unveiling a new site to friends, family, and colleagues, you might receive constructive criticisms instead of constant kudos. Grrrr. You mutter a few choice epithets under your breath, but then you realize that, hey, they're right. The changes really would make your pages look better. So, conscientious webmeister that you are, you begin the long and laborious process of opening all the pages and editing the dozens of tags that determine the look of each page. Sigh. There's got to be a better way.

If making large-scale changes to your site is getting you down, I have some good news. There's some web technology that will enable you to change fonts, colors, and other features for 2 or 102 pages with only a few keystrokes! This miraculous bit of techno-trickery is called a style sheet, and you learn how it works here in Part 3.

A Beginner's Guide to Style Sheets

In This Chapter

♦ Understanding style sheets

♦ Three methods of using style sheets

♦ Applying styles to sections, words, and phrases

♦ Numerous other style sheet shenanigans

This chapter gets your style sheet education off to an easy start by introducing you ever so gently to this brave new web world. You learn just what styles and sheets are, how they affect your pages, and why they're so darned useful. You also learn the basic methods for incorporating style sheets into your pages. Although I run through a few examples in this chapter, the real style sheet goods can be found in the next two chapters where I delve into the style sheet specifics for things like text, paragraphs, positioning, margins, and more.

What's a style, and what's a sheet?

If you've ever used a fancy-schmancy word processor such as Microsoft Word or WordPerfect, then you've probably stumbled over a style or two in your travels. In a nutshell, a style is a combination of two or more formatting options rolled into one nice, neat package. For example, you might have a "Title" style that combines four formatting options: bold, centered, 24-point type size, and an Arial typeface. You can then "apply" this style to any text and the program dutifully formats the text with all four options. If you later change your mind and decide your titles should use an 18-point font, instead, all you have to do is redefine the Title style. The program then trudges through the entire document and updates each bit of text that uses the Title style.

Styles in the Web Universe

In a web page, a style performs a similar function. That is, it enables you to define a series of formatting options for a given tag, such as <P> or <H1>. Like word processor styles, page styles offer two main advantages:

◆ They save time because you create the definition of the style's formatting once, and the browser applies that formatting each time you use the tag.

◆ They make your pages easier to modify because all you need to do is edit the style definition and all the places the style is used within the page get updated automatically.

Let's eyeball an example. The browser window in Figure 14.1 shows the following HTML file (see ssbefore.htm on the CD in this book), which contains just a single <H1> heading, and you can see the result in Figure 14.1:

```
<HTML>
<HEAD>
<TITLE>Style Sheets: Before</TITLE>
</HEAD>
<BODY>
<H1>Style Sheets: What's the Big Whoop?</H1>
</BODY>
</HTML>
```

Figure 14.1

A simple web page, showing just a single <H1> heading.

Now suppose you prefer to use bigger text in your heading. You can't change the size of <H1> headings directly, but you could do it by changing the SIZE attribute of the <FONT> tag, like this:

```
<FONT SIZE="7">
Style Sheets: What's the Big Whoop?
</FONT>
```

That's no big deal if you have only one or two headings, but what if you use dozens of them? Not only is it a pain to add those <FONT> tags, but it also makes your HTML source code more difficult to read.

A better solution is to create a style for the <H1> tag that tells the browser to use a larger font size for the <H1> text. The following HTML file (see ssafter.htm on the CD in this book) shows you one way to do it, and Figure 14.2 displays the results (I explain the specifics of this a bit later):

```
<HTML>
<HEAD>
<TITLE>Style Sheets: After</TITLE>

<STYLE>
H1 {font-size: 34pt}
</STYLE>

</HEAD>
<BODY>
<H1>Style Sheets: What's the Big Whoop?</H1>
</BODY>
</HTML>
```

Figure 14.2

Use a style to get a larger heading.

Note the new <STYLE> tag and, in particular, the following line:

```
H1 {font- size: 34pt}
```

What this tells the browser is that, each time it comes across the <H1> tag, it should format the text with a 34-point font size.

And it's easy to make a change if you decide that you want your heading even larger. For example, if you want to use a 72-point font size (what newspaper types called "Second Coming" type), you need only make a single change (see ssafter2.htm on the CD in this book):

```
<HTML>
<HEAD>

<STYLE>
H1 {font-size: 72pt}
</STYLE>

</HEAD>
<BODY>
<H1>Style Sheets: What's the Big Whoop?</H1>
</BODY>
</HTML>
```

Figure 14.3 shows how it looks with Internet Explorer.

Figure 14.3

Styles make it easy to change the formatting in your pages.

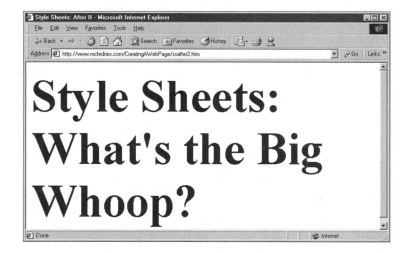

Combining formats into one easy-to-use bundle is a nifty time saver, and it's worth the price of admission alone. However, style sheets have a few other tricks up their digital sleeves, tricks that enable you to do things that are either difficult or downright impossible with your garden-variety HTML tags. For example, displaying text at a 72-point type size, as shown in the previous figure, is impossible under plain HTML. Here's a tiny sampling of some other style sheet sleight of hand you can do:

◆ You can set a background color or image for paragraphs or even single words.

◆ You can define a margin around your page.

◆ You can indent text precisely.

Sheets: Collections of Styles

So far so good, but what the heck is a sheet?

The term *style sheet* harkens back to the days of yore when word processors enabled you to store your styles in a separate document known as a style sheet. This is equivalent to what we usually call a template, today. As you'll see later on, it's possible to define all your HTML styles in a separate page and then tell the browser where that page is located, so it's a bit like those old style sheets (although *style file* might have been a better—and more fun—name). More generally, an HTML style sheet is any collection of styles, whether it exists in a separate page or within the current page (as in the earlier example with the <H1> tag).

What About Browser Support?

Style sheets have come a long way in the past couple of years. Once an obscure section of the HTML 4.0 standard, style sheets are now a much-traveled part of the Web design landscape. The reason style sheets have come into their own is simple: Most modern browsers support them.

Technically, style sheet support is built into Internet Explorer versions 3.0 and later, and Netscape Navigator versions 4.0 and later. However, that accounts for most browser traffic today (about 96 percent, as I write this).

Therefore, it's perfectly safe to go ahead and start learning and using style sheets right away. Those few style sheet-ignorant browsers that visit your pages ignore the extra tags (and you can use HTML comment tags to block out other style-related text), so no harm comes to your pages.

Some Style Basics

Before I show you how to implement style sheets, let's take a second to get a grip on just what a style looks like. As an example, let's put the style we used earlier under the microscope. Here it is again:

```
H1 {font-size: 34pt}
```

This is called a *style definition*, and here's a rundown of the various parts:

Page Pitfalls

I should warn you, however, that even though most browsers support style sheets, they have a nasty habit of supporting them in different and often unpredictable ways. I'll try to take this into account as we go along, but it's important to check your pages in different browsers to make sure everyone will see what you want them to see.

◆ The definition always begins with the HTML tag that you want the style to modify, without the usual angle brackets (< and >).

◆ The rest of the definition is ensconced inside those curly brackets—{ and }—which are known officially as *braces*.

◆ The first thing inside the braces is the name of the property you want to set, followed by a colon (:). In our example, the property is called `font-size`.

◆ Finally, after the colon, you type the value you want to assign to the property (34pt, in the example, where "pt" is short for "points").

Webmaster Wisdom

Besides applying multiple styles to a single tag, it's also possible to apply a single style to multiple tags. What you do is list the tags you want affected, separated by commas, before the opening brace ({). Here's an example:

```
P, OL, UL, DT, DD {font-
size: 10pt}
```

As a different example, suppose you want all your <TT> text to appear in a gray font. In style sheet land, font color is governed by the `color` property, so you'd set this style like so:

```
TT {color: gray}
```

Finally, you can set multiple properties in a single style by separating each property and value with a semicolon (;). In the following example, <H2> tags are displayed with purple, 20-point text:

```
H2 {color: purple; font-size: 20pt}
```

Three Sheets to the Web: Style Sheets and HTML

One of the most confusing things about style sheets is the sheer number of methods you can use to implement them. To help alleviate the confusion, this section shows you just three methods and explains exactly when you should use each method.

Method #1: The <STYLE> Tag

Probably the most straightforward way to implement a style sheet is to use the <STYLE> tag you saw in the earlier example. The idea is that you plop a <STYLE> tag and a </STYLE> end tag into your document, and then insert all your style definitions in between. The best place to put all this stuff is within the page header, like so:

Words from the Web

Style sheet mavens call the <STYLE></STYLE> method an **embedded** style sheet.

```
<HTML>
 <HEAD>

<STYLE TYPE="text/css">
<!--
Your style definitions go here
```

```
-->
</STYLE>

</HEAD>
<BODY>
The visible Web page stuff goes here
</BODY>
</HTML>
```

Note, too, that I tossed in the HTML comment tags, for good measure. This hides your style definitions from older browsers that don't know a style sheet from a rap sheet.

This method is best when you want to apply only a particular set of style definitions to a single page.

Method #2: Linking to an External Style Sheet

Style sheets get insanely powerful when you use an "external" style sheet. This is a separate file that contains your style definitions. To use these definitions within any web page, you simply add a special <LINK> tag inside the page header. This tag specifies the name of the external style sheet file, and the browser then uses that file to grab the style definitions.

Here are the steps you need to follow to set up an external style sheet:

1. Use your favorite text editor to create a shiny new text file.
2. Add your style definitions to this file. Note that you don't need the <STYLE> tag or any other HTML tags.
3. Save the file in the same directory as your HTML files, and use a "css" extension (for example, "mystyles.css"). This helps you remember down the road that this is a style sheet file. (The "css" stands for cascading style sheet.)
4. For every page in which you want to use the styles, add a <LINK> tag inside the page header. Here's the general format to use (where *filename.css* is the name of your external style sheet file):

   ```
   <LINK REL="stylesheet" TYPE="text/css" HREF="filename.css">
   ```

For example, suppose you create a style sheet file named mystyles.css and that file includes the following style definitions:

```
H1 {color: red}
TT {font-size: 16pt}
```

You'd then refer to that file by using the <LINK> tag shown in the following example (see ssextern.htm on the CD in this book):

```
<HTML>
<HEAD>
<LINK REL="stylesheet" TYPE="text/css" HREF="mystyles.css">
</HEAD>
<BODY>
<H1>This Heading Will Appear Red</H1>
<TT>This text will be displayed in a 16-point font</TT>
</BODY>
</HTML>
```

Why is this so powerful? Well, you can add the same <LINK> tag to any number of web pages and they'll all use the same style definitions. This makes it a breeze to create a consistent look and feel for your site. And if you decide that your <H1> text should be green, instead, all you have to do is edit the style sheet file (mystyles.css). Automatically, every single one of your pages that link to this file will be updated with the new style!

Webmaster Wisdom

The HREF part of the <LINK> tag doesn't have to be a simple filename. You can use a full URL, if need be. This is handy if you've set up your site with multiple directories, or if you want to link to an external style sheet file on another site. (I don't recommend the latter, however, because it takes your pages a bit longer to load because the browser has to go fetch the file.)

Method #3: Inline Styles

In the two style sheet methods we've looked at so far, the browser applies the style to *every* instance of whatever tag you specify in the definition. This is good because it ensures a consistent look throughout a page. But what in tarnation do you do if you want a particular instance of a tag to use a different style? For example, suppose you want all your <H1> headings to appear in a 24-point font, but you want the *first* <H1> heading to appear in a 36-point font. You can accomplish this by shoehorning the STYLE attribute right inside the tag you want to work with. (Among style sheet wonks, this is known as an *inline* style.) Here's an example (see ssinline.htm on the CD in this book):

```
<HTML>
<HEAD>
<TITLE>Style Sheets: Inline Styles</TITLE>
</HEAD>
```

```
<STYLE TYPE="text/css">
<!--
H1 {font-size: 24pt}
-->
</STYLE>

<BODY>
<H1 STYLE="font-size: 36pt">This Heading Uses 36-Point Type</H1>
<H1>This One Uses 24-Point Type</H1>
</BODY>
</HTML>
```

As before, I use the <STYLE> tag in the header to define a style for the <H1> tag.
Notice, however, that the first <H1> tag includes a STYLE attribute that specifies a different font size. (Notice, too, that you define the style slightly differently. That is, you use
quotation marks instead of braces.) Figure 14.4 shows the results.

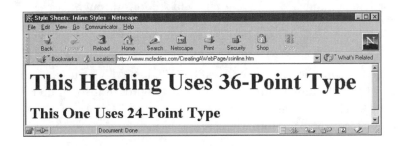

Figure 14.4

*Using inline styles lets you
set a style for individual tags
and thus override the default
style.*

Applying a Style to a Section

The <DIV> tag is used to divide your page into separate sections. It doesn't do a whole lot
by itself, although the browser usually inserts a line break (equivalent to a <BR> tag)
before the <DIV> tag and after the </DIV> end tag. However, by including the STYLE
attribute inside the <DIV> tag, you can apply an inline style to everything that's inside
one of these sections. Here's an example:

```
<DIV STYLE="font-size: 16pt">
<H1>This Is a 16-Point Heading</H1>
This here sentence will appear in a 16-point font.
<H2>So Will This Heading</H2>
</DIV>
```

In this case, everything between <DIV> and </DIV> gets formatted with the 16-point
font size style.

Applying a Style to a Word or Phrase

What if you want to apply a style only to a particular word or phrase? In most cases, you won't want to use <DIV> because it adds line breaks before and after the defined section. The solution is to use the <SPAN> tag. The idea is that you surround your word or phrase with <SPAN> and </SPAN>, and then toss the STYLE attribute inside the <SPAN> tag. Here's an example:

```
Apply the style right <SPAN STYLE="font-size: 20pt">now</SPAN>.
```

Working with Style Classes

Although I promised you earlier that I'd show you only three methods for implementing styles in your pages, I can't resist telling you about a fourth method that can be really handy: the *style class.* The style class was created to solve a common problem: What if you want to apply a specific style to a number of different tags and sections throughout the document?

Couldn't you just use inline styles?

Absolutely. However, what if you decide to change the style? Then you'd have to go through the entire page and edit all those inline styles. An easier approach is to set up a style class within your main style sheet (that is, either within the <STYLE> tag or within an external style sheet file). Here's the basic format to use:

```
.ClassName {style definitions go here}
```

Here, *ClassName* is a unique name (without any spaces) that you use for the class. Here are a couple of examples:

```
.TitleText {font-size: 20pt; color: Navy; text-align: center}
.SubtitleText {font-size: 16pt; color: Gray; text-align: center}
```

The TitleText class uses a font size of 20 points, navy text, and a center alignment; the SubtitleText class uses a font size of 16 points, gray text, and a center alignment.

To use these classes, add a CLASS attribute to the tags you want the styles applied to, and set it equal to the class name (without the dot). Here's a for instance:

```
<DIV CLASS="TitleText">This is the Title of the Document</DIV>
```

The advantage here is that if you decide to change this style, you need edit only the style class; after that, every tag that uses the class changes automatically.

Here's a page (see ssclass.htm on the CD in this book) that offers up a complete example.

```
<HTML>
<HEAD>
<TITLE>Style Sheets: Styles Classes</TITLE>
</HEAD>

<STYLE TYPE="text/css">
<!--
.TitleText {font-size: 20pt; color: Navy; text-align: center}
.SubtitleText {font-size: 16pt; color: Gray; text-align: center}
-->
</STYLE>

<BODY>
<DIV CLASS="TitleText">This is the Title of the Document</DIV>
<DIV CLASS="SubtitleText">This is the Subtitle of the Document</DIV>
</BODY>
</HTML>
```

Figure 14.5 shows how Internet Explorer interprets the classes.

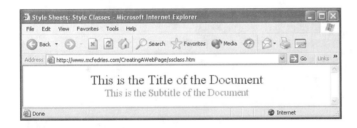

Figure 14.5

Use style classes for even more control over your styles.

The Least You Need to Know

- ◆ The basics. A *style* is a collection of formatting instructions for a given tag and a *style sheet* is a collection of styles.
- ◆ Embedded style sheet. This is a style sheet that resides inside a document and is defined by the <STYLE> and </STYLE> tags.
- ◆ External style sheet. This is a collection of styles that sits in a separate file. You let the browser know about the existence of this file by using the <LINK> tag:

  ```
  <LINK REL="stylesheet" TYPE="text/css" HREF="filename.css">
  ```

- ◆ Inline style. This is a style defined by adding the STYLE attribute inside the tag you want to affect.
- ◆ Style sections. Use the <DIV> tag to apply a style to all the tags and text between <DIV> and </DIV>. Use the <SPAN> tag to apply a style to all the text between <SPAN> and </SPAN>.

Sheet Music: Styles for Fonts, Colors, and Backgrounds

In This Chapter

- ◆ Fiddling with font sizes, families, and weights
- ◆ Indenting and aligning text
- ◆ Text formatting such as underlining and strikethrough
- ◆ Working with style sheet colors
- ◆ Getting a handle on background styles
- ◆ Lots of ways to use styles to gussy up your pages.

Okay, now that you know how to sew styles into your HTML creations, it's time to examine the specifics of the various styles available. This chapter examines style definitions for fonts, text, colors, and backgrounds.

Using Styles to Control Fonts

Earlier in the book (Chapter 3, "From Buck-Naked to Beautiful: Dressing Up Your Page," to be exact) I showed you how to use the <FONT> tag to adjust font properties such as the size and typeface. Well, anything the <FONT> tag can do, style sheets can do better. The next few sections show you why.

Font Size Styles

The <FONT> tag's control over the size of the font is limited, at best. Style sheets are vastly superior because they enable you to set the size of your text to just about anything you want.

Webmaster Wisdom

I cover most of the available style attributes in this chapter, but not all of them. For a complete list, see my Style Sheets Reference on the CD in this book or on my site: www.mcfedries.com/CreatingAWebPage/css.

Just so you know, the *font size* is a measure of the relative height used for each character. Although style sheets give you several ways to specify these heights, it's probably best to stick with *points*. To set the size, use the font-size style and set it to a number that ends with pt, like so:

```
P {font-size: 14pt}
```

There are also a half dozen predefined size values you can plug in: xx-small, x-small, small, medium, large, and x-large. Finally, you can also use the relative smaller and larger values to get text that's a bit smaller or a bit larger than the regular page text.

Webmaster Wisdom

Here's a list of the various types of units that are used in style sheets:

Unit	What It Represents
em	font-size (the current font size, as given by the font-size property)
ex	x-height (the height of the lowercase "x" in the current typeface)
px	pixels
in	inches
cm	centimeters
mm	millimeters
pt	points (there are 72 points to an inch)
pc	picas (one pica equals 12 points)

The following HTML file (see ss-size.htm on the CD in this book) tries a few different values on for, uh, size, and Figure 15.1 shows how the browser interprets them:

```
<HTML>
<HEAD>
<TITLE>Style Sheets: Font Sizes</TITLE>
</HEAD>
<BODY>

Our t-shirts are available in sizes
<SPAN STYLE="font-size: xx-small">xx-small</SPAN>,
<SPAN STYLE="font-size: x-small">x-small</SPAN>,
<SPAN STYLE="font-size: small">small</SPAN>,
<SPAN STYLE="font-size: medium">medium</SPAN>,
<SPAN STYLE="font-size: large">large</SPAN>,
<SPAN STYLE="font-size: x-large">x-large</SPAN>, and
<SPAN STYLE="font-size: xx-large">xx-large.</SPAN>
<DIV STYLE="font-size: small">
You can also special order t-shirts in
<SPAN STYLE="font-size: smaller">smaller</SPAN> or
<SPAN STYLE="font-size: larger">larger</SPAN> sizes.
</DIV>
Our biggest shirt is <SPAN STYLE="font-size: 24pt">Size 24</SPAN>.

</BODY>
</HTML>
```

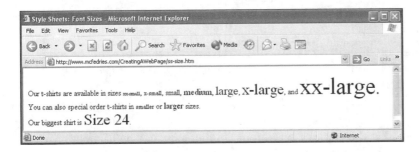

Figure 15.1

Styles enable you to set all kinds of different font sizes.

Font Family (Typeface) Styles

The *font family* represents the overall look associated with each character (it's more commonly known as the *typeface*). Unlike the other styles, there are no set values you can use. Instead, you normally specify several possibilities and the browser uses the first one that's installed on the user's computer. Here's an example:

```
TT {font-family: Courier, "Courier New"}
```

CAUTION **Page Pitfalls**

As with the <FONT> tag's FACE attribute (see Chapter 3), the reader sees only a specified typeface if it's installed on the reader's computer. If the typeface isn't installed, the reader sees only the browser's default typeface.

Notice that multiple-word family names must be enclosed in quotation marks. If you're using an inline style (the STYLE attribute), enclose multiple-word family names in single quotation marks, like so:

```
<SPAN STYLE="font-family: 'Comic Sans MS'">
```

There are also five so-called *generic* family names you can use:

- ◆ cursive   Displays text in a cursive font (such as Comic Sans MS), which is a flowing style reminiscent of handwriting.

- ◆ fantasy   Displays text is a fantasy font (such as Broadway), which is a decorative style.

- ◆ monospace   Displays text in a monospace font (such as Courier New), which means each character—from the wide "w" to the skinny "i"—is given the same amount of horizontal space. This is similar to the effect produced by the <TT> tag.

- ◆ serif   Displays text in a serif font (such as Times New Roman), which means each character has extra cross strokes (called *feet* in the typographic biz).

- ◆ sans-serif   Displays text in a sans serif font (such as Arial), which means each character doesn't have the extra cross strokes. (Although this is a two-word value, it doesn't require quotation marks because it's a built-in value.)

CAUTION **Page Pitfalls**

All of the version 4 and later browsers will render the monospace, serif, and sans serif families reliably. However, support for the cursive and fantasy families is spotty, so you should probably avoid them.

These are most often used at the end of a list of font families as a "catch all" value that will render the text the way you want if the user doesn't have any of the specific font families installed. For example, if you want to display sans serif text, you might set up your style like this:

```
.title {font-family: Arial, Helvetica, "MS Sans Serif", sans serif}
```

The following HTML file (it's ssfamily.htm on the CD in this book) puts a few families to the test. Figure 15.2 shows how they look with Internet Explorer 5 for Windows, and Figure 15.3 shows the results in Netscape 6 for the Macintosh.

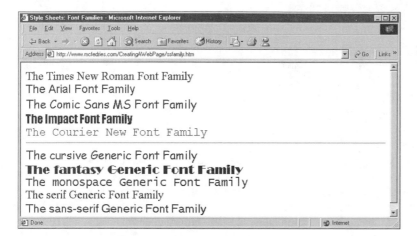

Figure 15.2

A few font families in Internet Explorer 5.

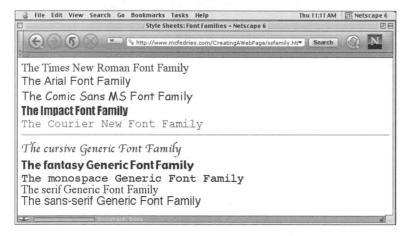

Figure 15.3

The same families in Netscape 6 for the Mac.

```
<HTML>
<HEAD>
<TITLE>Style Sheets: Font Families</TITLE>

<STYLE TYPE="text/css">
<!--
.family1 {font-size: 18pt; font-family: "Times New Roman"}
.family2 {font-size: 18pt; font-family: Arial}
.family3 {font-size: 18pt; font-family: "Comic Sans MS"}
.family4 {font-size: 18pt; font-family: Impact}
.family5 {font-size: 18pt; font-family: "Courier New"}
-->
</STYLE>

</HEAD>
```

```
<BODY>

<DIV CLASS="family1">The Times New Roman Font Family</DIV>
<DIV CLASS="family2">The Arial Font Family</DIV>
<DIV CLASS="family3">The Comic Sans MS Font Family</DIV>
<DIV CLASS="family4">The Impact Font Family</DIV>
<DIV CLASS="family5">The Courier New Font Family</DIV>
<HR>
<DIV STYLE="font-size: 18pt">
<DIV STYLE="font-family: cursive">The cursive Generic Font Family</DIV>
<DIV STYLE="font-family: fantasy">The fantasy Generic Font Family</DIV>
<DIV STYLE="font-family: monospace">The monospace Generic Font Family</DIV>
<DIV STYLE="font-family: serif">The serif Generic Font Family</DIV>
<DIV STYLE="font-family: sans-serif">The sans-serif Generic Font Family</DIV>
</DIV>

</BODY>
</HTML>
```

Font Weight Styles (Bolding)

The font weight controls the thickness of text. For example, the <B> tag renders text as bold by displaying thicker letters. As usual, however, style sheets give you much greater control. In this case, you use the font-weight style:

```
font-weight: value
```

Here, *value* can be either of the following:

- ◆ **A predefined weight** Use one of the following predefined values: normal, bold, bolder, or lighter. The latter two are relative values that make the text appear bolder or lighter than the surrounding text.

- ◆ **A specific weight** Use one of the following: 100, 200, 300, 400 (normal), 500, 600, 700 (bold), 800, or 900.

Page Pitfalls

Unfortunately, most browsers don't do much of anything when confronted with font weight values from 100 to 500 (as you can see in Figure 15.4). Also, the version 6 browsers seem to render the values from 600 to 800 in the same way.

Here's an example file (it's ssweight.htm on the CD in this book) that puts the font-weight style through its paces (Figure 15.4 shows what happens in Netscape 4):

```
<HTML>
<HEAD>
<TITLE>Style Sheets: Font Weights</TITLE>
</HEAD>
<BODY>

<DIV STYLE="font-size: 18pt">
The <SPAN STYLE="font-family: 'Courier New', Courier">font-weight</SPAN>
style uses the following values:<BR>
<SPAN STYLE="font-weight: 100">100</SPAN>,
<SPAN STYLE="font-weight: 200">200</SPAN>,
<SPAN STYLE="font-weight: 300">300</SPAN>,
<SPAN STYLE="font-weight: 400">400</SPAN>,
<SPAN STYLE="font-weight: 500">500</SPAN>,
<SPAN STYLE="font-weight: 600">600</SPAN>,
<SPAN STYLE="font-weight: 700">700</SPAN>,
<SPAN STYLE="font-weight: 800">800</SPAN>,
<SPAN STYLE="font-weight: 900">900</SPAN>
</DIV>

</BODY>
</HTML>
```

Figure 15.4

The various values for the font-weight style.

Font Style Styles (Italics)

If font-weight is the style sheet equivalent of the <B> tag, you might be wondering if there's an equivalent style for the <I> tag. Yup, there is, but it has the confusing name of font-style. Yeah, that's *real* descriptive. Anyway, it's very simple:

```
font-style: italic
```

Also, some fonts have an *oblique* style that looks sort of like italic, but it's really just the letters slanted to one side. If a particular font has an oblique version, you can use the following style to specify it:

```
font-style: oblique
```

Textstyles: More Ways to Format Text

Besides fiddling with fonts, style sheets offer a few other ways to format your page text. This section looks at four of them: indentation, alignment, underlining, and casing.

Indenting the First Line of a Paragraph

Many professionally typeset pages indent the beginning of each paragraph. The only way to do that in regular HTML is to string together a series of nonbreaking spaces ( ) at the start of each paragraph. With style sheets, however, it's no sweat because you just use the text-indent style. For example, the following page (see ssindent.htm on the CD in this book) includes a style sheet that tells the browser to indent the first line of every paragraph by half an inch, as shown in Figure 15.5.

```
<HTML>
<HEAD>
<TITLE>Style Sheets: Text Indents</TITLE>

<STYLE TYPE="text/css">
<!--
P {text-indent: 0.5in}
-->
</STYLE>
</HEAD>
<BODY>


<H3>Textstyles: More Ways to Format Text</H3>
<P>
Besides fiddling with fonts, style sheets offer a few other
ways to format your page text. This section looks at four of them:
indentation, alignment, underlining, and casing.
</P>
<H4>Indenting the First Line of a Paragraph</H4>
<P>
Many professionally-typeset pages indent the beginning of each
paragraph. The only way to do that in regular HTML is to string
together a series of non-breaking spaces (<TT>&#38;nbsp;</TT>) at the start of
each paragraph. With style sheets, however, it's no sweat because
you just use the <TT>text-indent</TT> style. For example, the following
page includes a style sheet that tells the browser to indent the
first line of every paragraph by half an inch.
</P>

</BODY>
</HTML>
```

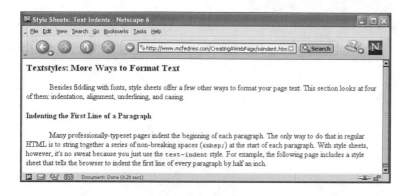

Figure 15.5

Use text-indent to indent the first line of a paragraph.

Webmaster Wisdom

If you want the entire paragraph indented instead of just the first line, you need to work with the various margin styles. I tell you about them in Chapter 16, "The Box Model: Styles for Dimensions, Borders, Margins, and More."

Aligning Text

To set the alignment of a section of text, use the `text-align` style:

```
text-align: alignment
```

Here, *alignment* can be one of the following four values:

- ◆ `left`   Aligns the text with the left side of the browser window.
- ◆ `center`   Centers the text within the browser window.
- ◆ `right`   Aligns the text with the right side of the browser window.
- ◆ `justify`   Aligns the text with both the left and right sides of the browser window.

The following page (see ssalign.htm on the CD in this book) gives these alignment values a test drive (see Figure 15.6):

```
<HTML>
<HEAD>
<TITLE>Style Sheets: Aligning Text</TITLE>
</HEAD>
<BODY>

<TABLE BORDER="1">
<TR>
<TH WIDTH="25%">
```

```
Left-aligned text
</TH>
<TH WIDTH="25%">
Centered text
</TH>
<TH WIDTH="25%">
Right-aligned text
</TH>
<TH WIDTH="25%">
Justified text
</TH>
</TR>
<TR>
<TD WIDTH="25%" STYLE="text-align: left">
Puns are little plays on words that a certain breed of person
loves to spring on you and then look at you in a certain
</TD>
<TD WIDTH="25%" STYLE="text-align: center">
self-satisfied way to indicate that he thinks that you must
think that he is by far the cleverest person on Earth
</TD>
<TD WIDTH="25%" STYLE="text-align: right">
now that Benjamin Franklin is dead, when in fact what you
are thinking is that if this person ever ends up in a
</TD>
<TD WIDTH="25%" STYLE="text-align: justify">
lifeboat, the other passengers will hurl him overboard by the end of
the first day even if they have plenty of food and water. &#150;Dave Barry
</TD>
</TR>
</TABLE>

</BODY>
</HTML>
```

Figure 15.6

The align values in action.

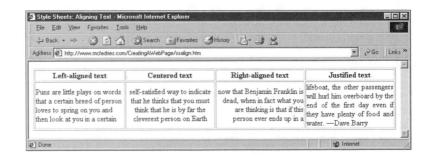

Using the Text Decoration Styles

One of the most common questions that readers ask me is "How can I display my links without an underline?" And my answer is "Use the text-decoration style on the <A> tag and set it to none":

```
A {text-decoration: none}
```

That's a nice trick, but the text-decoration style has a few others up its sleeve. Here's a complete list of the values you can use with this style:

- blink   This is a Netscape-only (version 4.0 and up) value, and it's the equivalent of the dumb <BLINK> tag.

- line-through   Formats text with a line through the middle (this is usually called *strikethrough* text). Most people use this style to represent text that's been "deleted" from a document.

- none   Formats text without any decoration.

- overline   Formats text with a line over the top. (Note that Netscape doesn't yet support this value.)

- underline   Formats text with an underline.

Here's some sample code that uses a few text decoration values (see ssdecor.htm on the CD in this book):

```
<HTML>
<HEAD>
<TITLE>Style Sheets: Text Decoration</TITLE>
</HEAD>
<BODY>
<H2 STYLE="text-decoration: none">None</H2>
<H2 STYLE="text-decoration: line-through">Line-through</H2>
<H2 STYLE="text-decoration: overline">Overline</H2>
<H2 STYLE="text-decoration: underline">Underline</H2>
</BODY>
</HTML>
```

Figure 15.7 shows how they look in Netscape 6 (which, by the way, is the first version of Netscape that supports the overline value).

Figure 15.7

Some text-decoration style examples.

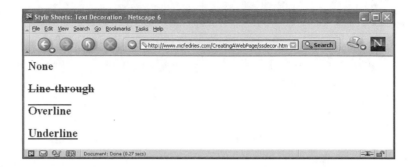

Working with Uppercase and Lowercase Letters

You can format text as all uppercase, all lowercase, or with only the first letter of each word as uppercase (this is often called *title case*). The style that accomplishes this goes by the unlikely name of text-transform. (Sheesh. Only a major league geek could come up with such a nonobvious name.) This style comes equipped with four values for your style pleasure:

- ◆ capitalize   Converts the first letter of every word to uppercase.
- ◆ lowercase   Converts every letter to lowercase.
- ◆ none   Leaves the text as is.
- ◆ uppercase   Converts every letter to uppercase.

Here's some code that demonstrates the various text-transform values (check out sstrans.htm on the CD in this book), and Figure 15.8 shows how it looks with Internet Explorer.

```
<HTML>
<HEAD>
<TITLE>Style Sheets: Text Transform</TITLE>
</HEAD>
<BODY>
<H2 STYLE="text-transform: capitalize">
I left my heart in Truth or Consequences, New Mexico</H2>
<H2 STYLE="text-transform: lowercase">
I left my heart in Truth or Consequences, New Mexico</H2>
<H2 STYLE="text-transform: none">
I left my heart in Truth or Consequences, New Mexico</H2>
<H2 STYLE="text-transform: uppercase">
I left my heart in Truth or Consequences, New Mexico</H2>
</BODY>
</HTML>
```

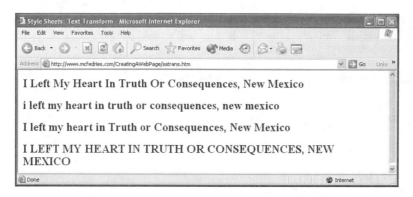

Figure 15.8

Examples of the ill-named text-transform style.

Coloring Your Web World with Color Styles

Using color within a style sheet is more or less the same as using the <FONT> tag's COLOR attribute (discussed in Chapter 3). In this case, you use the color style and set it to one of the weird six-digit RGB values, as in this example:

```
<SPAN STYLE="color: #FF0000">This text is red</SPAN>
```

The big advantage you get with style sheet colors is that you can finally get those unintuitive RGB values out of your life. That's because color names are part of the style sheet specification. These color names—semiofficially known as the *X11 color set*—enable you to use friendly monikers such as "red" and "yellow" instead of the obscure RGB values. There are 140 names in all and they cover most of the color spectrum, from AliceBlue to WhiteSmoke. In between are all kinds of fun names, such as PapayaWhip, DodgerBlue, and PeachPuff. Here's an example:

```
Try my <SPAN STYLE="color: LemonChiffon">Lemon Chiffon</SPAN> pie!
```

To help you get a handle on this riot of colors, I've put together a table of the various color names (along with the RGB equivalents, so you'll remember how much easier the names are to use). The file is called x11color.htm, and you'll find it on the CD in this book. Figure 3.7, shown earlier in this book, gives you a peek at this page.

Using Background Styles

As you learned back in Chapter 6, "A Picture Is Worth a Thousand Clicks: Working with Images," you can use the <BODY> tag to set up your page with either a background color (using the BGCOLOR attribute) or a background image (using the BACKGROUND attribute). Either way, the attribute you set applies to the entire page.

With style sheets, however, you can apply a background color or image to sections of your page, or even to individual words. The secret to this lies in two styles: `background-color` and `background-image`.

To set a background color, use either a color name or an RGB value:

```
background-color: blue
background-color: #0000FF
```

To specify a background image, use the following syntax:

```
{background-image: URL(filename)}
```

Here, *filename* is the name of the graphics file you want to use (or an URL that points to the file). The HTML code below shows a few examples of these styles (see ssback.htm on the CD in this book).

```
<HTML>
<HEAD>
<TITLE>Style Sheet Backgrounds</TITLE>
</HEAD>
<BODY>

<DIV STYLE="background-color: black; color: white">
The background style is great for setting off entire sections
of text using a different color. For example, this section
uses a black background with white text.
</DIV>

<DIV STYLE="background-color: skyblue; color: navy">
On the other hand, this section achieves a slightly different
effect by using a pleasant Sky Blue background with Navy text.
</DIV>

<P>You can also use the background style to
<SPAN STYLE="background-color: yellow">highlight individual words</SPAN>.
<P>

<DIV STYLE="background-image: URL(bg03.gif); font-size: 16pt">
<B>One of the most interesting ways to use the background style
is to specify a background image. The browser will tile the
image so that it fills the entire section, like this.</B>
</DIV>

</BODY>
</HTML>
```

Figure 15.9 shows this file displayed in Internet Explorer 5 (on the left) and Netscape Navigator 4 (on the right). Notice that Explorer paints the background color right across the screen (which looks nice), but Navigator just follows the text (which looks kind of ragged). To get the full effect, load the page ssback.htm into both Internet Explorer and Navigator on your own machine. Note that this is fixed in Netscape 6, which paints the background colors across the screen.

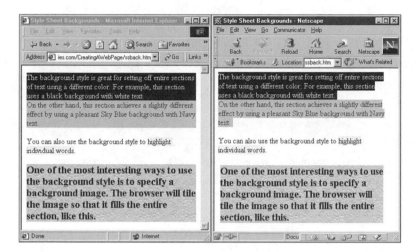

Figure 15.9

Some background styles. Internet Explorer and Navigator 4 display background colors slightly differently.

Another background style you might want to check out is background-repeat, which controls whether (and how) the browser tiles the background image to fill the window. There are four possible values:

- ◆ repeat   Tiles the background image to cover the entire browser window.
- ◆ repeat-x   Tiles the background image horizontally, only.
- ◆ repeat-y   Tiles the background image vertically, only.
- ◆ no-repeat   Doesn't tile the background image.

Also, Internet Explorer supports the background-attachment style. If you set this style to fixed, the background image remains in place when the user scrolls up and down the page. Set this style to scroll to revert to the usual background behavior (that is, the background image scrolls along with the text).

The Least You Need to Know

- That's about the size of it. To change the font size, use the `font-size` style and set it equal to a value in points (`pt`).

- Are you my typeface? To change the font typeface, use the `font-family` style and set it to the name of one or more typefaces. Be sure to enclose multiple-word typeface names in quotation marks.

- To boldly go … To create bold text, use the `font-weight` style and set it to either `bold` or one of the following values: `600`, `700`, `800`, or `900`.

- Italic spoken here. To create italic text, use the `font-style` style and set it to `italic`.

- If you intend to indent … To indent the first line of a paragraph, use the `text-indent` style and set it to the width of the indent.

- Adjusting your alignment. To align your text with the margins, use the `text-align` style and set it to one of the following: `left`, `center`, `right`, or `justify`.

- Links without lines. To format your links without the traditional underline, use the following:

  ```
  A {text-decoration: none}
  ```

- A splash of color. To create colored text, use the `color` style and set it to a color name or RGB color value.

- A new backdrop. To change the background of the page or some text, use either `background-color` (set it to a color name or RGB color value) or `background-image` (set it to `URL(`*filename*`)`, where *filename* is the name or address of the image file).

Chapter **16**

The Box Model: Styles for Dimensions, Borders, Margins, and More

In This Chapter

- ◆ Knocking some sense into the box model
- ◆ Setting the box dimensions
- ◆ Putting extra padding around the content
- ◆ Adding borders to the box
- ◆ Messing with the box margins
- ◆ Positioning the box precisely on the page
- ◆ How to wrap your page boxes in the style sheet equivalent of paper, bows, and ribbons

So far, you've learned what style sheets are and how to implement them (Chapter 14, "A Beginner's Guide to Style Sheets"), and you've learned some specific styles for fonts, text, colors, and backgrounds (Chapter 15, "Sheet Music: Styles for Fonts, Colors, and Backgrounds"). Style sheets are pretty useful little beasts, aren't they? They just give you so much more control over what your pages look like than plain old HTML.

This chapter takes this control up a notch by eyeballing quite a few more styles that cover things such as dimensions (the height and width of things), padding and margins (the amount of space around things), borders (lines around things), and position (where things appear on the page).

Thinking Outside the Box: Understanding the Box Model

Everything in this chapter is based on something called the style sheet *box model*. So let's begin by figuring out just what this box model thing is all about and why it's important.

In the geeky world known as Style Sheet Land, stuff inside a page is broken down into separate *elements*. In particular, there's a class of elements called *blocks*, and it includes those tags that start new sections of text: <P>, <BLOCKQUOTE>, <H1> through <H6>, <DIV>, <TABLE>, and so on.

In this strange world, each of these block elements is considered to have an invisible box around it (okay, it's a *very* strange world). This box has the following components:

- **Content**   This is the stuff inside the box (the text, the table, yadda, yadda, yadda).
- **Dimensions**   This is the height and width of the box.
- **Padding**   This is the space around the content. It's similar to the <TABLE> tag's CELLPADDING attribute that I told you about in Chapter 10, "Table Talk: Adding Tables to Your Page."
- **Border**   This is a line that surrounds the box and that marks the edges of the box.
- **Margin**   This is the space outside of the border. It separates the box from other boxes to the left and right, as well as above and below.
- **Position**   This is the location of the box within the page.

Figure 16.1 illustrates the basic structure of the box. The shaded area is the box itself.

Figure 16.1

The style sheet box model.

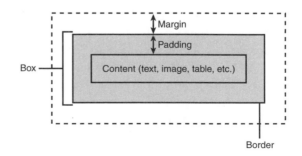

All the styles that you learned about in Chapter 15 dealt with formatting the box content. This chapter covers the five components that comprise the rest of the box: the dimensions, padding, border, margin, and position.

> ## Webmaster Wisdom
>
> Page knickknacks that don't create blocks—things like <B> and <I>—are called *inline elements*. You can use many of the style properties that I discuss in the rest of the chapter on inline elements, but I don't recommend it. The big problem is that Netscape 4 tends to convert inline elements to block elements if you try to apply block styles (such as a border or a margin). Note that Netscape 6 doesn't have this problem.

Box Blueprints: Specifying the Dimensions

The dimensions of the box are straightforward: the width property specifies how wide the box is, and the height property specifies how tall the box is. Note, however, that although Netscape 6 gets along fine with the height property, Netscape 4 doesn't support it (and will, in fact, crash horribly when confronted by it).

To set these properties, use either an absolute value in pixels (px) or a percentage of the browser's current width and height.

Here's some simple HTML code that tries out these two styles (see ssdimens.htm on the CD in this book). Note that I included a <STYLE> tag that sets the border property for the <P> tag so that you can easily see the dimensions of the resulting paragraphs (I discuss the border property in detail a bit later). Figure 16.2 shows what Internet Explorer 5 makes of the whole thing.

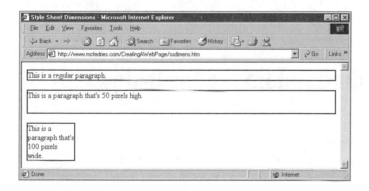

Figure 16.2

Some paragraphs with different dimensions.

```
<HTML>
<HEAD>
<TITLE>Style Sheet Dimensions</TITLE>

<STYLE TYPE="text/css">
<!--
P {border: thin solid}
-->
</STYLE>

</HEAD>
<BODY>

<P>This is a regular paragraph.
<P STYLE="height: 50px">This is a paragraph that's 50 pixels high.
<P STYLE="width: 100px">This is a paragraph that's 100 pixels wide.

</BODY>
</HTML>
```

CAUTION

Page Pitfalls

There are some browser peculiarities you have to worry about with the padding properties. In Netscape 4 and Internet Explorer 4 and later, the size of the block remains the same and the text inside the block is shoved aside to make room for the extra padding. In Netscape 6, however, the text remains the same and the block size is increased to make way for the new padding.

Also, it's possible to use a percentage value for the padding, but the value is interpreted differently in different browsers: With Internet Explorer, the percentage is based on the dimensions of the current block, but with Netscape, it's based on the current size of the browser window. Therefore, I suggest avoiding percentages altogether and using only absolute values.

Cushy Content: Adding Padding to the Inside of the Box

If you look at the previous figure, you can see that the text tends to cozy right up against the border of the box, particularly on the left and right. If your text is feeling claustrophobic, you can give it some extra elbowroom by increasing the amount of padding that surrounds the content within the box. Style sheets give you four padding properties to play with:

- ◆ `padding-top`   Adds space on top of the content.
- ◆ `padding-right`   Adds space to the right of the content.
- ◆ `padding-bottom`   Adds space below the content.
- ◆ `padding-left`   Adds space to the left of the content.

It's usually easiest to specify a value in pixels, like so:

```
P {padding-left: 10px}
```

There's also a shorthand property called `padding` that you can use to apply all four padding properties, in this order: padding-top, padding-right, padding-bottom, and padding-left. (To remember this order, start at the top and work your way clockwise around the other sides.) Separate each property with a space, like so:

```
DIV {padding: 10px 25px 10px 25px}
```

Note that if you specify just a single value, it applies to all four padding sides.

Here's some code (see sspaddng.htm on the CD in this book) that tries out each padding property on a few <DIV> sections. Figure 16.3 shows the result in Internet Explorer 6.

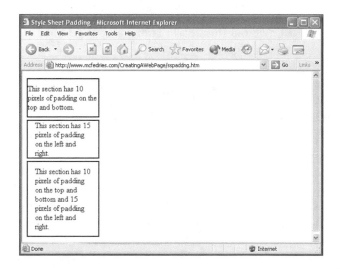

Figure 16.3

Trying out the padding properties.

```
<HTML>
<HEAD>
<TITLE>Style Sheet Padding</TITLE>

<STYLE TYPE="text/css">
<!--
```

```
DIV {border: thin solid;
   width: 100px;
   margin-bottom: 5px}
-->
</STYLE>

</HEAD>
<BODY>

<DIV STYLE="padding-top: 10px; padding-bottom: 10px">
This section has 10 pixels of padding on the top and bottom.</DIV>
<DIV STYLE="padding-left: 15px; padding-right: 15px">
This section has 15 pixels of padding on the left and right.</DIV>
<DIV STYLE="padding: 10px 15px 10px 15px">This section has 10 pixels of padding
on the top and bottom, and 15 pixels of padding on the left and right.</DIV>

</BODY>
</HTML>
```

The Box Revealed: Setting Borders

In the last couple of examples, I included borders so you could explicitly see the box in each element. So it's high time we checked out this border stuff to see what kind of fun you can have with it. The various border properties come in three flavors: width, style, and color.

The border width is controlled by the following five properties:

- `border-top-width` Specifies the width of the top border.
- `border-right-width` Specifies the width of the right border.
- `border-bottom-width` Specifies the width of the bottom border.
- `border-left-width` Specifies the width of the left border.
- `border-width` Specifies the width of all the borders, in this order: border-top-width, border-right-width, border-bottom-width, and border-left-width. Separate each property with a space, or use a single value for all four sides.

To set the width, use either an absolute value or one of the following predefined values: thin, medium, or thick.

The border style has five similar properties:

- `border-top-style` Specifies the style of the top border.
- `border-right-style` Specifies the style of the right border.

◆ `border-bottom-style` Specifies the style of the bottom border.

◆ `border-left-style` Specifies the style of the left border.

◆ `border-style` Specifies the style of all the borders, in this order: border-top-style, border-right-style, border-bottom-style, and border-left-style. As usual, separate each property with a space, or use a single value for all four sides.

Page Pitfalls

For borders to work properly, make sure you set at least the style. Also, Netscape 4's support of the border properties is flaky, so check your code (Netscape 6 appears to handle borders reasonably well).

The following table outlines the various values you can use for each border style property.

Table 16.1   Values for the Various Border Style Properties

Enter ...	To Get a Border That Uses ...
double	A double line
groove	A V-shaped line that appears to be etched into the page
inset	A line that appears to be sunken into the page
none	No line (that is, no border is displayed)
outset	A line that appears to be raised from the page
ridge	A V-shaped line that appears to be coming out of the page
solid	A solid line

For the border color, you can probably guess which five properties you can use:

◆ `border-top-color` Specifies the color of the top border.

◆ `border-right-color` Specifies the color of the right border.

◆ `border-bottom-color` Specifies the color of the bottom border.

◆ `border-left-color` Specifies the color of the left border.

◆ `border-color` Specifies the color of all the borders, in this order: border-top-color, border-right-color, border-bottom-color, and border-left-color. Separate each property with a space, or use a single value for all four sides.

You can set each border color property to one of the usual color values.

The following page (it's ssborder.htm on the CD in this book) demonstrates some of the border-width and border-style values. Figure 16.4 shows how they look in Internet Explorer.

Figure 16.4

Internet Explorer trying some border styles on for size.

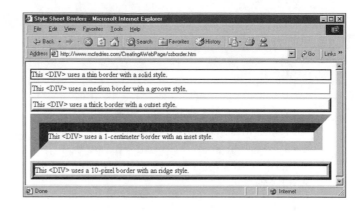

```
<HTML>
<HEAD>
<TITLE>Style Sheet Padding</TITLE>

<STYLE TYPE="text/css">
<!--
DIV {margin-bottom: 5px}
-->
</STYLE>

</HEAD>
<BODY>

<DIV STYLE="border-width: thin; border-style: solid">
This &lt;DIV&gt; uses a thin border with a solid style.
</DIV>

<DIV STYLE="border-width: medium; border-style: groove">
This &lt;DIV&gt; uses a medium border with a groove style.
</DIV>

<DIV STYLE="border-width: thick; border-style: outset">
This &lt;DIV&gt; uses a thick border with a outset style.
</DIV>

<DIV STYLE="border-width: 1cm; border-style: inset">
This &lt;DIV&gt; uses a 1-centimeter border with an inset style.
</DIV>

<DIV STYLE="border-width: 10px; border-style: ridge">
This &lt;DIV&gt; uses a 10-pixel border with an ridge style.
</DIV>

</BODY>
</HTML>
```

Webmaster Wisdom

If you want to format all the borders at once, here's a shorthand notation you can use:

```
{border: border-width border-style border-color}
```

Here, replace *border-width*, *border-style*, and *border-color* with values for each of those properties, like so:

```
{border: thin solid Gray}
```

Room to Breathe: Specifying Margins Around the Box

For our next style sheet trick, I show you how to use styles to specify margins. The default margins used by the browser depend on what element you're dealing with. For example, each new paragraph creates a bit of margin space above itself, and you always get a little bit of space at the top and bottom of the page, and on the left and right sides of the page. On the other hand, <DIV> sections don't use margins.

To control all this, use any of the following margin properties:

◆ `margin-top`   Specifies the size of the top margin.

◆ `margin-right`   Specifies the size of the right margin.

◆ `margin-bottom`   Specifies the size of the bottom margin.

◆ `margin-left`   Specifies the size of the left margin.

◆ `margin`   Specifies the size of all the margins, in this order: margin-top, margin-right, margin-bottom, and margin-left. Separate each property with a space, or use a single value for all four margins.

In each case, set the width to a specific value (such as 0px for no margin). The following HTML code (ssmargin.htm on the CD in this book) sets two different margins (see Figure 16.5):

◆ A <STYLE> block sets the margins of the <BLOCKQUOTE> tag to be 100 pixels on the left and right.

◆ The <BODY> tag's STYLE attribute sets the overall margins of the page to 0 for the left, top, and right. As you can see in Figure 16.5, Internet Explorer handles this perfectly, but Netscape 6 ignores the `margin-top` property (and Netscape 4 doesn't support messing with the <BODY> tag's margins at all).

Figure 16.5

Some margin styles in action in both Internet Explorer 6 and Netscape 6.

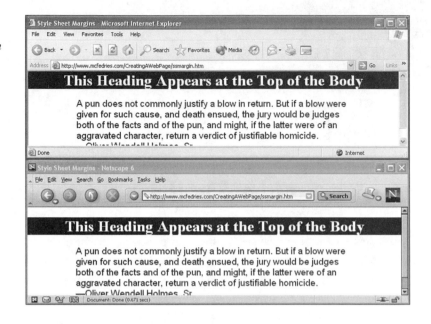

```
<HTML>
<HEAD>
<TITLE>Style Sheet Margins</TITLE>
</HEAD>

<STYLE TYPE="text/css">
<!--
BLOCKQUOTE {margin-left: 100px;
     margin-right: 100px;
     font-size: 14pt;
     font-family: Arial}
-->
</STYLE>

<BODY STYLE="margin-left: 0px;
     margin-top: 0px;
     margin-right: 0px;">

<DIV STYLE="background: black;
     color: white;
     text-align: center">
<H1>This Heading Appears at the Top of the Body</H1>
</DIV>

<BLOCKQUOTE>
A pun does not commonly justify a blow in return. But if a blow
were given for such cause, and death ensued, the jury would be
judges both of the facts and of the pun, and might, if the
```

```
latter were of an aggravated character, return a verdict of
justifiable homicide.<BR>
&#151;Oliver Wendell Holmes, Sr.
</BLOCKQUOTE>

</BODY>
</HTML>
```

Where the Box Goes: Working with Position Styles

Now that you've determined the structure and layout of your box, the last thing you have to decide is where to put it on the page. This might seem like a strange thing. After all, don't elements such as paragraphs and headings always go exactly where you put them on the page? In regular HTML they do, but style sheets, as you've seen so often, give you much more flexibility.

Your first chore is to decide how you want your element positioned. This is determined by, appropriately enough, the position property, which can take any of the following three values:

- ◆ position: absolute   When you use this value, you can toss the element anywhere you like on the page. For example, you could tell the browser to display a heading 100 pixels from the left and 50 pixels from the top.

- ◆ position: relative   This value first positions the element according to where it would normally appear in regular HTML. It then offsets the element horizontally and vertically, according to values you specify.

- ◆ position: static   This value positions the element according to where it would normally appear in regular HTML.

If you decide to set position to either absolute or relative, you then need to specify the exact position you want. For this you need to use some or all of the following four properties:

- ◆ top   The element's position from the top of the browser window (if you're using position: absolute) or below the element's natural position in the page (if you're using position: relative).

- ◆ right   The element's position from the right side of the browser window, if you're using position: absolute. Note that this value has no effect if you're using position: relative.

- ◆ bottom   The element's position from the bottom of the browser window, if you're using position: absolute. This value has no effect if you're using position: relative.

◆ left   The element's position from the left side of the browser window (if you're using position: absolute) or to the left of the element's natural position in the page (if you're using position: relative).

The following page (ssposit.htm on the CD in this book) tries out some absolute and relative positioning, and Figure 16.6 shows what happens in Netscape 4.

Figure 16.6

Use position styles to toss elements all over your page.

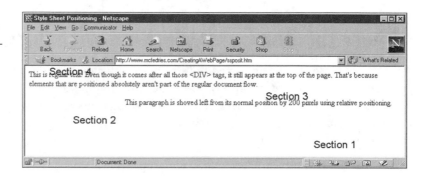

```
<HTML>
<HEAD>
<TITLE>Style Sheet Positioning</TITLE>
</HEAD>

<STYLE TYPE="text/css">
<!--
DIV {font-family: Arial;
   font-size: 16pt}
-->
</STYLE>

<BODY>

<DIV STYLE="position: absolute; left: 600px; top: 150px">Section 1</DIV>
<DIV STYLE="position: absolute; left: 100px; top: 100px">Section 2</DIV>
<DIV STYLE="position: absolute; left: 500px; top: 50px">Section 3</DIV>
<DIV STYLE="position: absolute; left: 50px; top: 0px">Section 4</DIV>
This is regular text. Even though it comes after all those &lt;DIV&gt;
tags, it still appears at the top of the page. That's because elements
that are positioned absolutely aren't part of the regular document flow.
<P STYLE="position: relative; left: 200px">
This paragraph is shoved left from its normal position by 200 pixels
using relative positioning.

</BODY>
</HTML>
```

Positioning in the Third Dimension

Style sheets understand not just the usual 2-D positioning, but also positioning in the third dimension. It sounds like science fiction, but all it really means is that you can "stack" elements on top of each other for interesting effects. The style property that controls this is called z-index. An element with a higher z-index value is displayed "on top" of an element with a lower z-index value. Here's an example (see sszindex.htm on the CD in this book):

```
<HTML>
<HEAD>
<TITLE>Style Sheet 3-D Positioning</TITLE>
</HEAD>

<STYLE TYPE="text/css">
<!--
DIV {font-family: Arial;
   font-size: 12pt}
-->
</STYLE>

<BODY>

<IMG SRC="home2.gif" STYLE="z-index: 0; position: absolute; left: 100px; top:
10px">
<DIV STYLE="z-index: 1; position: absolute; left: 10px; top: 30px">
<B>This text appears on top of the image.</B>
</DIV>

</BODY>
</HTML>
```

Figure 16.7 shows how it looks in the browser.

Figure 16.7

Use the z-index property to place one element "on top" of another.

The Least You Need to Know

◆ The bits of the box. The invisible box around each block element has six components: *content* (what's inside), *dimensions* (the height and width), *padding* (the space around the content), *border* (the line around the box), *margin* (the space outside the box), and *position* (where the box appears in the page).

◆ The box dimensions. Use the `height` and `width` properties.

◆ The box padding. Use the `padding-top`, `padding-right`, `padding-bottom`, and `padding-left` properties, or use the `padding` shortcut property.

◆ The box border width. Use the `border-top-width`, `border-right-width`, `border-bottom-width`, and `border-left-width` properties, or use the `border-width` shortcut property.

◆ The box border style. Use the `border-top-style`, `border-right-style`, `border-bottom-style`, and `border-left-style` properties, or use the `border-style` shortcut property.

◆ The box border color. Use the `border-top-color`, `border-right-color`, `border-bottom-color`, and `border-left-color` properties, or use the `border-color` shortcut property.

◆ The box margin. Use the `margin-top`, `margin-right`, `margin-bottom`, and `margin-left` properties, or use the `margin` shortcut property.

◆ The box position. Use `position: absolute` to place the element anywhere on the page; use `position: relative` to offset the element relative to its normal HTML position; use `position: static` to place the element in its normal HTML position. For the first two, position the element using the `top`, `right`, `bottom`, and `left` properties.

Part 4

Working with JavaScripts and Java Applets

At this point on your HTML learning curve, you know pretty much everything there is to know about making your pages look their best. From fonts to images to tables to style sheets, you've got the know-how to turn out well-buffed web pages. The problem, though, is that your pages just kind of sit there. Outside of adding a few animated GIFs, how can you make your pages seem more dynamic? You find at least part of the answer here in Part 4. These three chapters show you how to add a bit of "software" to your pages in the form of JavaScripts and Java applets. You'll see just how easy it is to display messages to the user, validate form content, store data about the user, and much more.

The Programmable Page: Adding JavaScripts to Your Pages

In This Chapter

◆ How to insert scripts into a page

◆ Using scripts to display messages to the surfer

◆ Writing text to the page on the fly

◆ Detecting the user's browser

◆ Everything you need to know to use JavaScripts on your pages

Way, way, back in Chapter 1, "A Brief HTML Primer," I took great pains to ensure you that the "Language" part of "Hypertext Markup Language" in no way meant that you had to learn a programming language to create a web page. You've seen so far that, thankfully, I wasn't lying.

Now, however, it's time to get ever so slightly acquainted with a *real* programming language. It's called *JavaScript* and you use it to add tiny little programs called *scripts* to your pages. You can use these scripts to pop up a welcome message whenever someone visits your site, display the current time, find out which browser a visitor is using, and tons more.

Does this mean you have to learn how to program in JavaScript? Well, no, not if you don't want to. You can always go the "black box" route where you simply add a script to your page without understanding exactly how the script does its thing. That's the approach I take in this chapter. You won't learn any programming here. Instead, I show you how to add a script to your page, and I run through a few examples of some useful scripts. (You'll see even more examples in the next chapter.)

Webmaster Wisdom

What's that? You *would* like to learn a bit of JavaScript? Well, good for you! It's actually not as hard as you might think, especially if you learn it using a book written by your favorite computer book author (that's me, silly). I have a book called *Special Edition Using JavaScript* (Que, 2001) that can teach you JavaScript even if you've never programmed before. To find out more about the book, please see the following website: www.mcfedries.com/UsingJavaScript.

Using the ‹SCRIPT› Tag

JavaScript code goes right inside the Web page, just like HTML tags. When a JavaScript-savvy browser (such as Netscape 2.0 and later and Internet Explorer 3.0 and later) accesses the page, the JavaScript code is executed and the program does its thing. For example, the program might check the time of day and display an appropriate welcome message, or you could embed a calculator right on the page.

JavaScripts reside between the <SCRIPT> and </SCRIPT> tags and always take the following form:

```
<SCRIPT LANGUAGE="JavaScript" TYPE="text/javascript">
<!--
The script commands go here.
//-->
</SCRIPT>
```

Note the use of HTML comment tags. These ensure that JavaScript-feeble browsers don't try to read the JavaScript commands.

Webmaster Wisdom

In the same way that HTML has comment tags that tell the browser to ignore the text and tags between them, programmers can also add comments to scripts. To do so, they insert two slashes (//) at the beginning of each line they want ignored. A common example is the line just above the </SCRIPT> end tag:

```
//-->
```

You have to put the comment slashes at the beginning to prevent JavaScript from trying to "execute" the end tag of the HTML comment (->).

Inserting the Script

Where you store the script in your page depends on what it does:

◆ If the script writes text to the page, you position the script where you want the text to appear.

◆ Otherwise, you position the script inside the page header (that is, between the <HEAD> and </HEAD> tags).

Using an External JavaScript File

Besides having your scripts snuggle up to your regular page tags, it's also possible in some cases to plop the scripts into a separate file. Although this is really only for advanced users who know what they're doing, it's worthwhile because it has three benefits:

◆ It makes it easier to reuse a script because you need to tell the browser only the name and location of the separate file. You don't have to insert the script itself into all your pages.

◆ If you need to adjust the script, you have to adjust it only in the separate file. Every page that accesses the script automatically uses the edited version.

◆ It makes your page's source code look less cluttered, so it's easier to read.

Webmaster Wisdom

This section on using an external JavaScript file is advanced stuff, so don't worry if it makes no sense to you now. Just skip over it and come back to it later, after you've had some experience working with JavaScripts.

The key thing about all this is that you can put only what are known as *functions* in the external file. A JavaScript function looks like this:

```
function Name() {
A bunch of programming statements go here.
}
```

Here, *Name* is the name of the function.

To tell the browser about the external file, add the SRC attribute to the <SCRIPT> tag. For example, if your functions are all in a file named scripts.js (it's traditional to use the .js extension for these files; they're just text files, however), you'd put the following into your page between the <HEAD> and </HEAD> tags:

```
<SCRIPT LANGUAGE="JavaScript" TYPE="text/javascript" SRC="scripts.js">
</SCRIPT>
```

Some JavaScript Examples

The real purpose of this chapter isn't so much to show you how to insert scripts (although that's clearly important). No, what I really want to do is give you a good supply of scripts to use, at no extra charge, in your own pages. To that end, the next few sections take you through quite a few JavaScripts that perform all manner of interesting and useful functions. (Remember, too, that you get even more script examples in the next chapter.)

Displaying a Message to the User

Let's begin with the simplest of all JavaScript functions: displaying a message to the user in a simple dialog box (also called a *pop-up box* or an *alert box*). Here's the JavaScript code that does the job:

```
alert("Insert your message here")
```

In other words, between the quotation marks you enter whatever message you want to display. For example, suppose you want to have a message pop up each time a user visits your home page. You can do that by inserting the following script between the </HEAD> and <BODY> tags (see jsalert1.htm on the CD in this book):

```
<SCRIPT LANGUAGE="JavaScript" TYPE="text/javascript">
<!--
alert("Welcome to my Web site!")
//-->
</SCRIPT>
```

Figure 17.1 shows what happens when the user loads your page.

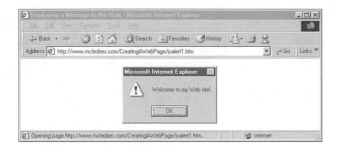

Figure 17.1

The JavaScript alert() statement displays a little dialog box like this one.

Writing Data to the Page

After displaying a dialog box message to the user, the second most common JavaScript chore is to write some data to the page. This is really powerful because it means that you can display *dynamic* text on your page. For example, you could write the current date and time (see the next section to learn how to do this).

The JavaScript statement that performs this magic is `document.write()`, which looks like this:

```
document.write("The stuff you want to write goes here.")
```

The idea is that you place this statement at the spot within your page that you want the text to appear.

For example, many web spinners like to include in their page the date and time that the page was last modified. This helps the surfer know whether he's dealing with recent data. JavaScript has a special statement called `document.lastModified` that returns the date and time that the file was last edited. Here's a script (see jswrite1.htm on the CD) that shows you one way to use it with `document.write()`:

```
<SCRIPT LANGUAGE="JavaScript"
TYPE="text/javascript">
<!--
document.write("This page was last edited on " + document.lastModified)
//-->
</SCRIPT>
```

Figure 17.2 shows how things shake out in Netscape.

Page Pitfalls

JavaScript is *really* finicky about uppercase versus lowercase letters. Therefore, when entering JavaScript statements, always use precisely the same combination of uppercase and lowercase letters that I show you. For example, you must use `document.lastModified` and not `Document.LastModified` or `document.lastmodified`.

Figure 17.2

*Use document.write() to add
text to your page on the fly.*

The text shown in the previous example is a bit plain. Can you put some fancy pants on it?

No problem. You can easily add HTML tags within the document.write() statement.
Here's a revised script (see jswrite2.htm on the CD in this book) that does just that:

```
<SCRIPT LANGUAGE="JavaScript" TYPE="text/javascript">
<!--
document.write("<FONT FACE='Arial' SIZE=+1><B>This page was last
➥edited on <TT>" + document.lastModified) + "</TT></B></FONT>"
//-->
</SCRIPT>
```

Webmaster Wisdom _____

This seems like a good time to remind you about the strange ➥ character that you
see in the jswrite2.htm code. Publishing types call this a *code continuation character.* All it means is that the current line and the line above it are to be considered a *single* statement. So if you're typing in the statement by hand, make sure
you keep everything on one line.

I added the <FONT>, <B>, and <TT> tags to produce the effect shown in Figure 17.3.

Figure 17.3

*There's no problem adding
tags within your
document.write() statements.*

> **CAUTION**
>
> ## Page Pitfalls
>
> One thing you have to watch out for in `document.write()` (and, indeed, in most JavaScript statements) is when you use quotation marks within quotation marks. In the previous example, I had to use <FONT FACE='Arial'> instead of <FONT FACE="Arial"> because `document.write()` already has its own double quotation marks ("), and it would seriously confuse things to use <FONT FACE="Arial">. Therefore, always use single quotation marks (') within JavaScript statements such as `document.write()`.

Hiding Your E-mail Address from a Spam Crawler

As you might know, *spam* is the whimsical name given to a nonwhimsical thing: unsolicited commercial e-mail messages. If you put up a web page and include your e-mail address on it somewhere, I'll bet you dollars to doughnuts that you'll start receiving more spam in your inbox. Why? Because programs called "spam crawlers" troll the web looking for pages containing e-mail addresses that they can harvest for their evil intentions. They look for "@" signs and "mailto" links.

You can foil spam crawlers by using a simple bit of JavaScript code to write your e-mail address to the page. Here's the code (see jsnospam.htm on the CD in this book):

```
<SCRIPT LANGUAGE="JavaScript" TYPE="text/javascript">
<!--
var addr1 = "mailto:"
var addr2 = "webpages"
var addr3 = "@"
var addr4 = "mcfedries.com"
document.write('<A HREF="' + addr1 + addr2 + addr3 + addr4 + '">')
document.write('E-mail Me!</A>')
//-->
</SCRIPT>
```

Place this script at the spot in the page where you want your mailto link to appear. Of course, you need to edit things for your own e-mail address. As you can see in Figure 17.4, what you end up with is a mailto link that works normally, as far as the surfer is concerned.

Figure 17.4

The JavaScript code creates a standard mailto link.

Putting the Date and Time into a Page

A similar example involves putting the current date and time into the page. The current date and time is produced by JavaScript's `Date()` statement. Here's a simple example that uses `Date()` (see jsdate1.htm on the CD in this book). Figure 17.5 shows Internet Explorer's interpretation.

Figure 17.5

This simple script inserts the current date and time.

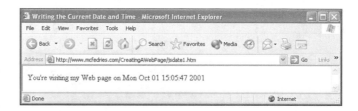

```
<SCRIPT LANGUAGE="JavaScript" TYPE="text/javascript">
<!--
document.write("You're visiting my Web page on " + Date())
//-->
</SCRIPT>
```

That's not bad, but the date and time display is a bit ugly. To get more control, you need to break out the various components of the date and time: the day of the week, the month, the hours and minutes, and so on.

Here's a quick summary of the JavaScript statements that do this:

- **getDay()** Returns a number between 0 and 6, where 0 is Sunday, 1 is Monday, and so on.

- **getMonth()** Returns the month number, where 0 is January, 1 is February, and so on.

- **getYear()** Returns the year component of a date. If the year is before 2000, it returns a two-digit year (such as 99); if it's in 2000 or later, Internet Explorer returns the four-digit year, but Netscape 4 and later subtract 1900 from the year (for example, 2001 returns 101).

- **getSeconds()** Returns the seconds component of a time.

- **getMinutes()** Returns the minutes component of a time.

- **getHours()** Returns the hours component of a time. Note that this is military time, so if it's 5:00 in the afternoon, it returns 17.

To use these statements, you must first store the current date in what programmers call a *variable*, like so:

```
d = new Date()
```

You can then apply one of the statements to this variable. Here's how you'd get the current day:

```
d.getDay()
```

Note, too, that after you go to all this trouble, then it becomes relatively easy to display a custom message to the user based on the current time. For example, you might want to add "Good morning!" if the current date and time is before noon.

Here's a long script that takes advantage of all this (see jsdate2.htm on the CD in this book).

```
<SCRIPT LANGUAGE="JavaScript" TYPE="text/javascript">
<!--
// Store the date in a variable
d = new Date()
dateText = ""

// Get the current day and convert it to the name of the day
dayValue = d.getDay()
if (dayValue == 0)
    dateText += "Sunday"
else if (dayValue == 1)
    dateText += "Monday"
else if (dayValue == 2)
    dateText += "Tuesday"
else if (dayValue == 3)
    dateText += "Wednesday"
else if (dayValue == 4)
    dateText += "Thursday"
else if (dayValue == 5)
    dateText += "Friday"
else if (dayValue == 6)
    dateText += "Saturday"

// Get the current month and convert it to the name of the month
monthValue = d.getMonth()
dateText += " "
if (monthValue == 0)
    dateText += "January"
if (monthValue == 1)
    dateText += "February"
if (monthValue == 2)
    dateText += "March"
if (monthValue == 3)
    dateText += "April"
```

```
if (monthValue == 4)
    dateText += "May"
if (monthValue == 5)
    dateText += "June"
if (monthValue == 6)
    dateText += "July"
if (monthValue == 7)
    dateText += "August"
if (monthValue == 8)
    dateText += "September"
if (monthValue == 9)
    dateText += "October"
if (monthValue == 10)
    dateText += "November"
if (monthValue == 11)
    dateText += "December"

// Get the current year
if (d.getYear() < 2000)
    dateText += " " + d.getDate() + ", " + (1900 + d.getYear())
else
    dateText += " " + d.getDate() + ", " + (d.getYear())

// Get the current minutes
minuteValue = d.getMinutes()
if (minuteValue < 10)
    minuteValue = "0" + minuteValue

// Get the current hours
hourValue = d.getHours()

// Customize the greeting based on the current hours
if (hourValue < 12)
    {
    greeting = "Good morning!"
    timeText = " at " + hourValue + ":" + minuteValue + " AM"
    }
else if (hourValue == 12)
    {
    greeting = "Good afternoon!"
    timeText = " at " + hourValue + ":" + minuteValue + " PM"
    }
else if (hourValue < 17)
    {
    greeting = "Good afternoon!"
    timeText = " at " + (hourValue-12) + ":" + minuteValue + " PM"
```

```
        }
else
    {
    greeting = "Good evening!"
    timeText = " at " + (hourValue-12) + ":" + minuteValue + " PM"
    }
// Write the greeting, the date, and the time to the page
document.write(greeting + " It's " + dateText + timeText)
//-->
</SCRIPT>
```

Whew! That's some script! It works quite nicely, though, as you can see in Figure 17.6.

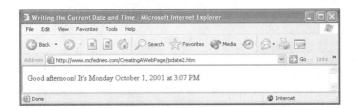

Figure 17.6

This page uses JavaScript to display the date and time and an appropriate message based on the time of day.

Understanding JavaScript Functions

In the examples you've seen so far, how did the browser know that it was supposed to run the JavaScript statements? Because the browser routinely scours the page for a <SCRIPT> and </SCRIPT> combo. If it sees one, it goes right ahead and runs whatever JavaScript statements are stuffed in there.

The exception to this is when the statements reside inside a JavaScript function. In that case, the browser ignores the function's statements. So how do they get executed? You have to put in a statement that says to the browser, "Hey, you! Run this function for me, will ya!" In geekspeak, this is known as *calling* the function.

Let's see a simple example. Instead of displaying a dialog box when the user loads your page, what if you want to display a message when the user *leaves* your page? The browser has already processed your page, so it doesn't do anything to it when the user leaves. Therefore, to execute some JavaScript code at that point, you have to create a function and then call it. Here's an example function called SayGoodbye():

```
function SayGoodbye() {
    alert("Thanks for visiting my Web site!")
}
```

Here's how it looks within the page (see jsalert2.htm on the CD in this book):

```
<HTML>
```

```
<HEAD>
<TITLE>Displaying a Message to the User, Part 2</TITLE>
</HEAD>

<SCRIPT LANGUAGE="JavaScript" TYPE="text/javascript">
<!--
function SayGoodbye() {
    alert("Thanks for visiting my Web site!")
}
//-->
</SCRIPT>

<BODY onUnload="SayGoodbye()">
<a href="/">Click here to leave this page and see the alert</a>
</BODY>
</HTML>
```

The thing to notice here is the special onUnload statement in the <BODY> tag. This tells the browser to execute the SayGoodbye() function when the user leaves ("unloads") the page.

So, to summarize, here's how the browser executes JavaScript statements:

◆ If the statements aren't within a function, the browser executes them as soon as the page loads.

◆ If the statements are within a function, the browser doesn't execute them until the function is called.

Displaying Messages in the Status Bar

Rather than tossing a dialog box-based message at the user, many HTMLists prefer a more subtle approach: displaying the message in the browser's status bar. To do this, use the self.status statement:

```
self.status = "Put your message here"
```

Here, *self* refers to the browser window. Here's a simple example (see jsstatus.htm on the CD in this book).

```
<SCRIPT LANGUAGE="JavaScript" TYPE="text/javascript">
<!--
self.status = "Welcome to my Web site!"
//-->
</SCRIPT>
```

Figure 17.7 shows how things look after the page is loaded into Internet Explorer.

Figure 17.7

Use the self.status statement to display a message in the browser's status bar.

One of the most requested JavaScript examples is a script that not only displays a message in the browser's status bar, but also scrolls the message from right to left. This is a complex procedure, as you can see in the next example, but you can safely ignore most of the code. You'll find everything on this book's CD in the file named jsscroll.htm, which also provides instructions for customizing the status bar message. Figure 17.8 shows the page in Netscape.

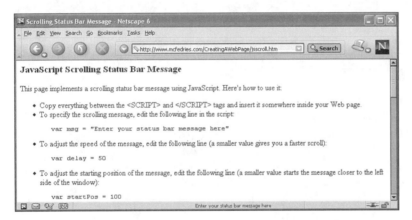

Figure 17.8

This page uses JavaScript to scroll a message along the browser's status bar.

```
<SCRIPT LANGUAGE="JavaScript" TYPE="text/javascript">
<!--
// Use the following three variables to set up the message:
var msg = "Enter your status bar message here"
var delay = 50
var startPos = 100

// Don't touch these variables:
var timerID = null
var timerRunning = false
var pos = 0

// Crank it up!
StartScrolling()
```

```
function StartScrolling(){
    // Make sure the clock is stopped
    StopTheClock()

    // Pad the message with spaces to get the "start" position
    for (var i = 0; i < startPos; i++) msg = " " + msg

    // Off we go...
    DoTheScroll()
}

function StopTheClock(){
    if(timerRunning)
        clearTimeout(timerID)
    timerRunning = false
}

function DoTheScroll(){
    if (pos < msg.length)
        self.status = msg.substring(pos, msg.length);
    else
        pos=-1;
    ++pos
    timerRunning = true
    timerID = self.setTimeout("DoTheScroll()", delay)
}
//-->
</SCRIPT>
```

Detecting the User's Browser

For the final example in this chapter, I show you how to determine which browser the user is surfing with. Why would you care? Well, you might want to send the surfer to a page that's been customized for her browser.

Webmaster Wisdom

My JavaScript page is also home to several other status bar scripts that display multiple messages, random messages, and more. See the following page for the appropriate links: www.mcfedries. com/JavaScript.

JavaScript offers two statements that return browser info:

- ◆ **navigator.appName** This returns the name of the browser.
- ◆ **navigator.appVersion** This returns the version number of the browser.

Here's a script (see jsbrowsr.thm on the CD in this book) that determines the browser name and version and then displays a custom message (shown in Figure 17.9).

Figure 17.9

This page displays the user's browser info.

```
<SCRIPT LANGUAGE="JavaScript" TYPE="text/javascript">
<!--
    var browserName = navigator.appName
    var browserVer = parseInt(navigator.appVersion);
    if (browserName == "Netscape")
        {
        alert("Welcome Netscape Navigator user!" + "\n\n" + "You are
        ➥using version " + browserVer)
        }
    else if (browserName == "Microsoft Internet Explorer")
        {
        var ver = navigator.appVersion
        var start = ver.indexOf("MSIE") + 5
        var end = ver.indexOf(";",start)
        browserVer = parseInt(ver.substring(start,end))
        alert("Welcome Internet Explorer user!" + "\n\n" + "You are
        ➥using version " + browserVer)
        }
    else
        {
        alert("Welcome " + browserName + " user!" + "\n\n" + "You are
        ➥using version " + browserVer)
        }
//-->
</SCRIPT>
```

Webmaster Wisdom

If you want to modify this script to send the user to another page based on his or her browser, use the `location.href` statement:

```
location.href = "url"
```

Here, *url* is the name or full URL of the page to which you want to send the surfer.

The Least You Need to Know

◆ The <SCRIPT> schtick. You insert scripts by using, not surprisingly, the <SCRIPT> and </SCRIPT> tags:

```
<SCRIPT LANGUAGE="JavaScript" TYPE="text/javascript">
<!--
The script commands go here.
//-->
</SCRIPT>
```

◆ Telling the script where to go. If your script writes text or tags to the page, insert the script at the exact spot where you want the text or tags to appear; otherwise, place the script inside the page header (that is, between the <HEAD> and </HEAD> tags)

◆ Writing tags as well as text. When you're using the document.write() method for inserting text on the fly, feel free to toss in a tag or two if you want to format the text.

More JavaScript Fun

In This Chapter

- ◆ Changing images on the fly with mouseovers
- ◆ Password-protecting your pages
- ◆ Using JavaScript to work with forms
- ◆ Setting up a drop-down list of links
- ◆ Calculating mortgage payments
- ◆ A whack of JavaScripts that'll have your visitors begging for more

The previous chapter showed you that although programming JavaScript is tough, just inserting a script or two into a page isn't a big deal. If you liked the examples I took you through in that chapter, wait until you see what I have in store for you here. By necessity, these are much more complex scripts, but you'll see that they do much more interesting things. Don't worry if some of the scripts look intimidating. Remember: You don't have to understand their inner workings to get them to work. Just follow my instructions and you'll have your JavaScript-enhanced pages up and at 'em in no time.

A Script for Mouseovers

Have you ever visited a site, sat your mouse over an image, and then seen that image magically transform into a different graphic? This neat effect is called a "mouseover" and it's all done with JavaScript.

There are several ways to go about this, but there's one method that's relatively simple and straightforward. You begin by entering a normal <IMG> tag, except that you name it by inserting the NAME attribute:

Webmaster Wisdom

The mouseover technique I show you in this section works in Netscape version 3.0 and later, as well as in Internet Explorer version 4.0 and later. This accounts for at least 95 percent of all users.

```
<IMG SRC="whatever.gif" NAME="somename">
```

For the example I'm using, I have two images:

- **mouseout.gif** This is the regular image that appears without the mouse pointer over it.
- **mouseovr.gif** This is the image that appears when the user puts the mouse pointer over mouseout.gif.

Here's the <IMG> tag (each attribute is on a separate line for easier reading):

```
<IMG SRC="mouseout.gif"
    WIDTH="157"
    HEIGHT="39"
    BORDER="0"
    NAME="mypicture">
```

As you can see, I've used mouseout.gif to start, and I've given the name "mypicture" to the <IMG> tag. Now you construct an <A> tag (mouseovers work only with images that are set up as links):

```
<A HREF="jsmouse1.html"
    onMouseover="mypicture.src='mouseovr.gif'"
    onMouseout="mypicture.src='mouseout.gif'">
```

There are two extra JavaScript attributes here: onMouseover and onMouseout. The onMouseover attribute says, essentially, "When the user moves the mouse pointer over the image named mypicture, change its SRC attribute to mouseovr.gif."

Similarly, the onMouseout attribute says, essentially, "When the user moves the mouse pointer off (out of) the image named mypicture, change its SRC attribute to mouseout.gif."

Here's how the whole thing looks (see jsmouse.htm on the CD in this book):

```
<A HREF="jsmouse1.html"
    onMouseover="mypicture.src='mouseovr.gif'"
    onMouseout="mypicture.src='mouseout.gif'">
<IMG SRC="mouseout.gif"
    WIDTH="157"
    HEIGHT="39"
    BORDER="0"
    NAME="mypicture">
</A>
```

Figure 18.1 offers two Internet Explorer windows showing the same page (jsmouse.htm). In the top window, I don't have the mouse over the image, so Internet Explorer shows mouseout.gif. In the bottom window, I've put my mouse over the image, so Internet Explorer displays mouseovr.gif.

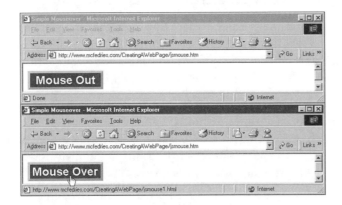

Figure 18.1

Internet Explorer showing the <IMG> tag without the mouse over it (top window) and with the mouse over it (bottom window).

Webmaster Wisdom _____

You might be wondering where the heck is the <SCRIPT> tag that I told you in the previous chapter you had to use for JavaScript. It's nowhere in sight because sometimes you can just enter a JavaScript statement directly, without needing a <SCRIPT> tag. For example, consider the following chunk from the <A> tag in this example:

```
onMouseover="mypicture.src='mouseovr.gif'"
```

The `onMouseover` part is called an *event*, and the rest of the line is an honest-to-goodness JavaScript statement. In other words, when the onMouseover event occurs (that is, when the user places the mouse over the image), the JavaScript statement is executed automatically.

Here are a few notes to keep handy when working with mouseovers:

◆ Don't use large images for your mouseover effects. When the user puts the mouse over the image for the first time, the browser delays while it downloads the mouseover image. If you use a large image, that delay can be several seconds or longer, which spoils the effect. Mouseovers are best used with images that weigh only a few kilobytes or so.

◆ If you have a larger image that you must use, or if you have a lot of mouseover images on your page, it's possible to "preload" images (that is, have the browser load the images and keep them waiting in memory when it first opens the page). I show you how this works in the following page: www.mcfedries.com/JavaScript/ mouseover3.html.

Creating a Password-Protected Page

Many readers have written to me over the years and asked how they can set up a page that can be accessed only if the user enters the appropriate password. "That depends," I always respond, "on how bulletproof you need your password to be." Here are a couple of things to consider when deciding how much password-protection you need for your page:

◆ If you have sensitive information that must be protected at all costs, ask your web hosting provider if it can establish a password-protected portion of your site. If that's not possible, you might need to hire a CGI programmer to create a password-protection script. There are also some password scripts available on the web. (See Chapter 12, "Need Feedback? Create a Form!" for some resources.)

◆ If your needs aren't so grandiose, then you can set up a reasonably strong password system using just a few dollops of JavaScript.

Hold on just a sec, mister! JavaScript stuff sits right inside the page. Won't someone be able to see the password if he looks at the page source code?

That's very perceptive of you. However, in the system that I show you, the password never appears in the JavaScript code! Why? Because the password is just the name of the protected page (minus the .htm or .html extension). Because it's just as hard to guess the name of a web page as it is to guess a password, you get basically the same level of protection.

CAUTION **Page Pitfalls**

For this password scheme to work, it's absolutely crucial to have a default page in the same directory as the password-protected page. Why? Well, recall that a default page is the one the server sends out if the user doesn't specify a page. For example, suppose the user enters the following address: www.yourserver.com/finances. Most servers use index.html as the default page, so the above is equivalent to the following address: www.yourserver.com/finances/index.html. If you don't include the default page in the directory, most web servers simply return a list of all the files in the directory! This would obviously defeat our password protection scheme.

The system I'm going to show you requires three parts:

◆ A page that has a link to the password-protected part of your site. I use a page titled jspwtest.htm (it's on the CD in this book) for this example.

◆ A page that asks the user for the proper password (this is jspass.htm on the CD).

◆ The password-protected page (this is idiot.htm on the CD). When you name this file, you must use lowercase letters only.

The next couple of sections show you how to set everything up.

Creating a Link to the Password-Protected Part of Your Site

You can send people to the password-protected page by including a link in one or more pages on your site. Other than the password-protected page itself, this is the only thing you need to create yourself. Here's the <A> tag to use:

```
<A HREF="javascript:GetPassword()">
```

As you can see, this link calls a JavaScript function named GetPassword(). Here's the code for that function (place this in the header section of the page that includes the link):

```
<SCRIPT LANGUAGE="JavaScript" TYPE="text/javascript">
<!--
function GetPassword()
{
    window.open("jspass.htm", "","width=225,height=70")
}
//-->
</SCRIPT>
```

All the GetPassword() function does is open a new window that contains the jspass.htm page. Figure 18.2 shows a page that uses this link and function (see jspwtest.htm on the CD in this book) and it shows the window that appears when you click the link.

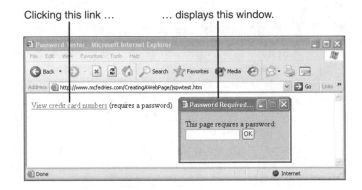

Figure 18.2

When you click this link, the GetPassword() function displays a window.

Understanding the Script That Processes the Password

The little window that shows up contains a simple form that asks the user to enter the password:

```
<FORM>
This page requires a password:<BR>
<INPUT TYPE="TEXT" NAME="pw" SIZE="15">
<INPUT TYPE="BUTTON" VALUE="OK"
onClick="SubmitPassword(this.form)">
</FORM>
```

There are two things to note here for future use:

- ◆ The text box is named pw.
- ◆ The button uses the JavaScript onClick event to run a function. That is, when the user clicks the button, the JavaScript function named SubmitPassword() is called.

Here's the code for the SubmitPassword() function:

```
<SCRIPT LANGUAGE="JavaScript" TYPE="text/javascript">
<!--

function SubmitPassword(frm)
{
    //
    // Get the value entered into the text box
    //
    var password = frm.pw.value
    //
    // Convert it to lowercase
    //
    password = password.toLowerCase()
```

```
    //
    // Add the .htm extension
    //
    var loc = password + ".htm"
    //
    // Make sure the user entered something
    //
    if (password != "")
    {
        //
        // If so, send the browser there
        //
        opener.location.href = loc
    }
    //
    // Close this window
    //
    window.close()
}

//-->
</SCRIPT>
```

> **Webmaster Wisdom**
>
> I give the details of a stur-
> dier version of this pass-
> word protection scheme in
> my book *Special Edition
> Using JavaScript* (www.
> mcfedries.com/UsingJavaScript).

Here's what happens:

1. The value in the pw text box is stored in the `password` variable.

2. The `password` value is changed to all lowercase letters (just in case the user entered any uppercase letters).

3. The .htm extension is tacked on to password. (You might need to change this to ".html" if your pages use that extension.)

4. If `password` isn't blank, the main browser window is sent to the password-protected page.

5. The little window is closed.

If you try out the example page that's on the CD in this book, enter **idiot** as the password.

JavaScript and Forms

In the previous example, you saw how I used a small form to get the password and then I used JavaScript to process that value. As you'll see over the next few sections, JavaScript is quite happy to work with forms for all kinds of things.

Making Form Fields Mandatory

One of the problems we webmasters face when constructing forms is getting our users to fill in all the required fields. We can augment the form with all kinds of notes that warn the user of the dire consequences that can result from leaving a field blank, but users have a way of ignoring these things.

A better approach is to use a little JavaScript know-how to make one or more form fields mandatory. That is, make it so the browser won't submit the form unless the user puts something in those fields.

For example, there isn't any way for my MailForm script (see Chapter 12) to detect the user's e-mail address, which means you have to rely on your readers to enter their e-mail address so that you can contact them. One thing you can do is use JavaScript to make your form's e-mail field mandatory.

To set this up, you first need to make two adjustments to your <FORM> tag:

♦ Add the NAME attribute and set it to whatever you want to name your form.

♦ Add the JavaScript onSubmit attribute, like so (here, *FormName* is the name you gave your form).

```
onSubmit="return Validate(FormName)"
```

Here's an example:

```
<FORM
    ACTION="http://www.mcfedries.com/scripts/formtest.asp"
    METHOD="POST"
    NAME="MyForm"
    onSubmit="return Validate(MyForm)">
```

The onSubmit event means that when the user clicks the form's Submit button, the function specified by onSubmit is executed before the form data is shipped out to the server. This enables you to check that a particular field has been filled in (or whatever). If it hasn't, the JavaScript can tell the browser not to submit the form.

You set up the rest of your form in the usual manner. You just need to pay attention to the names you supply each field because you use those names in the JavaScript procedure. Here's the example field I'll use:

```
<B>Please enter your e-mail address:</B><BR>
<INPUT TYPE="TEXT" SIZE="35" NAME="Email">
```

Here, at long last, is the script (see jsform1.htm on the CD in this book):

```
<SCRIPT LANGUAGE="JavaScript" TYPE="text/javascript">
<!--
function Validate(frm)
{
    //
    // Check the E-mail field to see if any characters were entered
    //
    if (frm.Email.value == "")
    {
        alert("Tsk tsk. Please enter an e-mail address.")
        frm.Email.focus()
        return false
    }
}
//-->
</SCRIPT>
```

What's happening here is that the `Validate()` function checks the value the user entered into the specified field (Email, in this case). If the value is empty (""), it means the user didn't enter a value. So the script displays an alert (see Figure 18.3), puts the cursor back in the Email field (this is called setting the "focus" in programming parlance), and then returns false, which tells the browser not to submit the form.

Figure 18.3

If the user doesn't enter anything in the text box, she sees this message.

To use this script on your own form, there are two things you need to adjust:

♦ The `if` statement checks the value of the form field named Email. When setting this up for your own use, you need to change `Email` to the name of your field.

♦ The same goes for the `frm.Email.focus()` statement. That is, you need to change `Email` to the name of your field.

Webmaster Wisdom

The user can easily thwart this script by entering a trivial value (such as a single letter) in the text box. My site offers a more sophisticated version of the script that checks to see if the user entered the @ sign (which is part of every e-mail address). See the following page: www.mcfedries.com/JavaScript/mandatory.html.

Confirming Form Data with the User

It's important that the data submitted in a form be as accurate as possible. However, lots of web surfers have short attention spans (present company excepted, of course), so they tend to fill in form data haphazardly. To help boost the accuracy of submissions, it's a good idea to display the entered data to the user before submitting it. If everything looks good, the user can submit the data; otherwise, he or she can cancel and make changes.

Before getting to the JavaScript, let's set up a sample form that includes the four main form controls: a text box, an option list, radio buttons, and a check box (see Chapter 12). Here it is (see jscheck.htm on the CD in this book):

```
<FORM
    ACTION="http://www.mcfedries.com/scripts/formtest.asp"
    METHOD="POST"
    NAME="MyForm"
    onSubmit="return CheckData(MyForm)">

Please enter your name:<BR>
<INPUT TYPE="TEXT" NAME="UserName">
<P>
Who is your favorite Beatle?<BR>
<SELECT NAME="Beatle">
<OPTION VALUE="George" SELECTED>George
<OPTION VALUE="John">John
<OPTION VALUE="Paul">Paul
<OPTION VALUE="Ringo">Ringo
<OPTION VALUE="Pete Best">Pete Best
<OPTION VALUE="Hunh?">Who the heck are the Beatles?
</SELECT>
<P>
Have you ever gotten jiggy with it?<BR>
<INPUT TYPE="RADIO" NAME="Jiggy" VALUE="Yes" CHECKED>Yes
<INPUT TYPE="RADIO" NAME="Jiggy" VALUE="No">No
<INPUT TYPE="RADIO" NAME="Jiggy" VALUE="Shhh">Not Telling
<P>
<INPUT TYPE="CHECKBOX" NAME="Spam">Send tons of spam?
<P>
<INPUT TYPE="SUBMIT" VALUE="Fire!">
</FORM>
```

Note, in particular, that I added the JavaScript onSubmit attribute to the <FORM> tag:

```
onSubmit="return CheckData(MyForm)"
```

This tells the browser that when the user submits the form, it must run the CheckData() JavaScript function. The return part means that the browser should examine the value returned by `CheckData()` to see whether the form submission should proceed or be cancelled. Here's the JavaScript:

```
<SCRIPT LANGUAGE="JavaScript" TYPE="text/javascript">
<!--
function CheckData(frm)
{
    //
    // Get the text box value
    //
    var tb = frm.UserName.value
    //
    // Get the selected option
    //
    var opt = frm.Beatle.options[frm.Beatle.selectedIndex].value
    //
    // Get the selected radio button
    //
    for (var i = 0; i < frm.Jiggy.length; i++)
    {
        if (frm.Jiggy[i].checked)
            var rb = frm.Jiggy[i].value
    }
    //
    // Get the check box value
    //
    if (frm.Spam.checked)
        var cb = "On"
    else
        var cb = "Off"
    //
    // Construct the message to display
    //
    var msg = "Your name: " + tb + "\n"
        + "Favorite Beatle: " + opt + "\n"
        + "Jiggy with it? " + rb + "\n"
        + "Send spam: " + cb + "\n"
    //
    // Show the data to the user
    //
    return confirm("Here is the form data you entered:" + "\n\n"
        + msg + "\n"
        + "Do you want to submit this data?")
}
//-->
</SCRIPT>
```

Webmaster Wisdom

In case you're wondering, all those "\n" things in the script are just the JavaScript code for starting a new line. This makes the displayed message easier to read.

Most of the function is spent getting the various form values. After that's done, a message containing all the values is constructed and then shown to the user via the `confirm()` statement. Figure 18.4 shows the dialog box that pops up. If the user clicks **Yes,** the `confirm()` statement returns `true`, and the form gets submitted; if the user clicks **No,** `confirm()` returns `false` and the form doesn't do anything.

Figure 18.4

When the user submits the form, he or she sees this confirmation message.

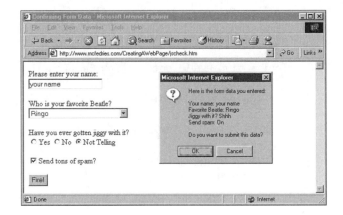

Creating a Drop-Down List of Links

After your site grows to a certain size, you run up against a daunting problem: How do you let surfers navigate to the various nooks and crannies of your site without cluttering each page with tons of links or a massive image map? My solution to this problem is the humble option list that you learned about in Chapter 12. Figure 18.5 shows what I mean. As you can see, the list contains all kinds of items that represent pages on my site. The surfer simply picks an item from the list and is immediately whisked to the selected spot. Best of all, it takes up just a small strip of space at the top of each of my pages.

As you've no doubt guessed by now, the secret behind this list legerdemain is JavaScript. This section shows you how easy it is to set up just such a list on your own site.

Let's begin with the list itself. You start by setting up a more-or-less standard selection list within a form:

```
<FORM>
<SELECT WIDTH="20" onChange="JumpToIt(this)">
</SELECT>
</FORM>
```

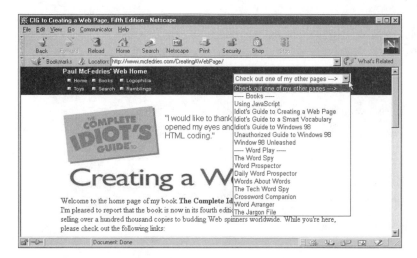

Figure 18.5

Each of my pages uses a drop-down list to help folks navigate my site.

There are two things you should note about this structure:

◆ The <FORM> tag is completely naked. That's okay because with this technique you never have to submit any form data to a server. That makes this method as lightning quick as a regular link.

◆ The <SELECT> tag houses the JavaScript onChange attribute. This tells the browser that whenever the list changes (that is, whenever the user selects a different item), it must run the JavaScript function named JumpToIt(). (The this part is a reference to the list itself that gets sent to the function.)

Now you need to populate the list with items that represent your pages. You do that with <OPTION> tags that take the following form:

```
<OPTION VALUE="URL">Item text
```

Here, replace *URL* with the URL of the page, and replace *Item text* with whatever text you want to appear in the list (such as the page title).

If you want to add nonactive items to the list (such as a "Select an item from this list" message or headings), use <OPTION> tags that take the following form:

```
<OPTION VALUE="None">Item text
```

Again, replace *Item text* with the text that you want to appear in the list. Here's the list structure with a few items added (there's a larger list in jslist.htm on the CD in this book):

```
<SELECT WIDTH="20" onChange="JumpToIt(this)">
<OPTION VALUE="None">Select a JavaScript resource from this list --->
<OPTION VALUE="http://www.mcfedries.com/UsingJavaScript/">SE Using JavaScript
```

```
<OPTION VALUE="http://www.javascripts.com/">JavaScripts.com
<OPTION VALUE="http://www.scriptsearch.com/">ScriptSearch
<OPTION VALUE="http://www.wsabstract.com/">Website Abstraction
<OPTION VALUE="http://javascript.internet.com/">The JavaScript Source
</SELECT>
```

Here's the JavaScript that is executed when the user selects a list item:

```
<SCRIPT LANGUAGE="JavaScript" TYPE="text/javascript">
<!--
function JumpToIt(list)
{
    var selection = list.options[list.selectedIndex].value
    if (selection != "None")
        location.href = selection
}
//-->
</SCRIPT>
```

The value of the currently selected list item is stored in the selection variable. If the value isn't "None," then the value is a URL, so the location.href property is set to that value, and away you go.

A Mortgage Calculator

For the final example, I show you a particularly powerful script that sets up a mortgage calculator. Figure 18.6 shows the calculator, which I created using form and table tags.

Figure 18.6

A mortgage calculator created using standard form and table tags. JavaScript makes the calculator calculate.

The calculator looks pretty enough, but can it calculate anything? Sure! Using the JavaScript below, you can actually compute the monthly mortgage payment based on the values you input.

```
<SCRIPT LANGUAGE="JavaScript" TYPE="text/javascript">
<!--
function checkForZero(field)
{
    if (field.value == 0 || field.value.length == 0) {
        alert ("This field can't be 0!");
        field.focus(); }
    else
        calculatePayment(field.form);
}


function cmdCalc_Click(form)
{
    if (form.price.value == 0 || form.price.value.length == 0) {
        alert ("The Price field can't be 0!");
        form.price.focus(); }
    else if (form.ir.value == 0 || form.ir.value.length == 0) {
        alert ("The Interest Rate field can't be 0!");
        form.ir.focus(); }
    else if (form.term.value == 0 || form.term.value.length == 0) {
        alert ("The Term field can't be 0!");
        form.term.focus(); }
    else
        calculatePayment(form);
}


function calculatePayment(form)
{
    princ = form.price.value - form.dp.value;
    intRate = (form.ir.value/100) / 12;
    months = form.term.value * 12;
    form.pmt.value = Math.floor((princ*intRate)/(1-Math.pow(1+
    [ccc]intRate,(-1*months)))*100)/100;
    form.principle.value = princ;
    form.payments.value = months;
}
//-->
</SCRIPT>
```

That's a complex chunk of code, to be sure, but luckily you don't have to understand how it works. The only thing you need to make sure of when using this script in another page, is that you use the same names for the form controls that I use in the example mortgage. htm file (which is, of course, on the CD in this book).

The Least You Need to Know

◆ Mind your mouseovers. When using mouseovers, keep your images small so that it doesn't take too long for the browser to download the second image.

◆ Premium password protection. If you have strict password needs, ask your web host or a CGI programmer to rustle you up some heavy-duty protection.

◆ Mandatory fields. If you have a field that the user *must* fill in, make that field mandatory by intercepting the submission using the onSubmit attribute.

◆ Ensuring accurate data. If you want users to enter the correct data into your form, show them the contents of each field before submitting the form. This gives the user a chance to cancel the submission if things don't look right.

Chapter **19**

Caffeinating Your Pages: Adding Java Applets

In This Chapter

- A bit of Java background
- How to put a Java applet inside a web page
- Some Java resources to check out
- A fistful of examples and just a few bad coffee puns

The JavaScript examples you messed with over the past couple of chapters added some programming "intelligence" to your pages. However, there's an even higher level of smarts you can confer on your web handiwork: a technology called Java. The idea behind Java is blindingly simple, but devilishly clever: When you access a Java-enhanced web page, your browser not only gets a page containing the usual HTML suspects, but it also receives a program. The browser (assuming it can tell a Java program from a Jackson Pollock, as most can) then runs the program right on the web page. So if the program is, say, a game of Hangman, then you're able to play Hangman right on the page. Now *that's* interactive!

This chapter gives you a bit of background on Java and then shows you how to add Java applets to your web pages.

Webmaster Wisdom

Java" and "JavaScript" sound kind of the same, so you might be wondering if they're related. Yes, they are, but only as distant cousins. The only thing they have in common is that the JavaScript programming language is basically a scaled-down version of Java. Other than that, they're completely different. The main difference is that you can construct JavaScript programs using a simple text editor, but creating Java programs requires a separate hunk of software called a *compiler*.

Java: A Piping Hot Mug of Browser-Based Programs

Java programs—or *applets*, as they're usually called—are written using the Java programming language developed by Sun Microsystems. Here are a few advantages that Java programs have over traditional software:

♦ The programs are sent to your browser and are started "behind the scenes." You don't have to worry about installation, setup, or loading because your browser takes care of all that dirty work for you.

♦ The programs are designed to work on just about any system. Whether you're running Windows, a Mac, or a Unix machine, Java programs run without complaint.

♦ Java is secure. When people hear about Java, their first concern is that some pimple-faced programmer who has succumbed to the dark side of The Force will send them a Java virus. But Java has built-in safeguards to prevent such attacks.

♦ Because you're always sent the latest and greatest version of the program when you access a site, you don't need to worry about upgrades and new releases.

So what do you need to start sipping some of this Java stuff? All you really need is a web browser that knows what the heck to do with any Java applet that comes its way. The latest versions of most browsers are now Java-jolted. Netscape has been Java-aware since version 2.0, and Internet Explorer has done Java since version 3.0. In other words, you shouldn't have any problems with Java applets, and most of the folks viewing your pages are able to work with whatever applets you purloin for your own use. (Having said that, let me backpedal a bit and mention that fresh installations of Internet Explorer 6 doesn't come with Java support installed. The first time Internet Explorer comes across an applet, it asks if you want to download Java. I suspect most people will say yes, but bear in mind that some people may opt to surf Java-free.)

Java applets come in all shapes and sizes, from tiny animations to full-blown software packages: word processors, spreadsheets, real-time stock quotes and portfolio management, high-end games, and much more. However, even the simplest Java doohickeys are exciting in their own way. This Java jazz is such a radical departure from typical web content that interacting with even the humblest applet is a revelation. So, in that spirit, let's visit a few sites that boast some Java functionality.

Our first example is a fun thing called the Random Sentence Generator, which I built myself. As you can see in Figure 19.1, you click the **Generate a New Sentence** button and the applet provides you with a new, random (and often hilarious) sentence. If you want to try this out for yourself, head for the following page: www. logophilia.com/WordPlay/random-sentence.html.

Words from the Web

Java-based animations tend to be simple or downright cheesy, so the web has spawned various uncomplimentary names for them, including **dancing baloney** and **craplets**.

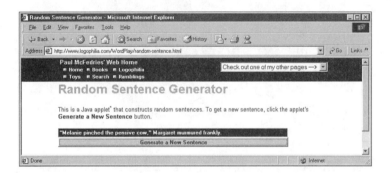

Figure 19.1

See semi-sensible sentences with the Random Sentence Generator Java applet.

Generating random sentences redefines the word "timewaster." If you're looking for more serious fun, there are thousands of Java-based games available. My own day isn't complete without a visit to the Word Game of the Day page on the Merriam-Webster site: www.m-w.com/game.

This page offers a link to the game, which is one of five Java-fueled word games that rotate each day. Figure 19.2 shows an example.

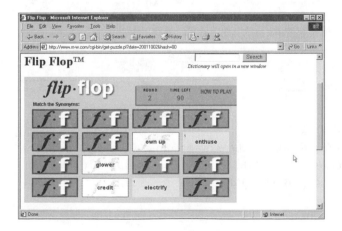

Figure 19.2

There's no shortage of Java games on the web.

How to Add a Java Applet to a Web Page

If you'd like to give your visitors some Java applets to play with, they're easy enough to add to your pages. The secret is the <APPLET> tag:

```
<APPLET CODE="file" WIDTH="x" HEIGHT="y">
Alternative text for non-Java browsers goes here.
</APPLET>
```

The critical chunk in this tag is the CODE attribute. The *file* part is the name of the "class" file that contains the Java code.

Example 1: A Java Clock

Here's an example:

```
<APPLET CODE="JavaTime.class" WIDTH="300" HEIGHT="60">
If you see this text, it means your browser doesn't support Java.
</APPLET>
```

The JavaTime.class file is a Java application I wrote myself. It implements a digital clock that displays the current date and time, as shown in Figure 19.3.

Figure 19.3

The JavaTime applet serves up the current date and time.

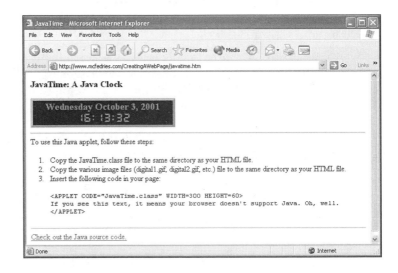

The <APPLET> tag also takes a few other attributes:

♦ **ALIGN** This attribute sets the alignment of the applet with respect to the text that surrounds it. You can use one of the following values: LEFT, CENTER, RIGHT, TOP, MIDDLE, or BOTTOM.

◆ **CODEBASE** You use this attribute to specify a different location for the Java files. For example, suppose you create a "classes" directory to store all your Java junk. Then you'd add CODEBASE="classes/" to the <APPLET> tag so that the browser knows where to look for the Java files.

◆ **HSPACE** This attribute sets a value (in pixels) for the amount of space that appears to the left and right of the applet.

◆ **VSPACE** This attribute sets a value (in pixels) for the amount of space that appears above and below the applet.

Webmaster Wisdom

The JavaTime applet is on this book's CD in the Chap19 directory. See the javatime.htm file for the full instructions on using this applet.

Example II: Using Parameters

Most of the Java applets you abscond with for your own devices will run "as is." In other words, you just copy the class file to your site, plop the appropriate <APPLET> tag into your page, and off you go.

However, many applets are customizable. They enable you to specify features such as the colors the applet displays, the contents of some controls, and so on. For these flexible applets, you specify your own custom settings by shoehorning <PARAM> tags between the <APPLET> and </APPLET> tags. The <PARAM> tag (short for *parameter*) uses the following format:

```
<PARAM NAME="name" VALUE="value">
```

Here, *name* is the name of the parameter and *value* is the custom value you want to use for the parameter. Let's make all this more concrete with an example. On the CD in this book, you'll find another Java applet that I built with my bare hands called JavaJump.class. (Look in the Chap19 directory.) As you can see in Figure 19.4, JavaJump consists of a drop-down list and a command button. The idea is that you select a page from the list and click the **Go!** button. The applet then tells the browser to go to that page.

Here's the code that sets up the applet (see javajump.htm on the CD in this book):

```
<APPLET CODE="JavaJump.class" WIDTH=250 HEIGHT=32>
<PARAM NAME="bgcolor" VALUE="0,0,0">
<PARAM NAME="pages" VALUE="3">
<PARAM NAME="url1" VALUE="CIG to Creating a Web Page;http://www.mcfedries.com/
➡books/cightml">
<PARAM NAME="url2" VALUE="Paul McFedries' Web Home;http://www.mcfedries.com/">
<PARAM NAME="url3" VALUE="Gamelan (Java Applets);http://www.gamelan.com/">
</APPLET>
```

Figure 19.4

JavaJump: Select a page from the list and then click Go! to jump to that page.

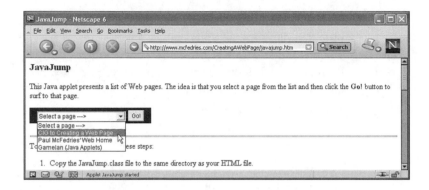

Figure 19.4

JavaJump: Select a page from the list and then click Go! to jump to that page.

Let's look at each <PARAM> tag in turn. The first one sets the background color of the applet:

```
<PARAM NAME="bgcolor" VALUE="red.green.blue">
```

Here, the VALUE parameter is set to three numbers (*red*, *green*, and *blue*), which are values between 0 and 255.

> **Words from the Web**
>
> The adjective *Javlovian* is used to describe the automatic response that causes marketing types to come up with only cute, coffee-related names for Java-based products (for example, Café, Roaster, Java Beans, Latte, and so on ad nauseum).

The second <PARAM> tag specifies the number of items that appear in the list:

```
<PARAM NAME="pages" VALUE="total">
```

The rest of the <PARAM> tags specify the list items and they use the following format:

```
<PARAM NAME="urlx" VALUE="Name;URL ">
```

Here, x is the item number (so your parameter names will be url1, url2, and so on), *Name* is the page name that appears in the list, and *URL* is the full URL of the web page.

Java Resources on the Web

If this short chapter has tickled your Java fancy and you want more, don't sweat it. The web is brim full to bursting with Java sites. Some of them are just so-so, but there are plenty of good ones. Here are some of my favorites (see javasite.htm on the CD in this book):

- **Developer's Daily** Designed with the Java programmer in mind, this site has links to tons of tutorials, FAQs, and applets. See www.devdaily.com.

◆ **FreewareJava.com**   This site includes hundreds of applets, Java courses, links to other sites, and much more. See freewarejava.com.

◆ **Gamelan**   This is "The Official Directory for Java" and remains one of the premier Java sites on the web. See softwaredev.earthweb.com/java.

◆ **JARS.COM**   This site bills itself as "The #1 Java Review Service," and I have no reason to doubt it. You'll find thoughtful reviews of hundreds of applets in dozens of categories. See jars.com.

◆ **The Java Boutique**   This is a first-rate site with lots of applets, programming tutorials, Java news, articles, forums, and more. See javaboutique.internet.com.

◆ **Netscape's Java Developer Central**   If you think you want to learn Java, this comprehensive site is a great place to start. See developer.netscape.com/tech/java/index.html.

◆ **ScriptSearch**   As I'm sure you've come to expect, this site has the Java goods, as well, with hundreds and hundreds of applets to play with. See www.scriptsearch.com.

◆ **Sun Microsystems**   I mentioned earlier that Sun Microsystems invented Java, so its site's a must-visit for news, documentation, discussions, and lots and lots of high-quality applets. See java.sun.com.

◆ **Webmonkey**   The famously simian site has a few nice Java tutorials and articles that are worth checking out. See www.hotwired.com/webmonkey/java.

◆ **Yahoo! Java Index**   This site contains a great listing of Java resources. See dir.yahoo.com/Computers_and_Internet/Programming_Languages/Java.

The Least You Need to Know

◆ The applet skinny. A Java applet is a miniprogram that gets loaded with the regular page riffraff and then runs right on the page.

◆ The <APPLET> tag. Here's the general shape of the <APPLET> tag (where *file* is the name of the .class file that contains the applet):

```
<APPLET CODE="file" WIDTH="x" HEIGHT="y">
Alternative text for non-Java browsers goes here.
</APPLET>
```

◆ Adding parameters. If the applet takes one or more parameters, you specify their details by using <PARAM> tags between <APPLET> and </APPLET>:

```
<PARAM NAME="name" VALUE="value">
```

Part 5

Rounding Out Your HTML Education

Okay, that's it; the show's over. Our box of HTML basics is now empty and all the shiny web page baubles, bangles, and bric-a-brac have been brought out for your consideration. It's true: your education on HTML fundamentals is over, finito, sayonara, done like dinner. You know it all. Been there, done that.

Well, so now what? Ah, now it's time for a bit of HTML finishing school. The next three chapters help bring everything together by running through a few semi-interesting web page technologies, giving you pointers on good HTML and web design style, and by offering you tons of links to websites that have resources or know-how that you'll find useful for the rest of your webmaster career.

Chapter

20

Web Page Doodads You Should Know About

In This Chapter

◆ How to let people search your site

◆ Putting up a chat room or bulletin board

◆ Getting the hang of server-side includes

◆ Making good use of HTML comments

◆ A passel of perks for your page-producing pleasure

Over the years, I've discovered that there are basically two types of web page artisans. On the one hand you have those people who are quite happy to cobble together their pages using just the basic HTML tags, with perhaps a style sheet or two and the odd bit of JavaScript thrown in for good measure. On the other hand, you have those folks whose mantra seems to be, "Okay, but what *else* can I do?" These page hounds are always on the lookout for shiny things they can tack on to their sites to entice visitors or impress their friends.

This chapter is dedicated to the latter group. For those intrepid souls, I've put together a list of extra accessories with which they can adorn their pages. These include search features, chat rooms, bulletin boards, and server-side includes (a technology I'll tell you about shortly).

The Searchable Site: Adding a Search Feature

If your site contains only a single page, or just a few pages, any visitor with a pulse ought to be able to find what he is looking for. (Assuming, of course, that you've set up the necessary links to your pages.) That may not be the case, however, if your site starts getting a bit big for its britches. Once you start talking about your total number of pages in the dozens or even the hundreds, then finding a specific tidbit on your site may become a real page-needle-in-a-web-haystack exercise.

To keep your visitors happy, there are resources out there in webland that you can use to add a searching component to your site, just like the big-time sites have. Even better, many of these search services are free. (Although there are some limitations. For example, there might be a maximum number of pages that can be indexed and you might be required to place an image or ad on your site.)

Before you start checking out specific search services, note that they all return a "results page" after the user runs a search. These results list all the pages on your site that match whatever criteria the user specified for the search. It's important to remember that these results will be useful only if you've done a bit of prep work in advance so that your site is search ready. This means setting up your pages just like you would if you were preparing for the major search engines to come calling: having descriptive titles on every page, using the "Description" and "Keywords" <META> tags, and so on.

Webmaster Wisdom

See Chapter 8, "Publish or Perish: Putting Your Page on the Web," for the details on setting up your site for search engines.

Page Pitfalls

Depending on the size of your site, search indexes can get quite large, so be prepared for them to usurp a decent-sized chunk of whatever disk space your web host has set aside for you.

Besides the results page, search features also usually include the following three components:

◆ **The search engine** This is the part that does the actual searching of your site. There are many different types of search engine, but there are two main types for you to consider: search hosting and CGI scripts. I discuss these in detail a bit later.

◆ **The search index** Before the search engine can run searches, it must first "crawl" through your site, reading the text of each page. As it goes along, it compiles a list of the words on each page (usually bypassing common words such as "the" and "and"). The words, along with pointers to the pages in which they appear, are stored in a file called an *index*. When the user searches for a particular word, the search engine looks up the word in the index, grabs a list of the pages in which that word appears, and then displays that list to the user.

♦ **The search form**   This is the form that your visitors use to enter their search criteria. Look for a search service that provides a prebuilt form (ideally, one that can be customized to blend in with your site design).

Your search for a good search feature should begin at home. That is, you should first ask your web hosting provider if it offers a search feature for its customers. If not, then it's time to hit the road. As I mentioned earlier, there are two main types of search features to consider: a CGI script and a search host.

The CGI route involves installing a script on your web host's server, either in your own CGI-BIN (if you have one) or the host's global CGI-BIN. Remember that most hosts will want to inspect a CGI script before they'll let you install it. To find a script, see my list of CGI resources in Chapter 12, "Need Feedback? Create a Form!"

A search host is a separate site that hosts not only the search engine, but also the search index. This type of search is marginally slower because the data has to go to and from the other server. However, it's the only way to go if your web host won't allow you to install a CGI program or Java applet, or if your disk space on the server is running low. Here are some search hosts to check out:

♦ **www.atomz.com**   This site has an "Express Search" product that's free for sites that have fewer than 500 pages. The only requirement is that you place an Atomz logo on the search results page. This is the most popular of the search servers.

♦ **www.freefind.com**   This service is free for sites that have up to 32 MB of data. You're required to place a banner ad (which will show ads for various products) on the search results page.

♦ **www.fusionbot.com**   The "Free Package" offered by this service lets you index up to 250 pages. The results page will have both a banner ad (with ads from FusionBot sponsors) and a FusionBot logo.

♦ **www.google.com/intl/en_extra/services/free.html**   The best search engine for the Web also offers a "SiteSearch Companion" for your site. The free version will index an unlimited number of pages, and the results page (on which Google reserves the right to display an ad) looks just like the regular Google page.

♦ **www.master.com**   This host has a "Search Your Site" feature, the free version of which is happy to index up to 5,000 pages, or 30 MB of data. You're required to display the Master.com logo on the results page.

Webmaster Wisdom

To help you check out the stuff in this chapter, I put together a page with links to the sites I mention. See doodads.htm on the CD in this book.

◆ **www.picosearch.com**   The free version of this service will index up to 1,500 pages, although you're required to place an ad for PicoSearch on the results page.

Talk Amongst Yourselves: Adding a Chat Room or Bulletin Board

Your site visitors can "talk" to you if you include a "mailto" link on your pages or if you set up a feedback form. But what if you want your visitors to be able to talk to each other? That may sound strange at first glance, but it's a great way to set up a kind of "community" on your site and to ensure that people keep visiting your site.

Like search features, chat rooms and bulletin board come in a number of different flavors, of which three are the most popular: Java applets and JavaScript (both of which are hosted on the remote server) and CGI script (which is usually installed on your own host). Here are some chat rooms and bulletin boards to check out:

◆ **boardserver.mycomputer.com**   This is a JavaScript-based bulletin board that's hosted on the BoardServer site. It costs (as I write this) US$19.95 per month or US$199 per year.

◆ **chat-forum.com/freechat**   This is a free Java-based chat service. You'll see banner ads or pop-up ads.

◆ **www.chattersworld.com/remote**   This is a free chat host service that offers a number of different chat rooms in various categories.

◆ **www.infopop.com**   This site offers the Ultimate Bulletin Board, a CGI script that you install on your web host. It costs (at the time of writing) US$125 for individuals.

◆ **www.multicity.com**   This site offers a free Java chat applet that's hosted on the Multicity site. The chat room displays a Multicity banner ad.

◆ **www.planetz.net/quickchat**   This site hosts a chat server and gives you a Java applet to place on your site.

Using Server-Side Includes to Insert Files in Your Pages

This section tells you about a clever little technology called server-side includes that enables you to include certain kinds of content automatically in your pages. As you'll see, this can save you *a lot* of time, particularly if you include similar content on all or most of your pages.

The Include Tag

One of the hallmarks of a good site is a consistent layout among your pages. I talk about this in more detail in the next chapter, but part of what this means is having certain elements appear on all or most of your pages. Here are some examples:

- Links to the major sections of your site.

- A "header" at the top of each page that includes a logo or some other image, the name of your site, and a motto or slogan.

- A "footer" at the bottom of each page that includes items such as your name, contact information, and a copyright notice.

Adding a snippet such as these to each of your pages isn't really a big deal. You just type it out once, copy it, and then paste the text into your other HTML files. Ah, but what if you make a change to the text or to a link? In that case, you have to open all your files and edit each one accordingly. That's no big thing if you have only a few pages, but what if you have 20 or 120?

To avoid the mind-numbing drudgery of having to edit a ridiculous number of pages each time you make a small change, consider using something called a *server-side include* (SSI). This involves two things:

- A small text file that contains any combination of text and tags.

- A special SSI tag that you place inside each of your pages. This SSI tag references the text file. What the tag does, essentially, is tell the web server to replace the tag with the entire contents of the text file.

What's the advantage here? Simply this: It means you need to edit only that lone text file. Since the server always replaces the SSI tag with the latest version of the text file, all your pages display the edited text automatically.

What's the catch? There are two:

- Your web host's server must be set up to handle SSI.

- You usually need to use the .shtml extension on any files that have the SSI tag. (SSI also works with ASP pages, which I discuss later in this chapter.)

CAUTION

Page Pitfalls

Remember that SSI requires the services of a server to work properly. If you view your page with the include tag on your own computer, you won't see the inserted file.

To use SSI requires two steps:

1. Create a new text file and use it to insert the tags and text that you want to insert into your pages. When you're done, be sure to upload this file to your web host directory.

2. In each HTML file that you want the text file inserted, add the special SSI tag that I've been blathering on about:

```
<!--#include file="TextFileName"-->
```

This is called the *SSI include tag*, and you need to replace *TextFileName* with the name of the text file from Step 1. Remember, as well, to position this tag *exactly* where you want the text file's contents to appear.

Let's give an example a whirl. Here are the contents of a text file named footer.txt (which you'll find on the CD in this book):

```
<HR>
<ADDRESS>
This page is Copyright &copy; 200?, your-name-here<BR>
company-name-here<BR>
company-address-here<BR>
Phone: (###) ###-####<BR>
Fax: (###) ###-####<BR>
Email: <A HREF="mailto:your-email-address-here">your-email-address-here</A>.
</ADDRESS>
<P>
Last revision: date-goes-here
<P>
Return to my <A HREF="home-page-URL-goes-here">home page.</A>
```

Now here's the code for a file named ssi.shtml (also on the CD in this book), which includes an SSI tag that references the footer.txt file:

```
<HTML>
<HEAD>
<TITLE>An SSI Example</TITLE>
</HEAD>

<BODY>
The regular page text and graphics go here.

<!--#include file="footer.txt"-->

</BODY>
</HTML>
```

As you can see in Figure 20.1, the server replaces the SSI tag with the contents of footer.txt.

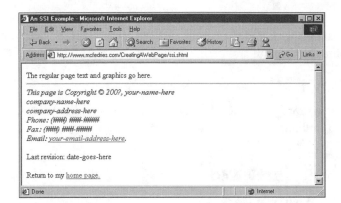

Figure 20.1

When the server trips over the SSI include tag, it replaces the tag with the entire contents of the file specified by the tag.

The Echo Tag

Most servers that support SSI also support a second SSI tag:

```
<!--#echo var="VariableName"-->
```

This is called the *SSI echo tag*, and you use it to "echo" or write a specific type of data to the page. The data that gets written depends on what you specify for the *VariableName*. For example, you can use the LAST_MODIFIED variable:

```
Last edited on <!--#echo var="LAST_MODIFIED"-->
```

Here, the server replaces the SSI echo tag with the date and time that the file was last modified:

```
Last edited on Friday, August 23 2002 03:02:59
```

Table 20.1 lists some of the more useful echo variable names (as well as a few that are only semi-useful).

Table 20.1   Some SSI Echo Tag Variables

Variable	What It Echoes
DATE_GMT	The current date and time at Greenwich (Greenwich Mean Time)
DATE_LOCAL	The current date and time on the server
DOCUMENT_NAME	The current page's server directory and name
DOCUMENT_URI	The URL of this page (less the host)
LAST_MODIFIED	The date and time this page was last modified
HTTP_REFERER	The address the user came from to get to the current page
REMOTE_ADDR	The IP address of the user

When you're using any of the date and time echo variables, the actual appearance of the output varies depending on the browser and the computer used by the surfer. Thankfully, you can control the appearance of the date and time by using the SSI config tag:

```
<!--#config timefmt="TimeFormat"-->
```

You place this tag immediately before your SSI echo tag, and you replace *TimeFormat* with any of the formats listed in Table 20.2.

Table 20.2   Some SSI Config Tag Formats

Format	What You Get
%a	The abbreviated weekday name
%A	The full weekday name
%b	The abbreviated month name
%B	The full month name
%c	The date and time format that's appropriate for the user's locale
%C	The default date and time format
%d	The day of month (from 01 to 31)
%H	The hour in 24-hour format (00 to 23)
%I	The hour in 12-hour format (01 to 12)
%j	The day of the year (001 to 366)
%m	The month of the year (01 to 12)
%M	The minute (00 to 59)
%p	A.M. or P.M.
%S	The second (00 to 59)
%U	The week of the year, where Sunday is the first day of the week (00 to 51)
%w	The day of the week (Sunday = 0)
%W	The week number of year, where Monday is the first day of the week (00 to 51)
%x	The date format for the user's current locale
%X	The time format for the user's current locale
%y	The year without the century (00 to 99)
%Y	The year with the century (for example, 2002)

Here's the code from a page that puts the SSI echo tag through its paces (see ssi2.shtml on the CD in this book).

```
<HTML>
<HEAD>
<TITLE>The SSI Echo Tag</TITLE>
</HEAD>

<BODY>
<B>Some useful (and semi-useful) echo variables:</B>
<TABLE BORDER="1">
<TR><TH>VARIABLE</TH><TH>What Gets Echoed</TH><TH>Description</TH></TR>
<TR><TD>DATE_GMT</TD>
<TD><!--#echo var="DATE_GMT"--></TD>
<TD>Current date and time at Greenwich (Greenwich Mean Time).</TD></TR>
<TR><TD>DATE_LOCAL</TD>
<TD><!--#echo var="DATE_LOCAL"--></TD>
<TD>Current date and time on the server.</TD></TR>
<TR><TD>DOCUMENT_NAME</TD>
<TD><!--#echo var="DOCUMENT_NAME"--></TD>
<TD>This page's server directory and name.</TD></TR>
<TR><TD>DOCUMENT_URI</TD>
<TD><!--#echo var="DOCUMENT_URI"--></TD>
<TD>URL of this page (less the host).</TD></TR>
<TR><TD>LAST_MODIFIED</TD>
<TD><!--#echo var="LAST_MODIFIED"--></TD>
<TD>Date and time this page was last modified.</TD></TR>
<TR><TD>HTTP_REFERER</TD>
<TD><!--#echo var="HTTP_REFERER"--></TD>
<TD>Address the user came from.</TD></TR>
<TR><TD>REMOTE_ADDR</TD>
<TD><!--#echo var="REMOTE_ADDR"--></TD>
<TD>IP address of the user.</TD></TR>
</TABLE>

<B>Formatting the date and time:</B>
<TABLE BORDER="1">
<TR><TH>TIMEFMT</TH><TH>What the Date and Time Look Like</TH></TR>
<TR><TD>%#c</TD>
<TD><!--#config timefmt="%#c"--><!--#echo var="LAST_MODIFIED"--></TD></TR>
<TR><TD>%c</TD>
<TD><!--#config timefmt="%c"--><!--#echo var="LAST_MODIFIED"--></TD></TR>
<TR><TD>%x</TD>
<TD><!--#config timefmt="%x"--><!--#echo var="LAST_MODIFIED"--></TD></TR>
<TR><TD>%#x</TD>
<TD><!--#config timefmt="%#x"--><!--#echo var="LAST_MODIFIED"--></TD></TR>
<TR><TD>%X</TD>
```

```
<TD><!--#config timefmt="%X"--><!--#echo var="LAST_MODIFIED"--></TD></TR>
<TR><TD>%a, %b %d, %Y</TD>
<TD><!--#config timefmt="%a, %b %d, %Y"--><!--#echo var="LAST_MODIFIED"--></TD>
</TR>
</TABLE>
</BODY>
</HTML>
```

Figure 20.2 shows how things look in the browser.

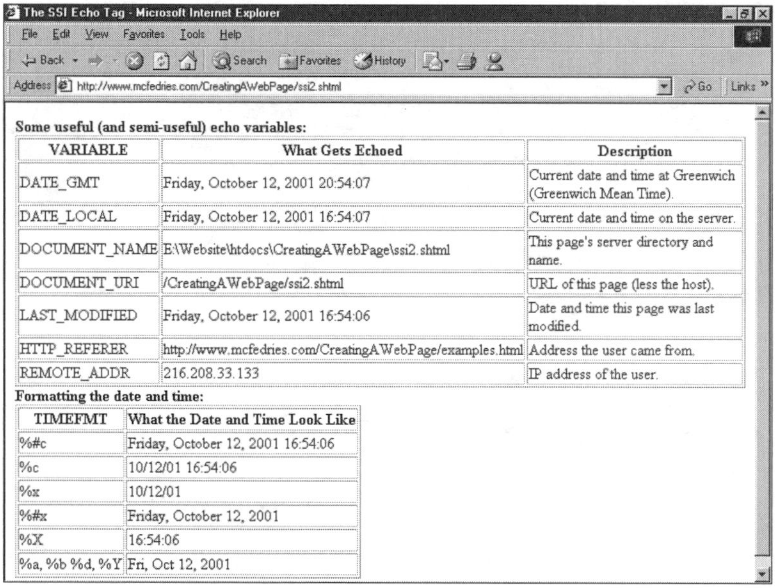

Figure 20.2

Some SSI echo tags.

Sneakily Hiding Text with HTML Comment Tags

In the lingo of HTML, a *comment* is a chunk of text that gets completely ignored by the browser. Yes, you read that right: When the browser comes upon a comment, it averts its electronic eyes and pretends that the comment doesn't even exist. What possible use could there be for such a thing? Here are a few:

◆ You can add notes to yourself in specific places of the page. For example, you can add a comment such as *Here's where I'll put my logo when I've finished it.*

◆ You can add explanatory text that describes parts of the page. For example, if you have a table that comprises the header of your page, you can add a comment before the <TABLE> tag such as *This is the start of the header.*

◆ You can skip problematic sections of your page. If you have a section that isn't working properly, or a link that isn't set up yet, you can convert the text and tags into a comment so as not to cause problems for the browser or the user.

◆ You can add a copyright notice or other info for people who view your HTML source code.

To turn any bit of text into a comment, you surround it with the HTML comment tags. Specifically, you precede it with <!-- and follow it with -->, like this:

```
<!--This text is a comment-->
```

To prove that this actually works, here's a simple page that includes a comment (see comment.htm on the CD in this book).

```
<HTML>
<HEAD>
<TITLE>A Comment Example</TITLE>
</HEAD>

<BODY>
This text isn't a comment.<BR>

<!--This text is a comment-->

This text isn't a comment, either.

</BODY>
</HTML>
```

Page Pitfalls

Although comment text isn't displayed in the browser, there's no problem seeing it if you simply view the page source code. Therefore, don't put sensitive information inside a comment tag.

As you can see in Figure 20.3, the text inside the comment tags isn't displayed by the browser.

Figure 20.3

Text that resides between the HTML comment tags is totally shunned by the browser.

The Least You Need to Know

◆ Search types. There are two main types of search component that you should consider: a search host and a CGI script.

◆ Chat room and bulletin board types. Most chat rooms and bulletin boards are hosted on remote servers and you place either a Java applet or some JavaScripts on your page. There are also CGI scripts that you install on your web host.

◆ The include tag. Use this tag to automatically insert the tags and test from a specified text file:

```
<!--#include file="TextFileName"-->
```

◆ The echo tag. Use this tag to insert data into a page, depending on the variable you specify:

```
<!--#echo var="VariableName"-->
```

◆ Hiding text from the browser. Use the HTML comment tags to force the browser to ignore a section of text:

```
<!--Hidden text goes here-->
```

Chapter 21

The Elements of Web Page Style

In This Chapter

◆ Prose prescriptions for web page writing

◆ Ideas for organizing your pages

◆ Tips on using graphics

◆ Things to keep in mind when dealing with links

◆ The do's and don'ts of world-class webcraft

With all that you've learned so far, you might be able to dress up your web pages, but can you take them anywhere? That is, you might have a web page for people to read, but is it a readable web page? Will web wanderers take one look at your page, say "Yuck!" and click their browser's Back button to get out of there, or will they stay awhile and check out what you have to say? Is your site a one-night surf, or will people add your page to their list of bookmarks?

My goal in this chapter is to show you there's a fine line between filler and killer—between "Trash it!" and "Smash hit!"—and to show you how to end up on the positive side of that equation. To that end, I give you a few style suggestions that help you put your best web page foot forward.

Content Is King: Notes About Writing

In earlier chapters, I've given you the goods on a number of web page techniques that most folks would shelve under "Eye Candy" in the HTML store. These include fonts, colors, animated images, image maps, style sheets, mouseovers, scrolling status bar messages, and Java applets. And while all of these things can and should be used by even the most sober of web page engineers, you should never forget one thing: It's the content, silly! This is the central fact of web page publishing, and it often gets obscured by all the glitz.

And, unless you're an artist or a musician or some other right-brain type, content means text. The vast majority of web pages are written documents that rely on words and phrases for impact. It makes sense, then, to put most of your page-production efforts into your writing. Sure, you'll spend lots of time fine-tuning your HTML codes to get things laid out just so, or tweaking your images, or scouring the web for "hot links" to put on your page, but you should direct most of your publishing time toward polishing your prose.

That isn't to say, however, that you need to devote your pages to earth-shattering topics composed with a professional writer's savoir-faire. Many of the web's self-styled "style gurus" complain that most pages are too trivial and amateurish. Humbug! These ivory tower, hipper-than-thou types are completely missing the point of publishing on the web. They seem to think the web is just a slightly different form of book and magazine publishing, where only a select few deserve to be in print. *Nothing could be further from the truth!* With the web, anybody (that is, anybody with the patience to muddle through this HTML stuff) can get published and say what she wants to the world.

In other words, the web has opened up a whole new world of publishing opportunities, and we're in "anything goes" territory. So when I say, "Content is king," I mean you need to think carefully about what you want to say and make your page a unique experience. If you're putting up a page for a company, the page should reflect the company's philosophies, target audience, and central message. If you're putting up a personal home page, put the emphasis on the personal:

- **Write about topics that interest you.** Heck, if *you* are not interested in what you're writing about, I guarantee your readers won't be interested, either.

- **Write with passion.** If the topic you're scribbling about turns your crank, let everyone know. Shout from the rooftops that you love this stuff—you think it's the greatest thing since they started putting "Mute" buttons on TV remotes.

- **Write in your own voice.** The best home pages act as mirrors that show visitors at least an inkling of the authors' inner workings. And the sure-fire way to make your page a reflection of yourself is to write the way you talk. If you say "gotta" in conversation, go ahead and write "gotta" in your page. If you use contractions such as

"I'll" and "you're" when talking to your friends, don't write "I will" and "you are" to your readers. Everybody—amateurs and professional scribes alike—has a unique writing voice; find yours and use it unabashedly.

Spelling, Grammar, and Other Text Strangers

Having said all that, however, I'm not proposing web anarchy. It's not enough to just slap up some text willy-nilly, or foist your stream-of-consciousness brain dumps on unsuspecting (and probably uninterested) web surfers. You need to shoot for certain *minimum* levels of quality if you hope to hold people's attention (and get them to come back for more).

For starters, you need to take to heart the old axiom, "The essence of writing is rewriting." Few of us ever say exactly what we want, the way we want, in a first draft. Before putting a page on the web, reread it a few times (at least once out loud, if you don't feel too silly doing it) to see if things flow the way you want. Put yourself in your reader's shoes. Will all this rambling make sense to that person? Is this an enjoyable read, or is it drudgery?

Above all, check and recheck your spelling (better yet, run the text through a spell checker, if you have one). A botched word or two won't ruin a page but, if nothing else, the gaffes will distract your readers. And, in the worst case, if your page is riddled with spelling blunders, your site will remain an eternally unpopular web wallflower.

Webmaster Wisdom

Correct spelling is important, so rather than trust your own sense of what's right, you ought to run your text through a handy spell checker. Most high-end word processing programs (such as Word) have one, and lots of HTML editors (such as Netscape Composer) are spell-check equipped. If there's no spell checker in sight, consider downloading a great little program called Spell Checker for Edit Boxes. It's free and it can be found here: www.quinion.com/mqa/index.htm.

Grammar ranks right up there with root canals and tax audits on most people's "Top Ten Most Unpleasant Things" list. And it's no wonder: all those dangling participles, passive voices, and split infinitives. One look at that stuff and the usual reaction is "Yeah, well, split *this!*" Happily, you don't need to be a gung-ho grammarian to put up a successful Web page. As long as your sentences make sense and your thoughts proceed in a semi-logical order, you'll be fine. Besides, most people's speech is reasonably grammatical, so if you model your writing after your speech patterns, you'll come pretty close. If you're not sure about things, ask some trusted and smart friends or family members to read your stuff and offer constructive criticism.

I should note, however, that this write-the-way-you-talk school of composition does have a few drawbacks. For one thing, most people get annoyed having to slog through too many words written in a "street" style; for example, writing "cuz" instead of "because," "U" instead of "you," or "dudz" instead of "dudes." Once in a while is okay, but a page full of that stuff will rile even the gentlest soul. Also, don't overuse "train of thought" devices such as "um," "uh," or the three-dot ellipsis thing ….

Webmaster Wisdom

Although you should always squash all spelling bugs before a page goes public, try to maintain a charitable attitude about other people's howlers. Although the lion's share of pages are written in English, not all the authors have English as their native tongue, so some pages include spelling that's, uh, creative. If an e-mail link is provided on the page, send a gentle note pointing out the slips of the keyboard and offer up the appropriate corrections.

More Tips for Righteous Writing

Thanks to the web's open, inclusive nature and its grass-roots appeal, there are, overall, few prescriptions you need to follow when writing your page. Besides the ideas we've talked about so far, here are a few other stylistic admonishments to bear in mind:

- **Keep exclamation marks to a minimum!** Although I told you earlier to write with passion, keep an eye out for extraneous exclamation marks! Yeah, you might be excited but, believe me, exclamation marks get old in a hurry! See?! They make you sound so darned perky! Stop!

- **DON'T SHOUT!** Many web spinners add emphasis to their epistles by using UPPERCASE LETTERS. This isn't bad in itself, but please use uppercase sparingly. An entire page written in capital letters is tough to read and it feels like you're shouting, WHICH IS OKAY FOR A USED-CAR SALESMAN ON LATE-NIGHT TV, but it's inappropriate in just about any other context (including the world of web-page prose). Instead, use *italics* to emphasize important words or phrases.

- **Avoid excessive font formatting.** Speaking of italics, it's a good idea to go easy on those HTML tags that let you play around with the formatting of your text (as described in Chapter 3, "From Buck-Naked to Beautiful: Dressing Up Your Page"). **Bold**, *italics*, and `typewriter text` have their uses, but overusing them diminishes their impact and can make a page tough to read.

◆ **Be good, be brief, be gone.** These are the "three B's" of any successful presentation. Being good means writing in clear, understandable prose that isn't marred by sloppy spelling or flagrant grammar violations. Also, if you use facts or statistics, cite the appropriate references to placate the doubting Thomases who want to check things for themselves. Being brief means getting right to the point without indulging in a rambling preamble. Always assume your reader is impatiently surfing through a stack of sites and has no time or patience for verbosity. State your business and then practice the third "B": Be gone!

The Overall Organization of Your Web Pages

Let's now turn our attention to some ideas for getting (and keeping) your web page affairs in order. You need to bear in mind, at all times, that the World Wide Web is all about navigation. Heck, half the fun comes from just surfing page-to-page via links. Because you've probably been having so much fun with this HTML stuff that you've created multiple pages for yourself, you can give the same navigational thrill to your readers. All you need to do is organize your pages appropriately and give visitors some way of getting from one page to the next.

What do I mean by organizing your pages "appropriately?" Well, there are two things to look at:

◆ How you split up the topics you talk about

◆ How many total documents you have

The One-Track Web Page: Keep pages to a single topic.

Although there are no set-in-stone rules about this site organization stuff, there's one principle that most people follow: one topic, one page. That is, cramming a number of disparate topics into a single page is not usually the way to go. For one thing, it's wasteful because a reader might be interested in only one of the topics, but he or she still has to load the entire page. It can also be confusing to read. If you have, say, some insights into metallurgy and some fascinating ideas about Chia Pets, tossing them together in a single page is just silly. (Unless you have a *very* strange hobby!) Make each of your pages stand on its own by dedicating a separate page for each topic. In the long run, your readers will be eternally thankful.

There's an exception to this one page-one topic rule for the terminally verbose: if your topic is a particularly long one, which means you end up with a correspondingly long page. Why is that a problem? Well, lengthy web pages have lots of disadvantages:

- Large files can take forever to load, especially for visitors accessing the web from a slow connection. (This becomes even worse if the page is full of images.) If loading the page takes too long, most people aren't likely to wait around for the cobwebs to start forming; they're more likely to abandon your site and head somewhere else.

- If you have navigation links at the top and bottom of the page (which I talk about later on), they aren't visible most of the time if the page is long. (Unless, of course, you're using frames on your page. Not sure what "frames" are? You can find out more about them by surfing back to Chapter 13, "Fooling Around with Frames.")

- Nobody likes scrolling through endless screens of text. Pages with more than three or four screenfuls of text are hard to navigate and tend to be confusing to the reader.

> **CAUTION**
>
> **Page Pitfalls** _____
>
> Some studies show that many web ramblers don't like to scroll at all! They want to see one screenful and then move on. This is extreme behavior, to be sure, and probably not all that common (for now, anyway). My guess is that many folks make a snap judgment about a page based on their initial impression. If they don't like what they see, they catch the nearest wave and keep surfin'.

To avoid these pitfalls, consider dividing large topics into smaller subtopics and assigning each one a separate page. Make sure you include links in each page that make it easy for the reader to follow the topic sequentially (more on this later).

For example, I have an e-mail primer on my site. It's a long article, so I divided it up into eight separate pages and then added navigation links to help the reader move from section to section. Figure 21.1 shows one of those sections.

Use your home page to tie everything together.

Most people begin the tour of your pages at your home page. With this in mind, you should turn your home page into a sort of electronic launch pad that gives the surfer easy access to all your stuff. Generally, that means peppering your home page with links to all your topics. For example, check out my home page shown in Figure 21.2. Through the various types of links, readers can get to any part of my site with just a click or two.

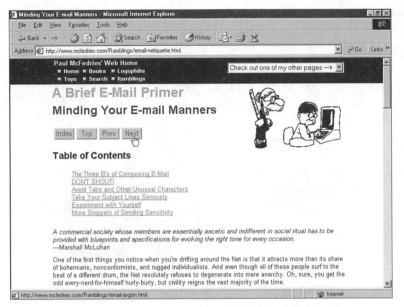

Figure 21.1

Break down long-winded topics into several pages with navigation links on each page.

Try to set up your home page so it makes sense to newcomers. For example, most people know that Yahoo! (www.yahoo.com) is a subject catalogue of sites, so the subject-related links on its home page make immediate sense. Most people's home pages aren't quite so straightforward. Therefore, include a reasonable description of your major links so visitors know what to expect.

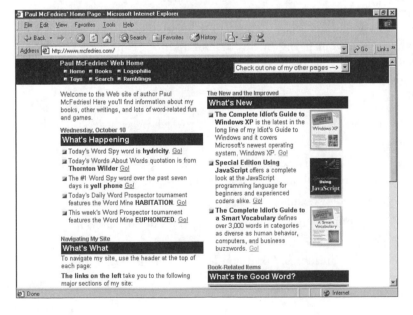

Figure 21.2

Surfers should be able to navigate to just about anywhere on your site from your home page.

For example, each page on my site contains a navigation header at the top of the page. On my home page I have a "What's What" section that explains how to use the navigation header, as shown in Figure 21.3.

Figure 21.3

For smoother surfing, include descriptions beside your home page links.

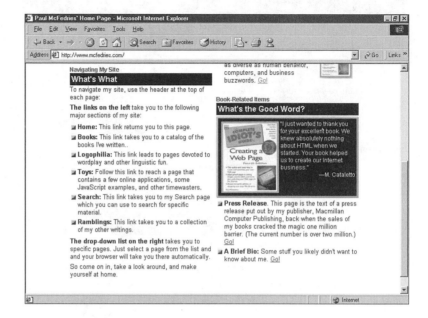

Use a consistent layout.

Another thing to keep in mind when designing your pages is consistency. When folks are furiously clicking links, they don't often know immediately where they've ended up. If you use a consistent look throughout your pages (or throughout a set of related pages), everyone will know that they're still on your home turf. Here are some ideas you can use to achieve a consistent look:

- ◆ If you have a logo or other image that identifies your site, plant a copy on each of your pages. Or, if you'd prefer to tailor your graphics to each page, at least put the image in the same place on each page.

- ◆ Preface your page titles with a consistent phrase. For example, "Jim Bob's Home Page: Why I Love Zima," or "Alphonse's CyberHome: The BeDazzler Page."

- ◆ Use the same background color or image on all your pages.

- ◆ If you use links to help people navigate through your pages, put the links in the same place on each page.

- ◆ Use consistent sizes for your headings. For example, if your home page uses the <H1> tag for the main heading and <H3> tags for subsequent headings, use these tags the same way on all your pages.

Figures 21.4 and 21.5 show you what I mean. The first is the home of my book *The Complete Idiot's Guide to a Smart Vocabulary*, and the second is the home of my book *The Complete Idiot's Guide to Windows XP*. As you can see, the two pages use an almost identical layout. So if you know how to get around in one site, you have no problem figuring out the other.

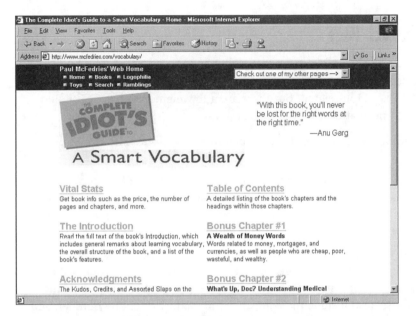

Figure 21.4

The home page of my book The Complete Idiot's Guide to a Smart Vocabulary.

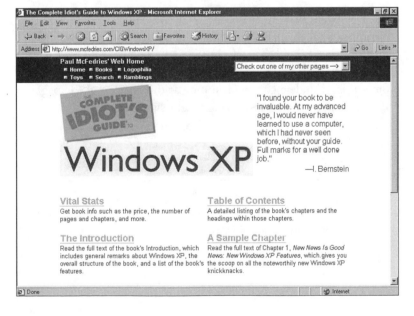

Figure 21.5

The home page of my book The Complete Idiot's Guide to Windows XP. *Note the consistent layout between the two pages.*

Organization and Layout Hints for Individual Pages

After you get the forest of your web pages in reasonable shape, it's time to start thinking about the trees, or the individual pages. The next few sections give you a few pointers for putting together perfect pages.

Elements to Include in Each Page

For each of your web pages, the bulk of the content that appears is determined by the overall subject of the page. If you're talking about Play-Doh, for example, most of your text and images will be Play-Doh related. But there are a few elements that you should include in all your pages, no matter what the subject matter:

♦ **A title:** A site without page titles is like a cocktail party without "Hi! My Name Is ..." tags.

♦ **A main heading:** Nobody wants to scour a large chunk of a page to determine what it's all about. Instead, include a descriptive, large heading (<H1> or <H2>) at the top of the page to give your readers the instant feedback they need. In some cases, a short, introductory paragraph below the heading is also a good idea.

♦ **A "signature":** If you're going on the web, there's no point in being shy. People appreciate knowing who created a page, so you should always "sign" your work. You don't need anything fancy: just your name and your e-mail address will do. If the page is for a business, also include the company name, address, phone number, and fax number.

♦ **Copyright info:** If the web pages you create are for your company, the company owns the material that appears on the page. Similarly, the contents of personal home pages belong to the person who created them. In both cases, the contents of the pages are protected by copyright law, and they can't be used by anyone else without permission. To reinforce this, include a copyright notice at the bottom of the page. Here's an example (the © code displays the copyright symbol):

```
The content of this site is Copyright &copy; 2002 Millicent Peeved
```

CAUTION

Page Pitfalls _____

Many webmeisters include some kind of "Under Construction" icon on pages that aren't finished (a few examples of the species are on this book's CD). This is fine, but don't overdo it. The nature of the web is that most pages are in a state of flux and are constantly being tweaked. (This is, in fact, a sign of a good site.) Scattering cute construction icons everywhere reduces their impact and annoys many readers.

- ◆ **The current status of the page:** If your page is a preliminary draft, contains unverified data, or is just generally not ready for prime time, let your readers know so they can take that into consideration.

- ◆ **A feedback mechanism:** Always give your visitors some way to contact you so they can lavish you with compliments or report problems. The usual way to do this is to include a "mailto" link somewhere on the page (as described in Chapter 5, "Making the Jump to Hyperspace: Adding Links").

- ◆ **A link back to your home page:** As I mentioned earlier, your home page should be the "launch pad" for your site, with links taking the reader to different areas. To make life easier for the surfers who visit, however, each page should include a link back to the home page.

Most of these suggestions can appear in a separate section at the bottom of each page (this is often called a *footer*). To help differentiate this section from the rest of the page, use an <HR> (horizontal rule) tag and an <ADDRESS> tag. On most browsers, the <ADDRESS> tag formats text in italics. Here's an example footer (look for footer.htm on the CD in this book) you can customize:

```
<HR>
<ADDRESS>
This page is Copyright &copy; 200?, your-name-here<BR>
company-name-here<BR>
company-address-here<BR>
Phone: (###) ###-####<BR>
Fax: (###) ###-####<BR>
Email: <A HREF="mailto:your-email-address-here">your-email-address-here</A>.
</ADDRESS>
<P>
Last revision: date/goes/here
<P>
Return to my <A HREF="home-page-URL-goes-here.htm">home page</A>.
```

Make your readers' lives easier.

When designing your web pages, always assume your readers are in the middle of a busy surfing session, and therefore won't be in the mood to waste time. It's not that people have short attention spans. (Although I'd bet dollars to doughnuts that the percentage of web surfers with some form of ADD—attention deficit disorder—is higher than that of the general population.) It's just the old mantra of the perpetually busy: "Things to go, places to do."

Words from the Web

A page that hasn't been revised in some time is known derisively as a **cobweb page**.

So how do you accommodate folks who are in "barely-enough-time-to-*see*-the-roses-much-less-stop-and-smell-the-darn-things" mode? Here are a few ideas:

♦ Organize your pages so people can find things quickly. This means breaking up your text into reasonably sized chunks and making judicious use of headers to identify each section.

♦ Put all your eye-catching good stuff at the top of the page where people are more likely to see it.

♦ If you have a long document, place anchors at the beginning of each section and then include a "table of contents" at the top of the document that includes links to each section. (I explain this in more detail in Chapter 5.)

♦ Add new stuff regularly to keep people coming back for more. You should also mark your new material with some sort of "new" graphic so regular visitors can easily find the recent additions.

Guidance for Using Graphics

As you saw back in Chapter 6, "A Picture Is Worth a Thousand Clicks: Working with Images," graphics are a great way to get people's attention. With images, however, there's a fine line between irresistible and irritating. To help you avoid the latter, this section presents a few ideas for using graphics responsibly.

For starters, don't become a "bandwidth hog" by including too many large images in your page. Remember that when someone accesses your Web page, all the page info—the text and graphics—is sent to that person's computer. The text isn't usually a problem (unless you're sending an entire novel, which I don't recommend), but graphics files are much slower. It's not unusual for a large image to take a minute or more to materialize if the surfer has a slow Internet connection. Clearly, your page better be *really* good if someone waits that long. Here are some ideas you can use to show mercy on visitors with slow connections:

♦ If your graphics are merely accessories, keep them small.

♦ If you have a large JPEG image, try *compressing* it so that it will download faster. To adjust the compression of a JPEG using Paint Shop Pro, open the image, select the **File, Save As** command, and then click the **Options** button in the Save As dialog box. In the Compression group, move the slider to the right to increase the compression, and then click **OK.** Save the file under a different name and then see how large the new file is. Remember that the higher the compression, the lower the image quality, so you might need to play around with the compression value to find an ideal value.

- If you have a large GIF image, the following sites offer services that will "optimize" the image for faster downloading: www.webreference.com/services/graphics and www.gifworks.com.

- Always use the <IMG> tag's WIDTH and HEIGHT attributes (see Chapter 6).

- Don't populate your home page with a single, massive "Enter My Site Here" image. Few things are as annoying as waiting forever for the image to download, only to find out that you're *still* not at the actual site. Grrr.

- It's acceptable to use graphics to get spiffy fonts because you can't be sure that surfers have the same font installed on their computers. However, don't rely on this too heavily, or your page could end up as nothing but a giant image!

Always bear in mind that a certain percentage of your readership is viewing your pages either from a text-only browser or from a graphical browser in which they've turned off image loading. If you're using an image as a link, be sure to provide a text alternative (by using the <IMG> tag's ALT attribute, as described in Chapter 6). For nonlink graphics, you can use ALT to describe the picture or even to display a blank. If you must use lots of images, offer people a choice of a text-only version of the page.

Finally, be careful if you decide to use a background image on your page. The Internet has lots of sites that offer various textures for background images. (I tell you about some of these sites in the next chapter.) Many of these textures are "cool," to be sure, but they're too "busy" to display text properly. For example, check out the page shown in Figure 21.6. Now *that* is the mother of all ugly backgrounds! (Lucky for you, the figure doesn't show the background in color; the actual texture incorporates various shades of sickly green.) For maximum readability, your best bet is to combine solid, light backgrounds with dark text.

Words from the Web

A web page that takes forever to load because it's either jammed to the hilt with graphics, or because it contains one or two really large images, is called a **JPIG**. An annoyingly large web page graphic that serves no useful purpose is known as a **vanity plate**.

Figure 21.6

Some background textures just aren't worth it!

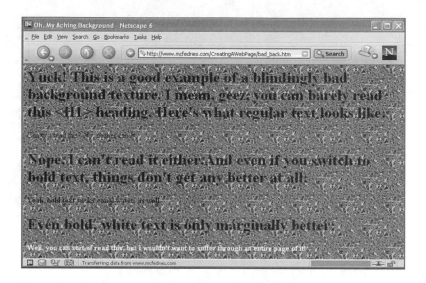

Link Lessons: Keeping Your Links in the Pink

To finish our look at web page style, here are a few ideas to keep in mind when using links in your pages:

◆ Make your link text descriptive. Link text really stands out on a page because browsers usually display it underlined and in a different color. This means the reader's eye is drawn naturally toward the link text, so you need to make the text descriptive. That way, it's easy for the reader to know exactly what they're linking to. Always avoid the "here" syndrome, where your link text is just "here" or "click here." The snippet below shows you the right and wrong way to set up your link text. Figure 21.7 shows how each one looks in a browser.

```
<H3>Wrong:</H3>
The Beet Poets page contains various odes celebrating our favorite edible
root, and you can get to it by clicking <A HREF="beetpoet.htm">here</A>.
<H3>Right:</H3>
The <A HREF="beetpoet.htm">Beet Poets page</A> contains various odes
celebrating our favorite edible root.
```

◆ If you're presenting material sequentially in multiple pages, create "navigational links" to help the reader move forward and backward through the pages. For example, each page could have a **Previous** link that takes readers to the previous page, a **Next** link that takes them to the next page, and a **Top** link that returns them to the first page. (See Chapter 9, "Images Can Be Links, Too," for a bit more detail on this.)

Webmaster Wisdom

You might be wondering why the heck you'd want to bother with **Previous** and **Next** buttons when most browsers have similar buttons built in (usually called **Back** and **Forward**). Well, they're not really the same things. For example, suppose you surf to a site and end up on a page that's in the middle of a series of pages. If you select the browser's **Back** button, you find yourself tossed back to the site you just bailed out of. If you select the page's **Previous** button, however, you head to the previous page in the series.

◆ For maximum readability, don't include spaces or punctuation marks either immediately after the <A> tag or immediately before the </A> tag.

◆ If you're planning a link to a particular page, but you haven't created that page yet, leave the link text as plain text (for example, don't surround it with the <A> and </A> tags). Links that point to a nonexistent page generate an error, which can be frustrating for surfers.

◆ If you move your page to a new site, leave behind a page that includes a link to the new location. Even better, set up the page to automatically redirect people to your new site. I showed you how to do this in Chapter 11, "Making Your Web Pages Dance and Sing."

◆ Try to keep all your links (both the internal and external variety) up-to-date. This means trying out each link periodically to make sure it goes where it's supposed to go. If you have a lot of links, try Xenu's Link Sleuth: home.snafu.de/tilman/xenulink.html.

◆ A deep link is a link to a page other than the site's home page. Many sites frown upon this because their home pages have banner ads or other material that they want all visitors to see. Some sites have been known to sue people who set up deep links to their pages. So if you want to use a deep link to a site, ask for permission first. If you don't get an answer, just link to the site's home page, to be safe.

Words from the Web

A link to a nonexistent page is called a **vaporlink**.

The Least You Need to Know

◆ Write the right way (for you). Spend the most of your site construction time working on the page text, and remember to write passionately and in your own voice about topics that interest you.

◆ A spoonful of grammar helps the web page go down. The easy road to acceptably grammatical pages is to write the way you speak and to double-check your prose for sense and sensibility. Also, be sure to eliminate all spelling errors (which may mean running the text through a spell checker).

◆ Organizing your site. Keep your pages short and confined to a single topic wherever possible, use your home page as your site's home base, and use a more-or-less consistent layout on all your pages.

◆ The seven bones in a web page skeleton. Your pages should include most or all of the following: a title, a main heading, signature text, a copyright notice, the current page status, a feedback form or link, and a link back to your home page.

◆ Go easy on your visitors. This means setting up each page so that things are easy to find, putting good stuff at the top of the page, creating a table of contents for long pages, and adding new things regularly.

◆ A guide to good graphics. Keep nonessential images small, compress large JPEG and GIF images, include the <IMG> tag's WIDTH, HEIGHT, and ALT attributes, and be *very* careful about the image you use as your page background.

◆ Thinking about linking. Make your link text descriptive (don't use "click" or "click here"), set up navigation links for a series of pages, don't link to nonexistent pages, keep your external links up-to-date, and ask for permission before setting up a deep link to another site.

Some HTML Resources on the Web

In This Chapter

- ◆ Where to go to get great graphics, sounds, and videos
- ◆ HTML style guide sites
- ◆ Web page access counters, without programming!
- ◆ Sites that double-check your HTML
- ◆ HTML-related mailing lists and newsgroups
- ◆ A cornucopian compendium of cool HTML resources

The web is many things: It's a file repository, a communications medium, a shopping mall, a floor wax, a dessert topping, and a forum for all manner of kooks, crackpots, nut cases, and nincompoops. But the web is mostly an information resource. Everywhere you go, some kind soul has contributed a tidbit or two about a particular subject. Of course, *you* might not be interested in, say, the mating habits of the Andorran Cow, but it's a good bet that some surfer somewhere is.

What you *are* interested in, to be sure, is HTML. Now here's the good news: There are dozens, nay hundreds—okay billions—of HTML resources scattered throughout the web. The bad news, though, is the usual web gripe: How do you find what you need quickly and easily? This is where your purchase of this book—a savvy and prudent investment on your part—really pays off. Why? Because this chapter takes you through the best of the web's HTML resources. I show you great online locales for things like graphics and style guides, HTML checkers, HTML-related newsgroups and mailing lists, and lots more.

Graphics Goodies I: The Three B's (Buttons, Bars, and Bullets)

The CD that comes with this book is loaded with a few hundred bullets, buttons, bars, and icons for sprucing up your web pages. They do for a start, but you might want to check out other images to give your page just the right touch. The next few sections show you a few of my favorite web-based graphics stops. (Before we start, though, a caveat: Most of the graphics you find in these sites are free, as long as you don't use them commercially. Things change, of course, so you should always read the fine print before grabbing a graphic to use on your page.)

This section gets you going with some sites to check out for the buttons, bars, and other little accessories that add character to a page:

Webmaster Wisdom

To make surfing all these sites even easier, I've included a hypertext document on this book's CD that includes links to every site mentioned in this chapter. Look for the file named resource.htm.

- ◆ **Celine's Original .GIFs** This site includes a nice collection of images created by Celine herself. If you use one of her images, she'll even put a link to your page on her graphics page. See www.specialweb.com/original.

- ◆ **Ender Design: Realm Graphics** This is one of the best places to go for a wide variety of quality icons, balls, bullets, and more. And, if you're feeling gung-ho, you might want to use one of the few graphics-related documents (GIF versus JPEG, selecting a background, and more). See www.ender-design.com/rg.

- ◆ **GifsNow** GifsNow (formerly netCREATORS) has oodles of images organized in dozens of categories. See gifsnow.com.

- ◆ **GraphXKingdom** This site has a few bullets and things, but its forte is its large collection of icons and clip art, handily arranged by category. See www.graphxkingdom.com.

- **Image-O-Rama**   This site includes a large collection of graphics, especially the three B's. There's also an "Other Stuff" page that has a few cool icons, as well as a good collection of animated GIFs. See members.aol.com/dcreelma/imagesite/image.htm.

- **IconBAZAAR**   This site includes the usual portfolio of web page wonders, plus a few interesting variations on the standard themes. See www.iconbazaar.com.

- **Jelane's Free Web Graphics**   This site has a great collection of graphical gadgets created by Jelane Johnson. Particularly interesting are the "families" of graphics that offer buttons and arrows and other images that use a common design. See www.erinet.com/jelane/families.

- **McFedries.com Image Archives**   This is a collection of images that were distributed in earlier versions of this book. See www.mcfedries.com/graphics/archives.html.

- **Pixel Warehouse**   This site includes lots of public domain images, and a well-crafted set of custom graphics that offer unique takes on the standard categories. See matrixvault.com/PW.

- **Yahoo!'s Icon Index**   This site includes a seemingly endless list of sites that have collections of icons, bullets, and other images for web pages. See www.yahoo.com/Arts/Design_Arts/Graphic_Design/Web_Page_Design_and_Layout/Graphics/Icons.

Graphics Goodies II: Yet Another B—Background Textures

I don't like background images myself, but lots of web welders swear by them. If you want to give them a try, you might find a few files at some of the sites mentioned in the last section. You can also find lots of *textures* (as background images are often called) in the following locations:

- **Absolute Background Textures Archive**   This site claims to be "The Largest Collection of Free Background Textures on the Internet." I don't know if that's true, but with over 3,000 backgrounds on display, I can't imagine a bigger collection. See www.grsites.com/textures.

- **The Background Boutique**   This site boasts a very nice collection of custom graphics in both regular and bordered styles. See www.theboutique.org.

- **Backgrounds By Marie**   A wonderful collection of textures, including some nice margined backgrounds. Thanks, Marie! See www.artistic-designers.com/bkgds.

- **Dr. Zeus' Textures**   At this site you can find some truly unique and way-out images. Most of them are totally useless for displaying text, but they sure look wild! See www.best.com/~drzeus/Art/Textures/Textures.html.

- **Free-Backgrounds.com**   This site's name says it all: hundreds of high-quality backgrounds free for the taking. See www.free-backgrounds.com.

- **Netscape's Background Sampler**   This site has a truckload of textures from the folks who started all this background nonsense in the first place. See www. netscape.com/assist/net_sites/bg/backgrounds.html.

- **Pattern Land**   "Where all your pattern fantasies come true!" I bet you didn't even know you had pattern fantasies. See www.netcreations.com/patternland.

- **Silk Purse Backgrounds**   This site has an unusual collection of images. They're copyrighted by the author, but they can be used for nonprofit purposes. See www.silkpursegraphics.com/backgrnd.html.

- **The Wallpaper Machine**   This interesting site displays a different background each time you refresh the page. When you see one that you like, grab it for use on your own pages. See www.cacr.caltech.edu/cgi-bin/wallpaper.pl.

- **Yahoo!'s Background Index**   If none of the previous pages suits your fancy, Yahoo! has a list of a few dozen sites that feature background images. See www. yahoo.com/Arts/Design_Arts/Graphic_Design/Web_Page_Design_and_Layout/ Graphics/Backgrounds.

Graphics Goodies III: Rolling Your Own Graphics

If you don't have the time or the talent for creating graphics, don't sweat it because there are lots of sites on the Web that are happy to create images for you. This section tells you about a few of them:

- **3D Text Maker**   This site helps you to create 3-D text in a specific font, color, and size. You can create animated text using a number of different effects. See www.3dtextmaker.com.

- **CoolText**   Use this site to create custom text logos where you can define the font, foreground and background colors, and the effect (such as "burning" letters). See www.cooltext.com.

- **Fantabulous Icon-O-Matic**   This is a simple icon generator. It's not all that "fantabulous," if you ask me, but it's a decent tool to get you started. The site also has a "Ribbon-O-Matic" feature that generates ribbons of the kind that people pin all over their shirts and jackets these days. See www.webgurus.com/matic/ iconomatic.html.

◆ **GUISTuff** This site offers a large and interesting set of "styles," which are collections of buttons, bars, and other site graphics. Each image in a style is rendered in a consistent theme (such as "Chrome" or "Laser") and is ready to be customized with your text or other enhancements. See www.guistuff.com.

◆ **PixelSight** This site enables you to create your own icons and buttons. See www.pixelsight.com.

Sites for Sounds

Back in Chapter 11, "Making Your Web Pages Dance and Sing," I showed you how to turn your web page into a multimedia machine by adding sounds. If you don't have a ready supply of audio material on hand, here's a list of some sites that'll get you started:

◆ **The Daily .WAV** This site posts a new WAV file each weekday. It also has an extensive archive of WAV and MIDI files. See www.dailywav.com.

◆ **EarthStation1** This site claims to be "The Internet's #1 Audio/Visual Archive," and judging by the massive number of sound and video clips they have on hand, I for one am not going to doubt them. See www.earthstation1.com.

◆ **FindSounds** You won't find any sound files archived on this site. Instead, you use it to search the web for a particular sound effect. You can specify the sound format you want, the quality of the recording, and more. See www.findsounds.com.

◆ **SoundAmerica** This site has thousands of sound clips from all walks of life, including cartoons, movies, TV, and more. It also has a nice collection of MIDI music. See www.soundamerica.com.

◆ **Whoopie!** With a name like that, a site better be good—real good. And this one certainly is (see Figure 22.2). Here, you can find links to all kinds of sound, MIDI, and video files, as well as pointers to plug-ins and helper applications. See www. whoopie.com.

◆ **Yahoo!'s Audio Index** Lots of links to audio and music sites, including sites that offer audio archives. See www.yahoo.com/Computers_and_Internet/ Multimedia/ Audio.

The Big Picture: HTML Reference Pages

Few folks have the time or inclination to memorize all the HTML tags and attributes, much less all the style sheet styles and properties. So it's a good thing I created a couple of reference sites that offer a complete list of the tags and styles:

Webmaster Wisdom

Note that both of the references mentioned here are also available on this book's CD.

♦ **The Complete Idiot's HTML Tag Reference** This site (see Figure 22.1) offers a complete list of the HTML tags, the attributes that go with each tag, the values those attributes can take, the browser support, and more. See www.mcfedries. com/CreatingAWebPage/tags.

♦ **The Complete Idiot's Style Sheets Reference** This site (see Figure 22.2) runs through all of the properties associated with each style. (Note that there are two views: by property and by category.) It tells you the values you can apply to each property and it tells you which browsers support each property. See www. mcfedries.com/CreatingAWebPage/css.

Figure 22.1

A sample page from the Complete Idiot's HTML Tag Reference.

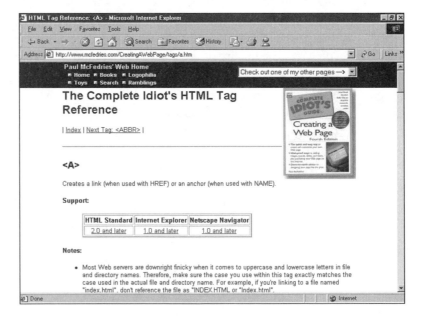

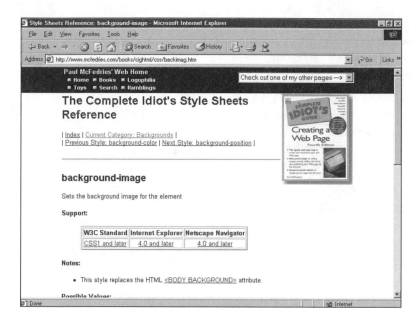

Figure 22.2

A sample page from the Complete Idiot's Style Sheets Reference.

A Guide to HTML Style Guides

Although I talked about HTML style in Chapter 21, "The Elements of Web Page Style," I didn't have room to cover everything. Fortunately, there's no shortage of web wizards who are only too happy to give you their two-cents worth. Here's a list of some of the better ones.

♦ **Art and the Zen of Web Sites**   This is a thoughtful article on how best to approach and design a site (although its extreme length violates one of the cardinal principles of good design!). See www.tlc-systems.com/webtips.shtml.

♦ **Composing Good HTML**   This site includes a guide by Eric Tilton that's a bit on the advanced side. It has a good section on common errors that crop up in HTML documents. See www.ology.org/tilt/cgh.

♦ **HTMLTips**   This site includes a nice compendium of articles in categories such as design and graphics. See www.htmltips.com.

♦ **The Sevloid Guide to Web Design**   Arranged in a tips and tricks format, this site offers over 100 pointers on good web design. See www.sev.com.au/webzone/design.asp.

♦ **Style Guide for Online Hypertext**   This is a friendly manual on good web page design by no less an authority than Tim Berners-Lee, the fellow who invented the World Wide Web. See www.w3.org/hypertext/WWW/Provider/Style/Overview.html.

◆ **Top Ten Ways to Tell If You Have a Sucky Home Page** This is a tongue-in-cheek (sort of) look at the ten worst things you can do in a web page. (Number 11? Using dumb words like "sucky"!) The site also has a "Sucky to Savvy" page that offers tips for avoiding the dreaded "sucky" label. See jeffglover.com/sucky.html.

◆ **Web Pages That Suck** What is it with this word "suck"? Anyway, the premise of this fun site is simple: Learn good site design by checking out (and, usually, laughing at) sites that feature bad design. See webpagesthatsuck.com.

◆ **WEB WONK** This page offers a few handy tips on making pages look their best. See www.dsiegel.com/tips/index.html.

◆ **Webmonkey Design Collection** This site includes a series of articles with loads of great tips and ideas about designing sites. See www.hotwired.com/webmonkey/design.

◆ **What Is Good Hypertext Writing?** This site is an excellent guide (though a bit on the pedantic side) to web page writing and editing. See www.cs.tu-berlin.de/~jutta/ht/writing-html.html.

◆ **Yale Style Manual** This is a stuffy but exhaustive guide to all aspects of site design. See info.med.yale.edu/caim/manual.

Counter Check: Tallying Your Hits

Okay, you've labored heroically to get your pages just right, a web server is serving them up piping hot, and you've even advertised your site shamelessly around the Internet. All that's left to do now is wait for the hordes to start beating a path to your digital door.

CAUTION

Page Pitfalls _____

Counters are fun, and they're certainly a handy way to keep track of the amount of activity your page is generating. There are, however, three counter-related caveats you should know about:

◆ The counter program sits on another computer, so it takes time for the program to get and send its information. This means your page loads a little slower than usual.

◆ If the computer that stores the counter program goes "down for the count" (sorry about that), the count won't appear on your page.

◆ Counters are notoriously fickle beasts that tend to reset themselves to 0 whenever they feel like it.

But how do you know if your site is attracting hordes or merely collecting dust? How do you know if you've hit the big time, or just hit the skids? In other words, how do you know the number of people who've accessed your pages? Well, there are two ways you can go:

◆ **Ask your hosting provider.** Many companies can supply you with statistics that tell you the number of "hits" your site has taken.

◆ **Include a counter in your web page.** A counter is a little program that increments each time some surfer requests the page.

Creating a counter program is well beyond the scope of a humble book such as this (insert sigh of relief here). However, a few community-minded programmers have made counter programs available on the web. Happily, you don't even have to copy or install these programs. All you have to do is insert a link to the program in your page, and the counter is updated automatically whenever someone checks out the page. This section provides you with a list of some counter programs to try:

◆ **The Counter.com**   This is a free counter that doesn't require placing an ad on your site. See www.thecounter.com.

◆ **eXTReMe Tracker**   This is a great service that offers a wide range of tracking options. See www.extreme-dm.com/tracking.

◆ **FastCounter**   This is a basic counter that's easy to set up (several different styles are available) and that sends reports to you via e-mail. See www.bcentral.com/services/fc.

◆ **The WebCounter**   This is a nicely implemented, no-frills counter. Note that busy sites (those getting more than 1,000 hits a day) have to pay a subscription fee to use this counter. See www.digits.com.

◆ **Yahoo!'s Access Counter Index**   As usual, Yahoo! has a long list of sites that supply counters. See dir.yahoo.com/Computers_and_Internet/Internet/World_Wide_Web/Programming/Access_Counters.

Passing Muster: Page Checkers

Everybody who designs web pages—pros, hobbyists, and rookies alike—has had the unpleasant experience of loading a page into a browser and then seeing the unexpected. It might be an image that doesn't appear, a table that's not centered, or even a page that displays *nothing*, despite the fact that you *know* there's lots of text and tags in there somewhere. More often than not, the culprit in these malformed pages is something simple: a missing quotation mark, the lack of an end tag, or a misspelled tag name.

It can be tough to spot these kinds of errors, so if you're having trouble, it's a good idea to submit your page to *page checker*, a service that validates the HTML code on your page. It looks for things like improper or unknown tags, mismatched brackets, and missing quotation marks, and it lets you know if things are awry. Best of all, many (but not all) of these services are free. It's the easy and cheap way to good HTML mental health! Here are a few you might want to try out:

> **Webmaster Wisdom**
>
> These services tend to be overly critical, so don't feel as though you have to act on every suggestion. Just look for and fix the obvious errors and leave the nitpicky stuff for people who don't have lives.

- ◆ **Bobby**   This service is a bit different from the others I present in this list. Bobby's job is to scan your page and then tell you if people with disabilities (such as impaired eyesight) might have problems viewing or reading your page. If it finds any problems, Bobby offers suggestions for improving the accessibility of the page. See www.cast.org/bobby.

- ◆ **NetMechanic's Browser Photo**   This unique service sends you "photos" that show you how your page looks in various browsers, browser versions, operating systems, and screen sizes. See www.netmechanic.com/browser-index.htm.

- ◆ **NetMechanic's HTML Toolbox**   This service not only checks your page for HTML errors, it also tells you if your page contains broken links, and it tells you the approximate load time for the page. See www.netmechanic.com/toolbox/html-code.htm.

- ◆ **W3C HTML Validation Service**   This validation service is courtesy of the World Wide Web Consortium (W3C), the folks who create and maintain the HTML standard (among others), so you can be sure they know what they're talking about. See validator.w3.org.

- ◆ **W3C CSS Validation Service**   This is another service from the W3C. This one focuses on validating your style sheets. See jigsaw.w3.org/css-validator/validator-uri.html.

- ◆ **Web Site Garage**   This excellent service performs all the usual checks, plus it looks for broken links, browser incompatibilities, and even spelling errors. See websitegarage.netscape.com.

- ◆ **Weblint**   This is one of the best checkers (because it picks the lint off your web pages). Place your page address or your HTML code into one of the boxes near the bottom of the screen, click **Check it,** and Weblint goes to work. After a few seconds, a new page appears with a complete analysis of your page. See www.unipress.com/cgi-bin/WWWeblint.

HTML Mailing Lists

HTML is a huge topic these days, so there's no shortage of HTML-related chinwagging and confabulating on the Net. If you're stumped by something in HTML, or if you're looking for ideas, or if you just want to commune with fellow web fiends, there are mailing lists and Usenet newsgroups to welcome you with open arms.

Here are a few mailing lists you might want to subscribe to:

◆ **ADV-HTML**   This is a moderated mailing list for intermediate-to-advanced HTML hounds. To subscribe, send a message to listserv@bama.ua.edu. In the message body, enter **SUBSCRIBE ADV-HTML.**

◆ **CIGHTML**   As I mentioned in the Introduction, this is a mailing list that I've set up exclusively for people smart enough to have purchased this book. You and your peers get to discuss HTML tips and pitfalls, ask questions, and get semisage advice from yours truly. To subscribe, send a message to the listmanager@mcfedries.com. In the Subject line of the message, type **join cightml.**

Webmaster Wisdom

The HTML Writers Guild (www.hwg.org/) maintains quite a few mailing lists. To see a list of them, head for the following page: www.hwg.org/lists/archives.html.

◆ **HTML-Haven**   www.designsbydaybreak.com/html/html-haven.html. This is a general discussion list for novices and experts, alike. To subscribe, send a note to html-haven-subscribe@yahoogroups.com.

Using Usenet Discussions

Usenet also has tons of HTML and web authoring discussions. Here's a rundown:

◆ **comp.infosystems.www.authoring.html**   This busy group is chock-full of HTML tips, tricks, and instruction.

◆ **comp.infosystems.www.authoring.images**   This group focuses on using images in web pages.

◆ **comp.infosystems.www.authoring.misc**   This is a catchall group that covers everything that doesn't fit into the other groups.

◆ **comp.infosystems.www.authoring.site-design**   This group concentrates on big picture issues of overall site layout and design.

◆ **comp.infosystems.www.authoring.stylesheets**   This group looks at the ins and outs of those new-fangled style sheet things you learned about back in Part 3, "High HTML Style: Working with Style Sheets."

◆ **comp.infosystems.www.authoring.tools**   This newsgroup looks at HTML editors and other web page authoring tools.

A List of HTML Lists

To finish off our look at HTML resources on the Net, this section looks at a few all-purpose, everything-but-the-kitchen-sink sites. The following pages offer one-stop shopping for links that cover all aspects of web page production:

◆ **Essential Links to HTML**   This is a nice collection of links to high-quality sites. See www.el.com/elinks/html.

◆ **Haznet's Fallout Shelter**   This Webmaster Resource Clearinghouse" is chock full of links to great sites. Its unique feature is a "Geiger Meter" that rates each link. See www.hudziak.com/haznet.

◆ **HTML Writers Guild**   This is the semi-official headquarters for webmeisters from around the world. Besides lots of links, you can also find tutorials, news, classes, and much more. See www.hwg.org.

◆ **HyperText Markup Language**   This is the W3C's home for the HTML specs that I mentioned earlier. It also includes a list of HTML links. See www.w3.org/MarkUp.

◆ **Nuthin' But Links**   This includes a long list of HTML links, as well as other Internet- and computer-related links. See nuthinbutlinks.com.

◆ **WebMonkey**   HotWired has put together this useful site that's filled to the gills with resources, tutorials, and much more. See hotwired.lycos.com/webmonkey.

◆ **Yahoo!'s HTML Index**   This is an absurdly impressive (bordering on overkill) list of HTML resources from the bottomless Yahoo! library. See dir.yahoo.com/Computers_and_Internet/Data_Formats/HTML.

The Least You Need to Know

This chapter showed you some of the "in" places to go on the Net for web page resources, materials, and discussions. We looked at sites for graphics and backgrounds, sound and video files, HTML style guides, hit counters, page checkers, mailing lists, Usenet newsgroups, and more.

The next part of the book shows you how to use all your hard-won HTML knowledge to do something really radical: make money!

Part 6

Show Me the Money: Turning Your HTML Skills Into Cash

This final section of the book gets downright mercenary by showing you how to convert your web page prowess into cold, hard cash. You'll learn three different "get-rich-click" schemes. The first (Chapter 23) tells you how to lose your amateur status and become a professional web designer. The second (Chapter 24) gives you the scoop on using your page popularity to make money by putting up banner ads and joining affiliate marketing programs. The third (Chapter 25) gives you a step-by-step tutorial on setting up your site for e-commerce—selling actual goods and services from your humble web home.

Turning Pro: Becoming a Paid Web Designer

In This Chapter

- Getting a web design business off the ground
- How to set rates
- Learning about contracts, advertising, and certification
- Proof that the "M" in HTML really stands for money, moolah, and mucho dinero

Dear Paul,

Just want to let you know that I am actually getting paid to design and produce websites, and it's all your fault for writing your HTML book.

—Patsy West (www.Websitewiz.com)

That's a real note sent to me from a real reader of the book. And it's no fluke, either, because I've received dozens of similar messages from readers over the years. I'm not at all surprised, because web page designing is one of *the* hottest fields right now. People who know how to cobble together web pages are in great demand and are being snapped up by companies large and small. If you've read the whole book and if you have at least a bit of design skills, then you, too, can get a job as a web page producer.

This chapter gives you some tips and pointers on becoming a paid page purveyor. My focus here is on setting up a freelance web design business. You learn how to set up your business, how to find contracts, what to charge, and more.

Getting Started: Your Business Plan

If you want to do this freelance web design business thing right, then there's one step that you shouldn't skip: creating a business plan. This doesn't mean you have to forge a 50-page tome with all kinds of charts and economic analyses. No, all you really want is to get a handle on the type of business that you're creating and running. To that end, you need to ask and answer 10 basic questions:

◆ **What's my goal?** It's tough to get anywhere if you don't have a final destination in mind. You need a concrete, realistic goal: to be able to quit the corporate rat race; to save up enough for the family vacation; to pay my way through school.

◆ **What's my target market?** Although general web design is still a reasonable area to shoot for, your chances of success improve immensely if you can target one or more smaller markets. Do you have a particular field of expertise? Are there particular kinds of websites you design better than others?

> **Webmaster Wisdom**
>
> If your interest lies more in "going captive"—getting a full-time job as a corporate web spinner—read this chapter anyway. For one thing, it helps immensely if you have a page "portfolio" that you can show to prospective employers. For another, many full-time page designers got their start by doing a great job on a freelance project for a company.

◆ **What's my name/domain?** Think long and hard about the name you want to use. Lots of rookie web weavers seem to change their business name every six months or so, which is no way to build your "brand." As soon as you've thought of a great name, *immediately* go to Network Solutions (www.networksolutions.com) or some other registration service (such as godaddy.com or register.com) and register the corresponding domain name. Having a "dot com" domain instantly makes your business look more solid and respectable. You think anyone's going to give money to someone with a 100-character long URL from GeoCities? I don't think so.

◆ **What are my expenses?** This is crucial, particularly because your income might take a while to build. Do you need to upgrade your computer or your Internet connection? Do you need other equipment, such as a scanner or a digital camera? What about software such as HTML editors or graphics programs? If you don't know JavaScript or CGI, will you have to hire someone to program for you? Or will you buy a bunch of books and figure things out yourself? Break everything down into two categories: startup costs and ongoing expenses. For the latter, don't forget living expenses such as food and shelter.

◆ **What will I charge?** This is one of the most important questions, and it's also one of the toughest to answer. See "Getting Paid: Web Design Rates" later in this chapter.

◆ **How will I allocate my time?** Come up with realistic estimates for how long it takes you to forge various kinds of pages: simple text-only pages, heavily designed graphics pages, and so on. You also need to budget time for client discussions, accounts receivable, and other business-related tasks.

◆ **What will my income be?** After you've settled on your rates and allocated your time, you can then come up with a realistic projection of your income.

◆ **Do I need professional help?** No, not a psychiatrist! I'm talking here about an accountant and a lawyer. An accountant can help you to set up books and can tell you whether some expenses are deductible (particularly if you work out of your home). You need a contract for each job, and a lawyer can help you create one that suits you and your business. (See "Legalese: Notes About Contracts" later in this chapter.)

◆ **How will I promote my business?** This isn't a better mousetrap you're building, so people won't automatically beat a path to your web door. You need to advertise not only online, but also in the real world, too. (See "Getting the Word Out: Advertising and Promotion" later in this chapter.)

◆ **What about customer service?** No matter how you look at it, web design is a service business. Therefore, you need to be prepared to offer a high level of customer service. Think about your policies regarding project updates, post-project follow-up, handling complaints, and so on.

Getting Paid: Web Design Rates

What you charge for your services is obviously a critical part of your business success (or lack thereof). If you charge too much, people won't hire you; if you charge too little, you'll leave money on the table (at best) or fail due to lack of profits (at worst). Unfortunately, the web design business is still wet behind its electronic ears, so there are no set rates. In any case, what you charge depends on a number of factors:

Webmaster Wisdom

It's a rare web designer who has the Big Four skills: HTML, writing, graphics, and programming. If you lack one or more of these assets, you can always hire someone to work with you on a project-by-project basis.

◆ **Your level of experience:** The more the monetarily merrier.

◆ **What skills you have:** Someone with good writing, graphics, or programming skills can charge more than someone who just knows HTML inside and out.

◆ **The type of client:** You can get away with charging more to a corporation than you could to a Mom and Pop shop or a nonprofit organization.

◆ **What type of page you're creating:** You should charge one (lower) price for simple text pages or for converting existing documents to HTML; you should charge another (higher) price for pages that require creative writing, custom graphics, or programming.

◆ **How much consulting is involved:** You can boost your rate if a job requires long consultations with the client.

With all that in mind, the next question to think about is how you want to charge the client: by the hour or by the project?

Per-hour pricing is the most common, particularly for new web designers. Before delving into this, you should be familiar with one crucial concept: *billable hours*. These are hours that you actually work on a project. They don't include activities such as selling the client in the first place, eating lunch, or blowing away nasty aliens in a rousing game of Quake. With that in mind, coming up with that all-important hourly rate is tough. Here are two ways to go about it:

◆ **See what other designers are charging.** Visit the sites of other page designers and check out their rates. See what kinds of sites they've produced. If you think you can do as good a job, then you might be able to charge the same amount.

CAUTION

Page Pitfalls

Although you don't want to include nonproductive time in your billable hours, be diligent about tracking even small blocks of time where you do real work. You'd be surprised to see how five minutes here and ten minutes there really add up.

◆ **Use the expenses-and-profits method.** With this method, you calculate your average weekly expenses, add the amount of profit you'd like, and then divide by the weekly billable hours. For example, suppose your weekly expenses work out to $600. If you want to make a minimum 25 percent profit (a not unreasonable figure), then you need to add another $150, for a total weekly nut of $750. If you figure your week has 30 billable hours, then you'd set your rate at $25 per hour.

Webmaster Wisdom _____

Yahoo! maintains a huge list of website designers. Here's where to find it: dir.yahoo.com/Business_and_Economy/Business_to_Business/Communications_ and_Networking/Internet_and_World_Wide_Web/Web_Site_Designers.

You can also get a bit of pricing data from the following:

- ◆ Real Rate Survey: www.realrates.com/survey.htm
- ◆ Software Salary Calculator: www.cybercoders.com/developer/ salary_calc/default.asp
- ◆ About.com Web Design Pricing and Salaries: webdesign.about.com/cs/ pricingsalaries

Note that all the links in this chapter can be found in the file pro.htm on the CD in this book.

After you've gained enough experience, you might consider moving to a per-project fee. This means that you charge a single fee for all the work you do in a particular project. Most web designers I've talked to say they usually make much more profit this way than they do using an hourly rate. However, going this route isn't for rookies in the field:

- ◆ You need to have top-notch skills. Per-project contracts are usually for a large number of pages, and you won't get those kinds of contracts unless your portfolio is of the highest quality.

- ◆ You need to be very experienced so that you can estimate with some exactitude just how long the project will take. You won't help your cause if you charge $1,000 for a project that you thought would take you 20 hours, and it ends up taking you 100 hours.

- ◆ These kinds of projects are really sellable only to large businesses.

Legalese: Notes About Contracts

Having a contract for each project is something that new web designers rarely think about. However, it's absolutely crucial because it helps ensure that you get paid; it prevents your client from suing your pants off because of a misunderstanding; it specifies copyright issues; and it outlines everyone's rights and responsibilities.

By far the best advice I can give you in this area is this: *See a lawyer!* Although I give you a few good resources to check out in a sec, don't fool yourself into thinking you can do this on your own. By all means put together a contract that makes sense for your business, but make sure you run it by a lawyer who is versed in this type of thing. I guarantee you'll be glad you did.

With that out of the way, the following is a list of resources devoted to web design contracts and legal issues:

◆ **Ivan Hoffman's Articles for Web Site Designers and Site Owners** Mr. Hoffman is *the* expert on legal issues involving creative adventures, including website design. This page is loaded with truly useful data on web design contracts, copyrights, and much more (see Figure 23.1). See www.ivanhoffman.com/web.html.

Figure 23.1

Ivan Hoffman's site is loaded with useful legal links.

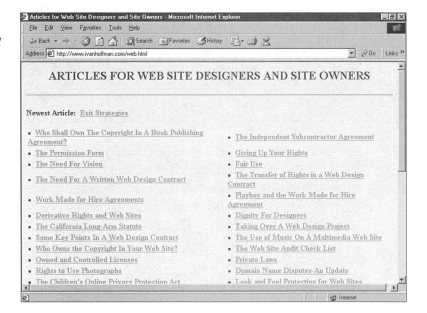

◆ **HTML Writers Guild Sample Contract** This site shows a very basic contract that offers a good place to start. See ftp://ftp.hwg.org/pub/archives/docs/legal/consult.txt.

◆ **Web Developer's Contract Swap File** This site is a great resource with tons of links to contract info. See provider.com/contracts.htm.

Webmaster Wisdom

Make sure your clients understand (put it in writing, too!) that any design or content changes that aren't in the contract result in extra charges.

◆ **Website Design Contract** This site has an elaborate design contract by Ralph Wilson. See www.wilsonweb.com/worksheet/pkg-con.htm.

◆ **Website Development Agreements: Planning and Drafting** This site offers an exhaustive (and often intimidatingly technical) look at the issues involved in creating web design contracts. See www.digidem.com/legal/wda.

Getting the Word Out: Advertising and Promotion

With site design being such a growing concern, you better believe that there are thousands of like-minded souls out there competing for those client bucks. To help your business stand out from the herd, you need to blow your own horn by doing a little advertising and promotion.

By far the best marketing tool in existence is a little thing called word of mouth. Impressed clients naturally sing your praises to other people, and that recommendation might be all some soul needs to come knocking on your door. In other words, the most effective advertising is to do the highest quality work, meet your deadlines, operate responsibly and ethically, and offer great customer service.

There are also plenty of other things you can do to spread the gospel of you even further afield. Here are some ideas for online promotion:

◆ Include at the bottom of all your e-mail messages a brief (nothing too elaborate) "ad" about your business. Even just the URL of your business home page is good. (Remember, too, that most e-mail programs can be set up to automatically tack on a "signature" to the bottom of each outgoing message.)

◆ Join mailing lists and participate in newsgroups and discussion lists related to your area of expertise.

◆ Be sure to use <META> tags on your pages so search engines index your site (see Chapter 8, "Publish or Perish: Putting Your Page on the Web"). When constructing your keywords, use words and phrases related to the market or markets in which you specialize. This helps differentiate your site.

◆ Even with <META> tags, don't assume all search engines will find you. Register your site with the major search engines directly.

◆ Make sure your contact information is present and easy to find on your web pages.

◆ Write articles for other sites or online magazines. Along similar lines, you could create your own e-newsletter that offers site tips, business ideas, and whatever else you think might interest prospective customers.

◆ Look for sites that list local businesses in your area and register your business with them.

◆ Get all your friends and relatives to link to your site.

◆ Make sure your own site is always up-to-date and well-designed. Nothing turns off a prospective client more than an ill-maintained business home page.

◆ At the bottom of every client page, put a small, tasteful logo that links back to your site. (Make sure your client is okay with this.)

◆ Show samples of your work on your site.

You don't have to restrict all your promotion efforts to cyberspace. Here are some ideas for advertising your business in the real world:

◆ Get business cards or flyers made up and plaster them around town in grocery stores, community centers, and other appropriate public spaces.

◆ Check to see if local businesses have a web presence. If not, send them a proposal.

◆ Create free pages for churches, charitable organizations, community groups, and schools.

◆ Chat up the nerds at the local computer or electronics store. Be sure to leave them a stack of business cards so that they can refer people your way.

◆ Advertise in community newspapers.

◆ Give talks or presentations to local computer user groups, community groups, clubs, or even the Chamber of Commerce.

Webmaster Wisdom

If you decide to start your own web design shop, or even if you're seriously thinking about it, you'd do well to check out a mailing list called hwg-business. It's run by the HTML Writers Guild and it covers most aspects of running a web design business. You can find out more about it here: www.hwg.org/lists/hwg-business/index.html.

Street Cred: Web Design Certification

As I said in the previous section, getting your new business noticed is vital if you want a steady stream of contracts. One good way to do that and to assure prospective clients that you really know what the heck you're doing is to get some kind of web design certification. There are tons of certification programs available, but the following are among the most respected:

Page Pitfalls

When you examine web certification programs, beware of hidden costs and fees. If a program seems reluctant to tell you how much it will cost, the chances are that it's very expensive and you should consider looking elsewhere.

◆ **Association of Internet Professionals** This is more of an umbrella group that exists to, in a sense, "certify the certifications." See www.association.org.

◆ **Association of Web Professionals** This site offers three programs—Certified Web Designer, Certified Web Manager, and Certified Web Technician (see Figure 23.2). See www.a-w-p.org/cert.htm.

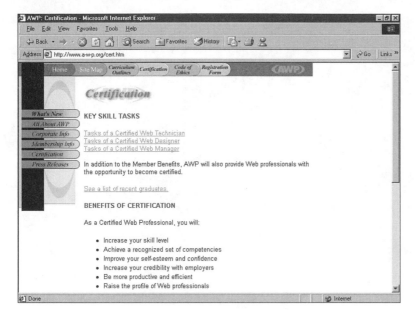

Figure 23.2

The Association of Web Professionals offers several different web certification programs.

- ◆ **Penn State** This site offers a Web Professional Certificate Program. See http://webpro.psu.edu/.
- ◆ **World Organization of Webmasters** This site offers a Certified Professional Webmaster program. See www.joinwow.org.

The Least You Need to Know

- ◆ Make a plan, Stan. Putting together a solid business plan will get your new venture off to the proper start.
- ◆ How do you rate? When deciding what to charge, take into account your level of experience, your skills, the client, and the types of pages you'll be cranking out. Be sure you're familiar with what other designers are charging.
- ◆ See a lawyer! Put together a web design contract you're comfortable with and then wave it in a lawyer's face to make sure it passes legal muster.
- ◆ This is no time to be shy. Advertise the heck out of your new business. When jobs do come your way, do high-quality, professional work to get the old word-of-mouth advertising working for you.
- ◆ Build up your bona fides. Consider getting some kind of certification or accreditation so that people know that *you* know what the heck you're doing.

Chapter 24

Joint Ventures: Working with Ads and Affiliate Programs

In This Chapter

- ◆ Why web ads still work
- ◆ Understanding ad jargon
- ◆ Pointers for selecting a banner exchange or ad network
- ◆ Understanding affiliate programs
- ◆ Choosing an affiliate program that's right for you
- ◆ More ways to turn your site into a money-making machine

The previous chapter showed you how to get started as a professional web page cobbler. But what if you like your day job, or are a student and don't have time to go into full-time webmastering? An alternative is to turn your home page into an electronic money machine. One way you can do that is by selling ad space on your site. On a slightly more ambitious level, there are all kinds of affiliate programs available on the web that will pay you cash. Neither method will make you rich, but they're a great way to earn some extra income and they don't require a ton of work. This chapters explains both money-making methods.

Making It a Banner Year: Putting Ads on Your Site

Web page advertising has gotten a bad rap or two over the past couple of years:

Bad Rap #1: You shouldn't put ads on your site because they'll just annoy your visitors.

I think that most web surfers have learned to live with ads (even if they don't exactly *like* them), so nobody's going to shun your site just because of a few page promos. (Although there *are* ways to truly annoy your readers; I talk about some of them a bit later.)

Bad Rap #2: Okay, if people ignore ads, doesn't that prove that web advertising is dead?

Nope. For one thing, we all still see *tons* of ads on sites, right? If they weren't working, we wouldn't see them. This whole notion of the death of web ads is a myth. What *is* dead is the idea of basing a company's income entirely on web advertising. That's why you see fewer freebies on the web these days. Companies are generating revenue not only from advertising, but also from fees, subscriptions, content licensing, and other e-commerce economics. In other words, businesses are still making money from web advertising, they're just not making *all* their money that way.

As an individual, you don't have to worry about diversifying your web-based income. (I'm assuming here that you have a day job.) All that matters is that, yes, it's still possible to make a bit of extra cash doing the web advertising thing.

Some Ad Lingo You Should Know

The waters of the web advertising business are infested with brain-bending buzzwords and sanity-sapping jargon. To survive, you first need to learn the lingo so that you know what the devil these people are jabbering on about. Here's a short lexicon of the most important terms you need to know:

♦ **above the fold**   Refers to an ad that the user sees without having to scroll down. (This is newspaper jargon, where it refers to stories that appear in the top half of the front page.) Ads that don't appear until the user scrolls down are described as being *below the fold.*

♦ **action**   Occurs when the user clicks an ad to visit the advertiser's site, and then performs some action such as purchasing a product, filling in a form, registering, subscribing, or whatever.

♦ **ad format**   The dimensions of the ad. There are eight standard formats that have been defined for web ads (see Figure 24.1):

Dimensions (height × width)	Format Name
468 × 60 pixels	Full banner
234 × 60 pixels	Half banner

Dimensions (height × width)	Format Name
392 × 72 pixels	Full banner with navigation
120 × 240 pixels	Vertical banner
125 × 125 pixels	Square button
120 × 90 pixels	Button 1
120 × 60 pixels	Button 2
88 × 31 pixels	Micro bar

There are also seven new formats that you're starting to see more of:

120 × 600 pixels	Skyscraper
160 × 600 pixels	Wide skyscraper
180 × 150 pixels	Rectangle
300 × 250 pixels	Medium rectangle
250 × 250 pixels	Square pop-up
240 × 400 pixels	Vertical rectangle
336 × 280 pixels	Large rectangle

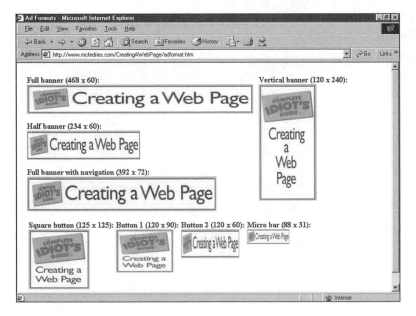

Figure 24.1

Examples of the eight standard ad formats used in web ads.

◆ **banner ad**   An ad that appears in a web page as a rectangular, clickable image.

◆ **click-through**   When the user clicks an ad.

- **click-through ratio (CTR)**   The rate at which users click an ad. It's calculated by dividing the number of *click-throughs* by the number of *impressions.*

- **cost-per-action (CPA)**   How much an ad costs per action.

- **cost-per-click (CPC)**   How much an ad costs per click-through. This is calculated using the CTR and the CPM (see the next item): CPC = CPM ÷ CTR * 1,000.

For example, if your CPM is $20 and your CTR is 1 percent, then the CPC is $2. This is also called the *cost-per-visitor.*

- **cost-per-thousand (CPM)**   How much an ad costs per thousand *impressions.* For example, if you charge $100 for an ad and that ad gets 5,000 monthly impressions, the CPM is $20.

- **impression**   An instance of an ad being displayed to a user. For example, if a person views one of your pages that has an ad and then a second person views the same page, you chalk up two impressions. Similarly, if one person views that page and then refreshes the page, that would also count as two impressions because the ad was displayed to the user twice. This is also called an *ad view.*

- **interstitial**   An ad that appears in a separate browser window, especially one that appears while the regular page is loading.

- **page view**   An instance of an entire page displayed to a user. This is usually differentiated from a *hit,* which refers to any request to the web server for data. So "hits" includes not only the request for the HTML file, but also any other files in the page, including images, sounds, applets, external style sheet or JavaScript files, and so on. Advertisers don't care about hits, only page views.

- **pop-under**   An ad that appears in a separate browser window that gets displayed "under" the user's current browser window.

- **pop-up**   An ad that appears in a separate browser window that gets displayed "on top of" the user's current browser window.

- **run-of-site**   This means that an ad can appear on any page of your site and not just a specific page (such as your home page).

- **unique users**   The number of separate individuals who have viewed a page or ad.

Selling Your Ad Space

Once you've decided to give up a chunk of your page real estate for an ad or two, you need to make a decision about how you go about attracting advertisers. That means deciding which of the following approaches best suits both you and your site:

- **Banner exchange network**   This is a free network in which sites submit their banner ads and agree to display the banner ads from the other sites in the network. This benefits you not with a direct monetary gain, but by sending more traffic to your site, which means you can make more money in other ways (such as selling stuff or selling ads). The network also sends out ads from paying customers, which is how the network makes its money.

- **Ad network**   This is a company that contracts with a number of advertisers and so generates a pool of ads. It then uses an "ad server" to distribute those ads to sites that have signed up with the ad network. Your site typically gets a percentage of whatever revenue the ad network generates (typically 40 to 60 percent).

- **Direct selling**   This is where you contact advertisers directly and ask them if they want to advertise on your site.

Choosing a Banner Exchange or Ad Network

There are thousands of banner exchange and ad networks on the loose. How do you choose one that's right for you? Here are some things to look for:

- **Credit ratio:** On a banner exchange network, this is the number of ad impressions that your site has to generate in order to have one of your ads displayed by someone else. The usual ratio is one half, which means that your ad gets displayed once for every two impressions you generate.

- **Payment:** Does the ad network use CPM or CPC to determine how much you get paid? Are there different rates for different ad formats? How do they pay you (check, PayPal, and so on)? Is there a minimum payment? For example, most networks won't send payment unless your account is at or above some minimum amount (such as US$50).

- **Minimums:** Does the network require a minimum number of monthly impressions or a minimum click-through ratio?

- **Image specifications:** Does the banner exchange network have any specific requirements for the image files you use as an ad? For example, it may want only GIFs or JPEGs, it may require file sizes to be a certain number of kilobytes or less, or it may not allow animated GIFs.

- **Ad formats:** What types of ad formats does the network serve, and can you choose the formats that are served to your site? For example, if you think your site visitors will hate pop-unders (most people do), then avoid a network that serves them (or doesn't allow you to choose a different format).

- **Ad position:** Does the network require that ads be positioned above the fold?

- **Multiple ads:** Does the network restrict the number of ads that can appear on the page?

◆ **Site type:** Does the network restrict the type of sites it deals with? For example, many networks won't serve ads to sites on free servers, sites where the proprietors don't own their domain names, sites that are composed only (or mostly) of chat rooms, bulletin boards, or links to other sites. Also, many banner exchange networks are geared to sites with specific types of content (such as business or sports).

Here are some sites that discuss and rate banner exchange and ad networks:

◆ **Adbility**   This site lists ad networks, and you get a comment about each network, some payment info, and other data that varies widely, depending on the network. See www.adbility.com/show.asp?cat_id=168.

◆ **AdsWise**   This site offers reasonably detailed reviews of both banner exchanges and ad networks. See www.adswise.com.

◆ **BannerTips**   This site offers a few short reviews of banner exchange networks, but its strong suit is the excellent collection of articles on banner design, tips, and advertising. See www.bannertips.com/exchangenetworks.shtml.

◆ **ClickQuick.com**   This is a nice site that offers in-depth reviews of a number of ad networks. See www.clickquick.com/subcat.asp?S=15.

◆ **Free Banner Exchange MegaList**   This site has tons of banner exchange listings, and each one tells you the focus of the network, whether it allows animated GIFs, the ad format, the maximum file size, and the credit ratio. There's also a brief comment about each network. See www.bxmegalist.com.

◆ **ReallyFirst.com**   Here you'll find thousands of banner exchange and ad networks. Each listing has a simple "star" rating and a short description from the network itself. See www.reallyfirst.com/Ad_Networks.

Webmaster Wisdom

I've gathered the links in this chapter and tossed them into the file named ventures.htm on the CD.

Ad It Your Way: Selling Ad Space Yourself

If you have a very popular site, then you ought to consider selling your ad space on your own. It's a lot more work, but you'll make five or even ten times the money you would using an ad network. The key word here is "popular." There's no point at all in going down this road if your site generates only a few hundred or a few thousand page views each month. A bare minimum would be 25,000 monthly page views, and your selling life will be much easier if your site can generate 100,000 page views or more.

Don't despair if your site doesn't generate this kind of traffic. You may still be able to sell ads with less traffic *if* your site content is targeted at a very specific audience. For example, if your site has high-quality content on cars and the car industry, you may be able to sell ad space to some dealerships or even to a manufacturer.

How do you go about getting advertisers? There are two basic methods:

- Contact companies or organizations that you think might have some interest in advertising on your site.

- Put up your own "This Space For Rent" banner. Link it to a "rate card" page that sets out your ad rates and terms, describes your audience, and gives any other information that you think may be of interest to potential advertisers.

Here are a few tips to bear in mind when putting ads on your site:

- **Keep ads down to a dull roar.** Don't paste multiple ads all over your pages. This will not only detract from your content, but will also make the ads less effective.

- **Avoid large ads.** Ads that are large (in terms of kilobytes) may take a long time to download, especially over a slow link.

- **Avoid annoying ads.** You may not have much choice about the kinds of ads that companies send your way. However, if you do have a choice, keep annoying ads to a minimum. By "annoying" I mean ads that contain pointless animations or dialog boxlike images, as well as pop-ups and pop-unders.

- **Place ads out of the way.** Ads are ideally positioned on the edges of your page: the top, bottom, left, or right. Don't position ads within the text of your page.

- **Rotate ads.** If you have multiple ads, get yourself a script that rotates the ads with each page view. This makes it more interesting for your visitors and ensures that the impressions are properly doled out.

- **Target ads.** Wherever possible, display ads for products that might be of interest to your visitors. If you have a "book club" page, for example, don't display an ad for the World Wrestling Federation.

Words from the Web

The **NASCAR effect** is the effect produced by a site that displays a large number of logos or advertising images. For those not familiar with the term, NASCAR is a U.S.-based association devoted to professional car racing (it's an acronym for National Association of Stock Car Automobile Racing). Almost all the cars are garishly festooned with sponsor logos, hence the underlying meaning of this phrase.

Partners in Cyberspace: Working with Affiliate Programs

An *affiliate program* (also sometimes called a referral program) is a partnership with a site that sells stuff. The basic idea is that you put on your page a link to a specific product from the selling site. If someone clicks your link and ends up purchasing the product, you get a piece of the action—typically, a percentage of the selling price.

For example, the granddaddy of all affiliate programs is the Associates Program run by Amazon.com (see Figure 24.2). In the books portion of the program, if someone purchases a book after linking to Amazon through your site, you get a "referral fee," which is usually a cool 15 percent of the purchase price. So, if someone buys a $30 book, your cut is $4.50. It redefines the phrase "easy money"!

Figure 24.2

Amazon.com's Associates Program pays you boffo bucks for sending paying customers its way.

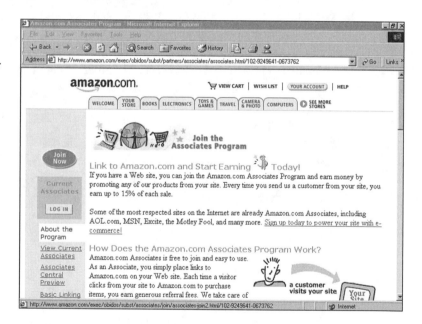

Even better, there are affiliate programs available for more than just books. There are programs for CDs, videos, computer software and hardware, food, liquor, furniture, and even cars. This means you can select a program that fits in with the type of site you have.

Setting Up an Affiliate Program

Setting up an affiliate program typically requires these steps:

1. Go to the site offering the program and sign up for it.

2. Create a "store" on your site. This doesn't have to be anything elaborate, although most programs also offer program-related graphics and other helping hands.

3. For each product you want to feature, set up a link to the specific product on the program site. You usually include some kind of code in the link address that identifies your site as the referrer.

4. Sit back and wait for the checks to come rolling in.

 **Webmaster Wisdom**

Although most affiliate programs are commission-based, some are based on other criteria. For example, some programs pay a flat fee for each *new* visitor who purchases something. Other programs offer click-through incentives that pay for each new visitor sent to the site.

Choosing an Affiliate Program

The hardest part about setting up an affiliate program is choosing one. There are hundreds available, and they all have different features. Here are a few things to watch for when choosing a program:

- **Commission rates:** These vary widely. Amazon's 15 percent is on the high end of the scale and most programs offer between 3 and 10 percent. Some programs offer a sliding scale where your commission goes up after the total sales attributed to your links goes over a certain amount.

- **Commission exceptions:** Some programs offer their highest commission rate only on certain items. Amazon, for example, offers only a 5 percent commission on its other products (such as CDs and videos). It's also typical to offer a reduced commission on products that are heavily discounted.

- **Direct versus general links:** Most programs pay a much higher commission if a sale was generated from a direct link to a product. (As opposed to linking to the program's home page, for example.)

- **The commission base:** Some programs base the commission on the selling price of the product, others base it on the profit earned by each sale.

- **Site restrictions:** Many programs reject sites that have "unsuitable" themes such as sex, violence, discrimination, or the promotion of illegal activities.

- **Check thresholds:** Many programs won't issue you a check until your commission reaches a certain threshold.

- **Exclusivity:** Some program agreements demand exclusivity, meaning that you can't also include a rival program on your site.

Whew! That's a lot to worry about. Fortunately, a few good people on the web have made it their full-time job to monitor and review these affiliate programs. The following are the sites that I think do the best job:

- **Adbility Affiliate Programs**   This site offers a comprehensive listing of affiliate programs, arranged by category. However, it's not as good as it used to be because it now gives only a minimal amount of information about each program. See www. adbility.com/show.asp?cat_id=171.

- **Affiliate World**   This site has a monthly "Top 20" feature that lists the best affiliate programs. You can also view programs by plan type (such as pay-per-sale and pay-per-click) and by category (such as books and music). There's also a monthly affiliate program newsletter, program guides and tips, and more. See www. affiliateworld.com.

- **Associate Programs Directory**   This directory has hundreds of programs broken down into dozens of categories. It includes ratings from program users as well as a free newsletter. See www.associateprograms.com.

- **Associate-It**   Associate-It has good reviews of a large number of programs, organized by category. It also allows program users to rate each program and to include their own reviews of the program. There's also a nice collection of articles on all aspects of setting up and running an affiliate store on your site. See www.associate-it.com.

- **CashPile**   This site has excellent reviews of thousands of affiliate programs. It also offers discussion boards, articles, tips, and even a "Commission Calculator" to help you figure out how much you'll earn. See www.cashpile.com.

- **i-revenue**   This site has capsule reviews of an impressive number of programs. It's also bursting at the seams with affiliate resources, including a newsletter, articles, discussion forums, and much more. See www.i-revenue.net.

- **Refer-It**   Refer-It lists hundreds of programs, which is good, but the descriptions are often written by the companies offering the programs, which is bad. Still, it's a good place to learn about commission rates and the number of affiliates associated with each program. See www.refer-it.com/main.cfm.

Affiliate Program Pointers

To close this section, here are a few pointers for getting the most out of affiliate programs:

- **Choose a program that fits.** Affiliate programs work best when you have lots of prospective buyers visiting your site. Therefore, you should always select a program that fits in with your site's theme. If you have a gardening site, for example, joining a CD-based program doesn't make much sense.

◆ **Sell your links.** You want people to not only click the program links, but also buy the item on the other end of the wire. You can encourage people to do that by selling the product on your end: writing a review, listing the product's features, and so on.

◆ **Make your "store" attractive.** Don't just slap up a few links. Use the HTML skills you've learned from this book to build a nice "store" that makes people come back for more. And don't forget to take advantage of whatever design help the affiliate program offers.

The Least You Need to Know

◆ Ads still work. Although a few doom-and-gloom types insist web advertising is dead, online ads are indeed alive and well and making people money. You may as well be one of them.

◆ Impressions and click-throughs. The most important terms you need to remember are *impressions*—the total number of times that users see an ad—and *click-throughs*—the total number of times that users click an ad.

◆ Choose your medium. If you want to attract more traffic to your site, choose a banner exchange network; if you have a reasonable amount of traffic, sign up with an ad network to start making money on your site right away; if you have a large amount of traffic, consider selling ads directly to merchants.

◆ Ad-vice. Keep images small, avoid annoying animations and pop-ups, keep ads out of your content, rotate ads for variety, and target ads to specific visitors wherever possible.

◆ Program study. Before signing up with an affiliate program, do some homework. This means studying commission rates, how commissions are generated, when you get paid, and what restrictions the program insists upon.

◆ Maximize your affiliation. Be sure to choose a program that fits in with the content of your site, encourage visitors to buy the products, and make your store an attractive place to shop.

25

Selling Stuff Online

In This Chapter

- ◆ Using an e-commerce hosting service
- ◆ Creating an order form for your site
- ◆ Processing orders
- ◆ Pointers to e-commerce tutorials

Have you got a widget you want to sell on the web? Whether it's a painting, a pencil sharpener, or a paperback, there's a big, fat wired market out there, just waiting to clamor for your product. You already know more than enough HTML to put together a classy catalog that shows your wares in their best light. But what happens when someone takes a shine to one of your trinkets and says, "I'll take it!"? Answering that question is the subject of this chapter. You'll learn about a few different ways to sell things online, including how to rent online retail space and how to cobble together an interactive order form that calculates the total automatically.

The No Muss Method: Renting Online Retail Space

In an ideal world, you'd do all your cyberselling directly from the comfy confines of your site. Unfortunately, doing this tends to be a complex and expensive business, so it's not for amateurs or the shallow-pocketed. Don't despair, though, because I'll discuss some ways to sell things on the cheap directly from your site a bit later in this chapter. You should also check with your web hosting provider to see if it offers some kind of e-commerce package or a "virtual store" that you can use.

Failing that, there are all kinds of businesses on the web whose job it is to host your online retail presence. This is a great way to go because the nasty details of things like shopping carts, payment authorization, and security are handled by the geeks at these companies. The rest of this section takes you through a list of the e-commerce hosting companies that have the best reputations (at least as I write this). Here are a few things to look for when comparing the various services:

- **Store limitations:** Most services place a limit on certain features, such as the number of products, the total disk space your pages use, and the amount of bandwidth your site serves. In most cases, you can increase those limits by spending more money.

- **Security:** Web shoppers are getting more savvy every day, so there are fewer people around who will knowingly give out their credit card number over a nonsecure connection. Therefore, you should shun any service that doesn't offer a secure shopping cart and credit card transactions.

- **Domain name:** Can you get your own domain name (such as www.yourdomain.com), or will you get a subdomain of the service (such as www.yourname.service.com)?

- **Residency requirement:** Lots of services require that you be a resident of a particular country. (Since most of the services are U.S.-based, they require a U.S. address.)

- **Reports:** What kinds of reports (orders, traffic, and so on) does the service send to you?

- **Setup fee:** Most sites charge a setup not only for hosting your site, but also for setting up a *merchant account*. The latter is required in order for you to handle credit card transactions.

- **Hidden fees:** Most sites (or the credit card services they use, such as Cardservice International) will charge you an extra monthly fee for such an account, and may also charge you extra fees for

Page Pitfalls

Remember that all prices quoted here are accurate as of when I hunted-and-pecked them into this chapter. Always double-check prices before signing up with any service.

each transaction. Some services also charge a "revenue share" fee that's a percentage of your monthly sales. Make sure you find out about these fees up front.

Here are a few companies that rent online retail space:

◆ **AT&T Small Business Hosting Services**   AT&T's small business hosting service combines web hosting with an e-commerce option (see Figure 25.1). You get a "wizard" to help you build your store, a shopping cart, real-time credit card processing, automatic tax and shipping calculations, and much more. Prices start at US$50 per month. See www.ipservices.att.com/products/productoverview.cfm?productid=sbhseo.

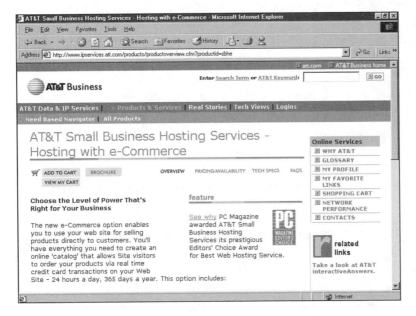

Figure 25.1

AT&T can host your site and toss in the necessary e-commerce doohickeys.

◆ **bCentral**   This Microsoft site offers a package called Commerce Manager that enables you to set up an online catalog. In this catalog you can enter product descriptions and images, inventory levels, product numbers, and more. bCentral will then list your cataloged products on various shopping and auction sites. It then handles the orders for you, including processing credit cards, security, and e-mail notification of orders. The price is US$24.95 per month, or US$224.95 per year. See www.bcentral.com/services/ cm/default.as.

Webmaster Wisdom

I've collected all of the resources I mention in this chapter and placed links for them in the file named selling.htm on this book's CD.

- **BigStep** This site offers a package called BigStep Store that includes a site-building service, Search Engine Manager (a site marketing tool), Catalog Manager (a tool for constructing a catalog of your products), a shopping cart, a merchant account to handle credit card transactions, and automatic tax and shipping calculations. A basic store (up to 25 items) will set up back US$44.95 per month, although a 30-day free trial is available. See www.bigstep.com.

- **BizBlast** This site's major feature is the StoreFront Wizard, an interactive tool that takes you step by step through the process of building an online store. The wizard creates a catalog of your products, and a customized shopping cart. You then upload your store to the BizBlast server, which supports secure credit card transactions, tax and shipping calculations, and more. A basic "Corner Store" supports up to 26 products for US$29.95 per month. See www.bizblast.com.

- **FreeMerchant** This site offers a web-based Store Builder for creating your online store, a secure shopping cart, credit card transactions, automatic tax and shipping calculations, and a Customer List Manager for maintaining a customer mailing list. And, sorry to say, despite the name, FreeMerchant is decidedly not free. The basic "Bronze" package will set you back US$39.95 a month, or US$399.95 a year. See www.freemerchant.com.

- **HostWay** Hostway offers quite a few e-commerce packages (see Figure 25.2), which start as low as US$24.95 per month (US$19.95 per month if you pay for a year in advance) for a 20-product store. All the packages offer a shopping cart, merchant account, and secure credit card transactions. See www.hostway.com/ecommerce/index.htm.

Figure 25.2

Hostway has e-commerce plans to suit most budgets.

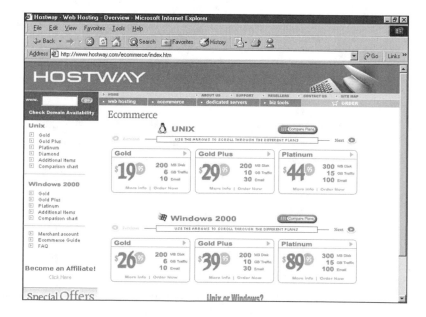

◆ **Yahoo! Storestore.yahoo.com**   This Yahoo! service offers a simple interface for building your store, a shopping cart, and secure credit card transactions. However, the big deal here is that you can choose to place your store in the Yahoo! Shopping section. Since this is one of the Web's most popular shopping sites, this gives you access to a huge number of potential customers. The basic price is US$49.95 per month.

The Do-It-Yourself Method: Selling Stuff from Your Site

If an e-commerce storefront seems like overkill for your small business, then perhaps you should think about doing things "in-house." I'm not talking here about building a full-fledged e-commerce system. As I explain a bit later, that's a tough row to hoe and it requires lots of know-how and money. Instead, this section aims to show you that it's not very hard to set up a simple yet functional order-taking system using your HTML smarts and just a smidgen of JavaScript.

Creating an Order Form

The first thing you need to create is an order form that your site visitors can use to specify what they want to purchase. This order form will have the following bits and pieces:

◆ A list of your products that includes the product name or description and the price of the product.

◆ Text boxes where the user can enter the quantity she wants to order for each item.

◆ Boxes that show the subtotal for each item (the price of the item multiplied by the quantity ordered).

◆ The overall total of the order.

◆ The user's personal data, including name, postal address, and e-mail address.

Figure 25.3 shows the top part of the form, which holds the list of products and the customer's order quantities. Note that the subtotals and order total are calculated automatically. That is, when the customer changes a quantity and moves to another field, the various totals are recalculated right away. Note, too, that things are set up so that the user can't edit the subtotal or order total fields. Figure 25.4 shows the bottom part of the form, which is where the user enters his or her personal data.

Webmaster Wisdom

If you have a large number of products, you may prefer to create a *shopping cart* that "remembers" customers' orders has they navigate through your site. That's a bit advanced for this book, but not for my book *Special Edition Using JavaScript* (Que, 2001), which devotes and entire chapter to creating a shopping cart.

Figure 25.3

The top part of the order form.

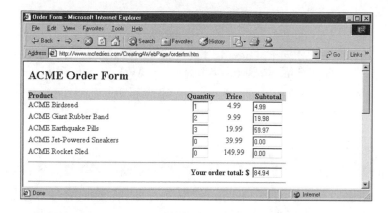

Figure 25.4

The bottom part of the order form.

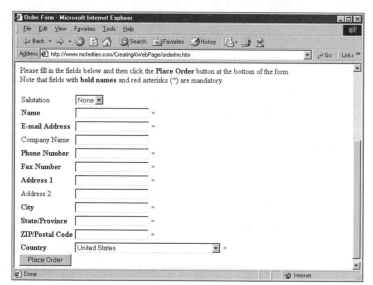

The order form is in a file named orderfrm.htm on the CD in this book. There are two things you need to know right up front before you can think about customizing this file to suit your own site:

- ◆ The product list and ordering boxes are arranged in a table that's written automatically to the page using JavaScript. The item names and prices can be customized.

- ◆ The rest of the order form is a basic HTML table that you can modify at will.

So the only bit of funny business here involves customizing the "database" of products. This is done as part of the script that sites near the top of the file. Here's the code that creates the database of products shown in Figure 25.1:

```
// Create the "database" of products
var database_records = new Array()
var i = 0
database_records[i++] = new database_record("ACME Birdseed", 4.99)
database_records[i++] = new database_record("ACME Giant Rubber Band", 9.99)
database_records[i++] = new database_record("ACME Earthquake Pills", 19.99)
database_records[i++] = new database_record("ACME Jet-Powered Sneakers", 39.99)
database_records[i++] = new database_record("ACME Rocket Sled", 149.99)
```

What's happening here is that you're storing some data about each product in the computer's memory. The key here is each line that begins `database_records[i++]`. Here's the general format of this statement:

```
database_records[i++] = new database_record("Product Name", Price)
```

Here, you replace *Product Name* with the name or short description of the product, and you replace *Price* with the item's price (don't include a dollar sign or any other monetary symbol).

Processing the Orders

The form from the previous section is designed to be e-mailed to you (using, for example, my MailForm service). Once you receive the form data, you may need to finalize the order total to include extra charges such as shipping, gift wrapping, and taxes. Once that's done, you have several choices:

- ◆ Contact the customer and ask him or her to send you a check or money order for the full amount.

- ◆ Use a third-party payment service such as PayPal (see www.paypal.com/) to arrange a cash transfer from the customer's account to yours.

- ◆ Contact the customer and ask for his or her credit card (or debit card) information and then use that info to process the payment.

How do you go about processing a credit card transaction? One easy way is to lease a *swipe terminal* that's normally used for swiping credit cards. You won't have access to the physical card, of course, but these terminals allow you to enter card numbers and expiration dates by hand. You can usually lease one for about US$30 per month.

The next step up from there is to contract with a third-party payment service to handle the dirty work of each credit card transaction. This is called a *payment gateway*. Many of the companies that I discussed at the start of this chapter also offer payment gateway services that let you add credit card processing to your pages.

There are also some companies that will handle credit card transactions for you. Here are a few to check out:

- **CCNow:** www.ccnow.com
- **iBill:** www.ibill.com
- **iFulfill:** www.ifulfill.com
- **Kagi:** www.kagi.com
- **VISAge Payment Service:** linz1.net/eCom/SecureServer.html

Page Pitfalls

Pay special attention to the transaction fees charged by these sites. Some of them can be quite exorbitant, and may mean the difference between making a profit or breaking the bank. Avoid sites that charge both a percentage of the selling price and a dollar amount per transaction.

When you're rummaging around in these sites, here are some things to compare so that you choose the best service for your needs:

- **Credit cards:** Which credit cards does the service handle?
- **Ordering:** How can you send the orders (online, fax, e-mail, and so on)?
- **Currencies:** Which currencies does the service support?
- **Setup fee:** How much does it cost to get your site set up with the service?
- **Transaction fees:** How much does the service charge per transaction?

Where to Learn About Big-Time E-Commerce

If you work for a medium- or large-sized company and some higher-up has told you to put together an in-house e-commerce system, things will get very complicated (and very expensive) in a hurry. A humble Idiot's Guide such as this is, unfortunately, not the place to delve into the details of planning for and setting up a full-blown e-commerce system. Fortunately, there are plenty of good e-commerce guides and tutorials available on the web. Here are some to check out:

- **About.com Electronic Commerce** This site offers a number of articles on various aspects of e-commerce, all put together with the quality that you've come to expect from the About.com family of sites (see Figure 25.5). See ecommerce.about. com.

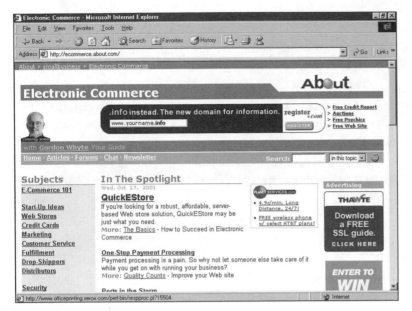

Figure 25.5

About.com's Electronic Commerce section.

◆ **Building Your First E-Commerce Site**   This site offers Building Your First E-Commerce Site, a very thorough guide that takes you step by step through the process of getting an e-commerce site up and selling. See ecommerce.internet.com/how/build/article/0,,10362_867521,00.html.

◆ **CNET Builder.com E-Business and Strategy**   This CNET site has tons of useful information, although the e-commerce tutorial is now outdated. See builder.cnet.com/webbuilding/0-3885.html.

◆ **Online-Commerce Introduction to E-Commerce**   This site offers Online-Commerce Introduction to E-Commerce, a simple guide that gives you the basics of how e-commerce works. See online-commerce.com/tutorial.html.

◆ **Webmonkey E-Commerce Tutorial**   The Webmonkey E-Commerce Tutorial is an excellent tutorial that is strong on the fundamentals, especially the all-important planning and preparation. See hotwired.lycos.com/webmonkey/99/04/index0a.html.

◆ **Web Developer's Journal E-Commerce Tutorial**   The Web Developer's Journal E-Commerce Tutorial isn't the best laid out article I've ever seen, but it's chock full of useful information. See www.webdevelopersjournal.com/columns/ecommerce1.html.

The Least You Need to Know

◆ Be secure. If you decide to opt for an e-commerce host, make sure it supports secure shopping carts and credit card transactions.

◆ Read the fine monetary print. Before signing on the digital dotted line for any service that offers credit card transactions, find out what fees you'll be charged. It's common to have to pay a monthly fee and a per-transaction percentage. However, watch out for other "administrative" fees.

◆ Contacting the customer. Just in case anything goes wrong, you should always ask the customer for contact information, particularly the customer's address and telephone number.

Appendix A

Speak Like a Geek Glossary

.asp The extension used with Active Server Pages files.

.cfm The extension used with ColdFusion files.

.cgi The extension used by a Common Gateway Interface script.

.php The extension used by a PHP script. (Alternatives are .phtml and .php3.)

.pl The extension used with Perl files.

404 Describes a person who is clueless. This comes from the following web server error message:

```
404 Not Found. The requested URL was not found on this server.
```

above the fold Refers to a web page ad that the user sees without having to scroll down. Ads that don't appear until the user scrolls down are described as being below the fold.

access counter See **counter**.

action Occurs when the user clicks an ad to visit the advertiser's site, and then performs some action such as purchasing a product, filling in a form, registering, subscribing, or whatever.

Active Server Pages (ASP) A web page technology that enables web designers to place scripts inside a page, and those scripts are executed by the web server before the page is sent to the user. Active Server Pages is used primarily on Microsoft operating systems, such as Windows NT and Windows 2000. See also **.asp** and **PHP.**

ad format The dimensions of a web page ad.

anchor   A word or phrase in a web page that's used as a target for a link. When the user selects the link, the browser jumps to the anchor, which might exist in the same document or in a different document.

applet   A Java program. See also **craplet** and **dancing baloney.**

arachnerd   A person who spends way too much time either surfing the web or fussing with his home page.

ASP   See **Active Server Pages.**

bandwidth   A measure of how much stuff can be stuffed through a transmission medium such as a phone line or network cable. Web hosting providers use this term to mean the amount of data that is sent to and from your site. Bandwidth is measured in bits per second.

banner ad   An ad that appears in a web page as a rectangular, clickable image.

Barney page   A page whose sole purpose in life is to capitalize on a trendy topic. The name comes from the spate of pages bashing poor Barney the Dinosaur that were all the rage a while back. Past Barney pages have been dedicated to O.J. and Princess Diana. Also known as a macarena page.

bit   The fundamental unit of computer information (it's a blend of the words "binary" and "digit"). Computers do all their dirty work by manipulating a series of high and low electrical currents. A high current is represented by the digit 1 and a low current by the digit 0. These 1's and 0's—or bits—are used to represent absolutely everything that goes down inside your machine. Weird, huh?

bits per second (bps)   A measure of bandwidth. Because it takes eight bits to describe a single character, a transmission medium with a bandwidth of, say, 8bps would send data at the pathetically slow rate of one character per second. Bandwidth is more normally measured in kilobits per second (Kbps—thousands of bits per second). So, for example, a 56Kbps modem can handle approximately 56,000 bits per second. In the high end, bandwidth is measured in megabits per second (Mbps—millions of bits per second).

body   The section of the web document in which you enter your text and tags. See also **head.**

bookmarks   In a web browser (particularly Netscape), a list of your favorite web pages, which you can set while you are surfing. To return to a page, just select it from the list. See also **favorites.**

bps   See **bits per second.**

browser   The software you use to display and interact with a web page.

byte   Eight bits, or a single character.

Century-21 site A website that has moved to a new location and now contains only a link to the new address.

CGI See **Common Gateway Interface.**

CGI Joe A programmer who specializes in the Common Gateway Interface (CGI) scripts that accept and handle input from most web page forms.

character reference Sounds like something you'd put on your resumé, but it's really an HTML code that lets you insert special characters in your web pages (such as é). See also **entity name.**

click-through When the user clicks an ad.

click-through ratio (CTR) The rate at which users click an ad. It's calculated by dividing the number of click-throughs by the number of impressions.

clickstream The "path" a person takes as they navigate through the World Wide Web.

client-side image map An image map where the links are processed by the browser instead of the server. See also **server-side image map.**

cobweb page A web page that hasn't been updated in a long time.

ColdFusion A product that enables a web designer to build and display web pages from a database.

comment Text in a web page file that doesn't get displayed to the user or processed by the browser. Webmasters use comments to annotate a page's HTML code to make it easier to read and understand, and also to force the browser to bypass problematic code.

Common Gateway Interface (CGI) A programming technology that enables a web server to accept data (usually from a form), process that data, and then send the browser some kind of result. See also **CGI Joe.**

cornea gumbo A web page that is an overdesigned, jumbled, soup of colors, fonts, and images.

cost-per-action (CPA) How much an ad costs per action.

cost-per-click (CPC) How much an ad costs per click-through. This is calculated using the CTR (see **click-through ratio**) and the CPM (see **cost-per-thousand**): $CPC = CPM \div CTR * 1,000$. For example, if your CPM is $20 and your CTR is 1 percent, then the CPC is $2. This is also called the cost-per-visitor.

cost-per-thousand (CPM) How much an ad costs per thousand impressions. For example, if you charge $100 for an ad and that ad gets 5,000 monthly impressions, the CPM is $20.

counter   A small script inserted in a web page that tracks the page's hits. Also referred to as an access counter.

craplet   A poorly designed, aesthetically unpleasing, or just generally useless Java applet. See also **dancing baloney.**

cyberscriber   A person who publishes something in an Internet forum (such as a web page or a Usenet newsgroup).

cyberspace   The place you "go" when you reach out beyond your own computer and interact with information or people on other computer systems. See also **meatspace.**

cybersquatting   The practice of obtaining and holding an Internet domain name that uses another company's registered trademark name.

cyberstyle   The writing style used in most online communications. This style is characterized by one or more of the following traits: frequent use of abbreviations, acronyms, and jargon; "street" slang (for example, using "cuz" instead of "because"); typos, misspelled words, and a general inattention to grammar and sentence structure; a rambling, stream-of-consciousness style.

cybersurfer   A person who surfs cyberspace.

dancing baloney   Web page-based animated images, Java applets, and other bells and whistles that are not only useless, but also detract from the overall quality of the page. See also **craplet.**

dead tree edition   The paper version of an online magazine or journal.

deep link   A web page link that points to a file within a site rather than to the site's home page.

dirt road   A frustratingly slow connection to a website. "Geez, that GIF still hasn't loaded yet? The web server must be on a dirt road." See also **JPIG.**

domain name   The part of your e-mail address to the right of the @ sign. The domain name identifies a particular site on the Internet.

e-commerce   The buying and selling of goods and services on the web.

e-tailer   A web-based retail operation.

egosurfing   Scanning the Internet's archives and search engines for mentions of your own name.

emotag   Mock HTML tags used in writing to indicate emotional states. "<FLAME>That guy on the mailing list is the rudest jerk I've ever had the misfortune of dealing with.</FLAME>"

entity name   An HTML code that lets you insert special characters in your web pages. See also **character reference.**

FAQ   The aficionado's short form for a Frequently Asked Question. The correct pronunciation is fack. See **Frequently Asked Questions list.**

favorites   In Internet Explorer, a list of web pages that you've saved for subsequent surfs. To return to a page, just select it from the list. See also **bookmarks.**

flash crowd   A sharp and often overwhelming increase in the number of users attempting to access a website simultaneously, usually in response to some event or announcement. See also **hit-and-run page** and **hot spot.**

flooded   A page rendered unreadable because of a poorly chosen background image. "I had to bail out of that page because the background was flooded with some butt-ugly tartan." See also **wrackground image.**

form   A web document used for gathering information from the reader. Most forms have at least one text field where you can enter text data (such as your name or the keywords for a search). More sophisticated forms also include check boxes (for toggling a value on or off), radio buttons (for selecting one of several options), and command buttons (for performing an action such as submitting the form).

frames   Rectangular browser areas that contain separate chunks of text, graphics, and HTML. In other words, you can use frames to divide the browser window into two or more separate pages.

Frequently Asked Questions list   A list of questions that, over the history of a newsgroup or website, have come up most often. If you want to send a question to a newsgroup or to a website's administrator, it's proper netiquette to read the group's FAQ list to see if you can find the answer there first.

FTP   File Transfer Protocol. This is the usual method for sending your HTML files to your web server. Note that it's okay to use FTP as both a noun (a method for transferring files) and a verb ("Your images aren't showing up because you forgot to FTP the graphics files to your home directory.").

geek   Someone who knows a lot about computers and very little about anything else.

GIF   Graphics Interchange Format. One of the two most commonly used graphics format on the web. See also **JPEG.**

grammar slack   The tolerance exhibited by most Internet users for small spelling and grammar errors.

greenlink   To use the web for monetary gain.

guru site   A website, put together by an expert on a particular subject, that contains a large amount of useful, accurate information on that subject.

hard launch   The release of a product or website for public consumption.

head   The top part of an HTML file. This is like an introduction to a web page. Web browsers use the head to glean various types of information about the page (such as the title). See also **body.**

hit   In general, a single access of a web page. That is, a hit is recorded for a particular web page each time a browser displays the page. Technically, however, it's a request to a web server for data. This means that a request for an HTML file is a hit, but so are any requests for supporting files, such as images, Java applets, external style sheet files, and so on. Therefore, many people prefer to use the more accurate term page view.

hit-and-run page   A web page that gets a huge number of hits and then disappears a week later. Most hit-and-run pages contain pornographic material and they get shut down when the website's system administrators figure out why their network has slowed to a crawl. See also **flash crowd, hot spot,** and **slag.**

home page   The main page of a website. See also **deep link.**

host   See **web server.**

hosting provider   A company that provides you with storage space (usually at a fee) for your web pages. The company runs a web server that enables other people to view your pages.

hot spot   A website that experiences a massive surge in traffic, usually in response to an event or promotion. See also **flash crowd** and **hit-and-run page.**

HTML   HyperText Markup Language. The collection of tags used to specify how you want your web page to appear.

HTML editor   A program that makes it easier to mark up a document by using menu commands and toolbar buttons to insert tags.

hypertext link   See **link.**

image map   A clickable image that takes you to a different link, depending on which part of the image you click. See also **client-side image map** and **server-side image map.**

impression   An instance of an ad being displayed to a user. For example, if a person views one of your pages that has an ad and then a second person views the same page, you chalk up two impressions. Similarly, if one person views that page and then returns to the page an hour later, that would also count as two impressions because the ad was displayed to the user twice. This is also called an ad view.

index   A list of words that appear in a site's web pages and that is used by a search engine to find all the pages that match a user's search query.

interstitial   An ad that appears in a separate browser window, especially one that appears while the regular page is loading.

inverse vandalism   Creating something for no other reason than the sheer fact that you *can* create it. Most web pages are acts of inverse vandalism.

invisible web   The collection of searchable websites whose content exists within databases and so can't be indexed by search engines. For example, see the Encyclopedia Britannica site (www.britannica.com).

ISP   Internet service provider. A company that offers access to the Internet.

Java   A programming language designed to create software (an applet) that runs inside a web page. Can also be used to create standalone applications such as word processors and spreadsheets. See also **craplet** and **dancing baloney.**

Javlovian   Describes the automatic response that causes marketing types to come up with only cute, coffee-related names for Java-based products (Cafe, Roaster, Java Beans, Latte, and so on ad nauseum).

JPEG   A common web graphics format developed by the Joint Photographic Experts Group. See also **GIF.**

JPIG   A web page that takes forever to load because it's either jammed to the hilt with graphics, or because it contains one or two really large images. See also **dirt road.**

Kbps   Kilobits per second (thousands of bits per second).

link   A word or phrase that, when selected, sends the reader to a different page or to an anchor.

link rot   The gradual obsolescence of the links on a web page as the sites they point to become unavailable.

Linux   An operating system used by many web servers. It's a variation of the **Unix** operating system.

macarena page   A web page capitalizing on a current fad. They are usually full of fluff and have a short life expectancy. See also **Barney page.**

Mbps   Megabits per second (millions of bits per second).

meatspace   The flesh-and-blood real world; the opposite of cyberspace.

mouse potato   The computer equivalent of a couch potato.

mousetrapping   A technique that forces a user to remain on a particular web page.

multimediocrities Lame web pages that are jam-packed with second-rate pictures, sounds, and applets.

NASCAR effect The effect produced by a website that displays a large number of logos or advertising images.

nooksurfer A person who frequents only a limited number of Internet sites.

notwork A downed network.

one-link wonder A web page that contains only a single useful link.

page jack To steal a web page and submit it to search engines under a different address. Users who run a search and attempt to access the page are then routed to another site.

page view An instance of a user viewing a web page. See also **hit.**

password trap A website that uses a legitimate-looking interface to fool users into providing their passwords.

Perl A programming language used to create CGI scripts. See also **.pl.**

PHP A web page technology that enables web designers to place scripts inside a page, and those script get executed by the web server before the page is sent to the user. PHP is used primarily on Unix or Linux servers. See also **.php** and **Active Server Pages.**

pixel shim A small, transparent, image (usually one pixel wide and one pixel tall) that Web page designers use to achieve exact placement of text and images.

plug-in A program that attaches itself to a web browser so that the functionality of the program then becomes an integral part of the browser.

pop-under An ad that appears in a separate browser window that gets displayed "under" the user's current browser window.

pop-up An ad that appears in a separate browser window that gets displayed "on top of" the user's current browser window.

portal site A website that combines a wide array of content and services in an effort to convince users to make the site their home page.

publish To make a web page available to the World Wide Web community at large.

read-only user A person who uses the Internet exclusively for reading web pages, e-mail, and newsgroups instead of creating her own content.

roadblock A web page that serves no other purpose other than to let you know that there is nothing available at the URL, but that something will be coming soon.

run-of-site This means that an ad can appear on any page of your site and not just a specific page (such as your home page).

search engine   A resource that indexes web pages and then enables the user to search for those pages that contain a particular word or phrase.

search jack   To include in a web page popular, but superfluous, search terms (such as "sex" or "Lewinsky") to appear in the results when people search for those terms.

server   A computer that sends out stuff. Check out **web server** for an example.

server-side image map   An image map where the links are processed by the server. See also **client-side image map.**

server-side include   A special HTML tag that enables the page designer to "include" an external text file or to "echo" certain types of data to the page.

shovelware   Content from an existing medium (such as a newspaper or book) that has been dumped wholesale into another medium (such as a web page).

skyscraper ad   An advertisement that runs vertically down the side of a web page.

slag   To bring a network to its knees because of extremely high traffic. "That Babe of the Week page has totally slagged the network." See also **notwork.**

spamdexing   To repeat a word dozens or even hundreds of times at the top of a web page. The word is usually indicative of the subject matter of the site, and repeating it so many times is an attempt to fool web search engines into thinking the site is a good representation of that subject. However, most search engines recognize this and refuse to index such a site.

stalker site   A website devoted to a celebrity, the content of which clearly indicates that the fan who created the site is obsessed with his subject.

sticky   Describes a website that encourages visitors to spend long periods of time visiting its various pages.

surf   To leap giddily from one web page to another by furiously clicking any link in sight; to travel through cyberspace.

tags   The HTML commands, in the form of letter combinations or words surrounded by angle brackets (< >). They tell a browser how to display a web page.

target   See **anchor.**

title   A short description of a web page that appears at the top of the screen.

typosquatter   A person who registers one or more domain names based on the most common typographical errors that a user might commit when entering a company's registered trademark name (for example, amazon.com).

ubiquilink   A link found on almost everyone's hotlist. "Yahoo! must be on every hotlist on the planet. It's a total ubiquilink."

Uniform Resource Locator   See **URL.**

unique users   The number of separate individuals who have viewed a page or ad.

Unix   An operating system used by many web servers. See also **Linux.**

URL   A web addressing scheme that spells out the exact location of a Net resource. For example, my home page's URL is http://www.mcfedries.com/.

vanity plate   An annoyingly large web page graphic that serves no useful purpose. See also **JPIG.**

vaporlink   A link that points to a nonexistent web page.

web cramming   A scam in which a person or small business accepts an offer for a free website, only to be subsequently charged a monthly fee on her phone bill.

web hosting provider   See **hosting provider.**

web rage   Anger caused by World Wide Web frustrations such as slow downloads, non-existent links, and information that is difficult to find.

web server   A computer that stores your web pages and hands them out to anyone with a browser that comes calling. Also known as a web host.

webology   The study of the content, structure, and interconnections of the World Wide Web.

wrackground image   A background image that ruins a page by making the text unreadable. See also **flooded.**

YOYOW   You own your own words. This refers to the copyright you have on the text in your web pages.

Frequently Asked Questions About HTML

This appendix presents a list of FAQs (frequently asked questions) about HTML. The questions are listed in the following categories: General HTML, Graphics, Publishing, Multimedia, Forms, Frames, and Page Design. A slightly longer list of FAQs is available on my website: www.mcfedries.com/ CreatingAWebPage/faq.html

General HTML Questions

How can I spell check my web page?

You have two choices for getting your spelling letter perfect:

* Compose your pages in a program that has a spell check feature. You can find such a feature in word processors (such as Word), HTML editors (such as Netscape Composer), or in text editors (such as UltraEdit: www.ultraedit.com or Notetab www.notetab.com).

* Use a spell check program such as Spell Checker for Edit Boxes (see www.quinion.com/mqa/index.htm).

The browser shows the tags I put into the page. What's wrong?

I explain how to solve this problem in Chapter 2, "Laying the Foundation: The Basic Structure of a Web Page." See the section titled "Help! The Browser Shows My Tags!"

Internet Explorer handles my link/graphic/whatever no problem, but Netscape doesn't. What's wrong?

The usual culprit here is a space that you've included in either a file name or a directory name. Netscape doesn't like spaces, so you need to rename your file or directory to remove the space. If you want to separate words in a file or directory name, a good substitute is the underscore character (_).

What's the difference between the .htm and .html file extensions?

There's no difference whatsoever. Both are legit HTML file extensions, and browsers process them equally. Note, however, that these extensions create separate files. For example, the files index.htm and index.html are distinct files.

How can I open a link in a separate browser window?

The usual method is to set the <A> tag's TARGET attribute equal to <SPAN STYLE="font-family: monospace">_blank</SPAN>:

```
<A HREF="whatever.html TARGET="_blank">New Window</A>
```

However, if you set the <A> tag's TARGET attribute equal to an undefined name—that is, it's not the name of a frame or one of the prefab names—then the browser opens a new window and assigns the TARGET value as the name of the new window.

For example, consider the following:

```
<A HREF="whatever.html" TARGET="LinkWindow">Click this!</A>
```

This opens a new window and displays the "whatever.html" page within that window. The browser assigns the name "LinkWindow" to that window. This means that you can load anything into that window just by referring to the same window name, like so:

```
<A HREF="another.html" TARGET="LinkWindow">Click this, too!</A>
```

This link displays the "another.html" page in the same window that the previous link opened.

How do I use a custom bullet in a bulleted list?

The solution I use is a two-column table, like so:

```
<TABLE>

<TR VALIGN="TOP">
<TD><IMG SRC="yourbullet.gif"></TD>
<TD>Bullet point 1 text goes here...</TD>
</TR>
```

```
<TR VALIGN="TOP">
<TD><IMG SRC="yourbullet.gif"></TD>
<TD>Bullet point 2 text goes here...</TD>
</TR>

etc.

</TABLE>
```

Is there a way to make table columns have a constant width?

Absolutely! Provided you're putting only text in each cell, then you have to do two things:

- ◆ Specify an exact width for each cell.
- ◆ Use our old friend spacer.gif, the transparent 1 × 1 pixel image (see Chapter 6, "A Picture Is Worth a Thousand Clicks: Working with Images").

For example, if you want a column to always be 100 pixels wide, use this:

```
<TD WIDTH="100">
Cell text goes here
<BR><IMG SRC="spacer.gif" WIDTH="100" HEIGHT="1">
</TD>
```

Instead of displaying the symbol represented by a character code or entity, I want to display the actual character code or entity. Is that possible?

Yes. All character codes and entities begin with an ampersand (&). So the easiest way to display the code is to remove the ampersand and replace it with the character code for the ampersand (&). For example, the character code for the copyright symbol (©) is ©. To display the code, you'd use the following:

```
&#38;#169;
```

How can I let surfers download a file from my site?

In most cases, you set up a regular link and point it to the file you want to be able to download. For example, suppose you have a file named mystuff.zip. To set up a download link, you'd use the following:

```
<A HREF="mystuff.zip">Download my stuff<A>
```

This assumes that you've uploaded mystuff.zip to your server and that the file is in the same directory as your HTML file. When the user clicks the link, the browser will display a dialog box asking whether the user wants to open the file or save it to his hard disk.

For files that get displayed in the browser (such as text files), you need to add instructions on your page that tell the user to load the file and then select the browser's **File, Save As** command.

Is there any way to specify a Subject line with a mailto link?

Most (but not all) browsers and e-mail programs let you specify the Subject line by adjusting the <A> tag as follows:

```
<A HREF="mailto:biff@isp.com?Subject=My Subject Line">
```

Replace *My Subject Line* with the actual Subject line you want.

What is ASP?

If you come across a page file name that uses the .asp extension, then you've come across a species of page known as an Active Server Page (ASP, for short). Most ASP files contain one or more scripts that are very similar to the JavaScripts that you learned about in Part 4, "Working with JavaScripts and Java Applets." However, they're vastly different:

- ◆ JavaScripts run when the browser loads the page or when the user initiates some action (such as submitting a form). In other words, JavaScripts are executed by the browser.

- ◆ An ASP script is executed by the server. That is, when the user requests an ASP file, the server first checks to see if it contains a script. If it does, it runs that script and then sends the file to the user's browser.

The big advantage you get with ASP is that you no longer have to worry about browser compatibility, as you do with JavaScript. Since the script runs on the server, it doesn't matter what browser the user is running. Also, since the script runs on the server, it's fairly easy to do things such as access a database, send an e-mail, and do other fancy tricks.

ASP is a Microsoft technology, so it's designed to run on Microsoft web servers, such as Internet Information Server. If you want to give ASP a whirl, you have to find a web host that supports it.

Note, too, that a similar technology called PHP also exists. However, PHP usually runs on Unix and Linux web servers.

What is XML?

XML (eXtensible Markup Language) is still pretty highfalutin stuff, and it's not really on the radar screens just yet (at least not for the likes of us). The basic idea is that XML enables the designer to create his or her own tags in such a way that an XML-smart browser knows what to do with those tags. This won't be a big deal for folks who just have straightforward pages. If you deal with databases or specialized fields (such as medicine or mathematics), however, you can create tags that describe database components or elements from your field of expertise. For example, a Math XML is already being proposed, and it'll enable math types to render equations and other elements that HTML just can't do. See www.w3.org/Math.

The problem with XML is that it requires some heavy-duty programming to "teach" the browser what each hand-built tag is supposed to do. For that reason, XML will remain a geeks-only technology for some time to come.

Finding nongeek info on XML is hard right now, but the following PC Magazine article isn't too bad: www.zdnet.com/pcmag/features/xml98/intro.htm.

Graphics Questions

Why don't my images appear when I view my page in the browser?

The fact that you're not seeing your images is probably due to one of the following reasons:

♦ If you're viewing your page on your home machine, the HTML file and the image files might be sitting in separate directories on your computer. Try moving your image files into the same directory that holds your HTML file.

♦ If you're viewing your page on the web, make sure you sent the image files to your server.

♦ Make sure you have the correct match for uppercase and lowercase letters. If an image is on your server and it's named "image.gif", and your IMG tag refers to "IMAGE.GIF", your image won't show up. In this case, you'd have to edit your IMG tag so that it refers to "image.gif".

Is it possible to change the color of the border that appears around images used as links?

The image link border color is the same as the regular link color. Therefore, you can change the border color by using the LINK, ALINK, and VLINK attributes in the <BODY> tag. For example, if you want a red border, you use this:

```
<BODY LINK="#FF0000" ALINK="#FF0000" VLINK="#FF0000">
```

When I'm using an image as a link, how do I remove the border around the image?

Add BORDER="0" to your <IMG> tag, as in this example:

```
<A HREF="something.html">
<IMG SRC="jiffy.gif" BORDER="0">
</A>
```

How do I create thumbnail images?

A thumbnail is just a smaller version of an existing image. What you need to do is load the original image into a graphics program and then use the program's **Resize** command to scale down the image to an appropriate size (which depends on the original image). Then use the program's **File, Save As** command to save the smaller image under a different name. I usually just add "-thumbnail" to the name. For example, if the original is mypic.jpg, I name the smaller version mypic-thumbnail.jpg.

To use the thumbnail, put it in your page with an <IMG> tag, and then set up that image as a link to the normal size file. Here's an example:

```
<A HREF="mypic.jpg">
<IMG SRC="mypic-thumbnail.jpg">
</A>
```

Webmaster Wisdom

This book's CD contains the necessary files for two of these image map programs: LiveImage and Mapedit.

How do I make an image map with weird shapes, not just the usual rectangle, circle, or polygon?

You need to create a *server-side* image map, which requires a special program. Here are some to check out:

◆ **Image Mapper:** www.coffeecup.com/mapper/

◆ **LiveImage:** www.liveimage.com/

◆ **Mapedit:** www.boutell.com/mapedit/

See also the following Yahoo! index:

www.yahoo.com/Computers_and_Internet/Internet/World_Wide_Web/Imagemaps.

How do I get those little banners to pop up when the user puts the mouse over an image?

Add ALT text to your <IMG> tag:

```
<IMG
SRC="vacation12.gif"
ALT="This is a picture of me getting mugged in Marrakesh">
```

Most modern browsers display that text as a banner when the mouse pointer sits over an image for a second or two.

When I use an image as a link, how do I remove the border around the image?

Add BORDER=0 to your <IMG> tag, as in this example:

```
<A HREF="something.html">
<IMG SRC="jiffy.gif" BORDER=0>
</A>
```

I'm an AOL user, and my uploaded images are distorted. What's the problem?

AOL compresses uploaded images, which causes problems for some files. There's a full explanation on the AOL Webmaster Info site: webmaster.info.aol.com.

When you get there, click **Graphic Info** and then **AOL Compression.**

How can I prevent people from stealing my web page images?

This is extremely difficult, if not impossible, to do. However, here are three things that can help:

♦ Put a strongly worded copyright message on all your pages.

♦ Disable the right-click functionality that most image thieves use to grab graphics. I have a script on my site that shows you how to do this: www.mcfedries.com/ JavaScript/NoRightClick.html.

♦ Add a "digital watermark" to your images. See the Digimarc Corporation: www. digimarc.com.

How do I reduce the size (in bytes) of a photo or other high-quality image?

The best thing to do to reduce the size of a photographic image is to convert it to the JPEG format. JPEG enables you to "compress" an image without losing much of the quality. In most cases, you can reduce the image size (in kilobytes) to a tenth of its original girth or less. I usually use Paint Shop Pro for this (it's on this book's CD):

1. Open the GIF image in Paint Shop Pro.
2. Select the **File, Save As** command to open the Save As dialog box.
3. In the **Save as type** list, choose the **JPEG - JFIF Compliant** item.
4. Click the **Options** button.
5. Enter a value (say, **50**) in the **Compression factor** box (or drag the slider below it back and forth).
6. Click **OK** to return to the Save As dialog box.
7. Click **Save.**

You'll probably need to try this whole procedure several times using different values for the compression in step 5. Start with 50 percent and work higher in, say, increments of 10 percent. After each save, check the right hand side of the status bar to see the size of the image in kilobytes (KBytes). Also, check the quality of the image in the browser. The idea is that you want to compress the image as much as possible while still maintaining acceptable quality.

How can I slice up a large image to put in a table or use as an image map?

The easiest way I know is to use the Picture Dicer program: www.ziplink.net/~shoestring/dicer01.htm.

How do I get text to wrap around an image?

Add one of the following to your <IMG> tag:

- ◆ **ALIGN="LEFT":** Aligns the image on the left side of the screen. Subsequent text wraps around the right side of the image.
- ◆ **ALIGN="RIGHT":** Aligns the image on the right side of the screen. Subsequent text wraps around the left side of the image.

Why does it take so long for my mouseover images to appear?

The first time you hover the mouse over an image, the browser has to download the new image from the server, which can take time. The easiest way to reduce that time is to use smaller images. If that's not practical, you can also "preload" all the images. This means that the images are loaded into memory when the page is loaded, so they appear immediately when the user places the mouse over the image. See the following mouseover tutorial to learn how to preload images: www.mcfedries.com/JavaScript/mouseover3.html.

Publishing Questions.

How can I get my own domain name?

Please see Chapter 7, "The Host with the Most: Choosing a Web Hosting Provider."

Why do I see only a list of my files when I plug my address into the browser?

In your directory, you need to have a file that uses your server's *default name*. I explain how this works in Chapter 7.

How do I register my site with search engines?

Once again, see Chapter 7 for the answer.

How do I copyright my page?

There's no official process you have to go through to copyright your web page text. According to copyright law (see lcweb.loc.gov/copyright/), as soon as your text is published in a fixed form (such as being uploaded onto your web server), then your copyright is automatically in place. To be safe, always include a copyright notice at the bottom of all your pages. The usual format is the word "Copyright", followed by the © symbol (use either © or ©), followed by the year of publication, followed by your name: Copyright © 2002 Paul McFedries.

Multimedia Questions

I have a MIDI version of a popular song. Is it okay to use it on my site?

Using MIDI variations of commercial music is definitely a copyright violation. As responsible webmeisters, we should use *licensed* MIDI music wherever possible. The following web page explains more about this and offers some licensed files: www.liveupdate.com/sounds.html

How can I get a MIDI file to play as a background sound in both Internet Explorer and Netscape?

It's okay to use both the <BGSOUND> and <EMBED> tags in the same document:

```
<BGSOUND SRC="earsore.mid" LOOP="INFINITE">
<EMBED SRC="earsore.mid" AUTOSTART="TRUE" HIDDEN="TRUE" LOOP="0">
```

Can I use a sound file with a mouseover instead of an image?

To play a sound in JavaScript, you set the <SPAN STYLE="font-family: monospace"> location.href</SPAN> property equal to the sound file you want to play, like so:

```
location.href="applause.au"
```

So with a mouseover, you'd tack this on to the end (note the semicolon in between):

```
onMouseover="books.src='books-on.gif'; location.href='applause.au'"
```

How do I create RealAudio or RealVideo files?

RealNetworks has a tools page that offers programs for creating streaming media: www.real.com/products/tools/index.html.

Why doesn't Netscape play sounds when I test my pages?

You might need to get the proper plug-in. Check out the Crescendo page: www.liveupdate.com.

Webmaster Wisdom

This book's CD is home to a copy of the Crescendo plug-in.

Forms Questions

What is this "cgi-bin" thing that I see all over the web?

"cgi-bin" is the name of a directory where CGI scripts and programs are stored.

How do I use a form's Submit button to create a link to another page?

Set up cute little miniforms that consist of just a single BUTTON control. You add the JavaScript <SPAN STYLE="font-family: monospace">onClick</SPAN> attribute and use it to set the location property to the address of the web page you want to load:

```
<FORM>
<INPUT
   TYPE="BUTTON"
   VALUE="Paul's Place"
   onClick="location='http://www.mcfedries.com/'">
</FORM>
```

Create a separate miniform for each link. Note, too, that you need to use a table if you want to line up the buttons side by each.

Is it possible to use JavaScript to take form data and record it on another page?

No, JavaScript can't create a page or add text to an existing page. This can be done only by using CGI or ASP.

How can I use an image instead of the usual SUBMIT button?

Use the <INPUT TYPE="IMAGE"> control:

```
<INPUT TYPE=IMAGE SRC="someimage.gif">
```

Replace *someimage.gif* with the name of the image file that you want to use. Two things to note:

◆ This type of button acts just like a SUBMIT button. That is, when the user clicks the image, the form is submitted to the server.

◆ When the user clicks the image, the browser sends not only the form data, but also the coordinates, in pixels, of the spot on the image where the user clicked. These are sent as "x" (the horizontal coordinate) and "y" (the vertical coordinate).

How do I get the e-mail address of a person who fills in my form?

Include a field in the form and ask the user to enter his or her e-mail address in that field. If you use my MailForm service (see Chapter 12, "Need Feedback? Create a Form!"), name this field "E-mail" or "E-mail." This ensures that when you reply to a MailForm message, your reply gets sent automatically to the address that the user filled in.

Can MailForm get the user's e-mail address automatically?

No, it can't.

I'm using your MailForm service, but it doesn't seem to work. Is it still available?

Yes, MailForm is still available. If you're not getting messages, check the following:

- The most common MailForm mistake is to misspell one of the hidden field names. For example, lots of people accidentally spell the "MFAddress" field as "MFAdress".
- Double-check that your e-mail address is correct in the MFAddress field.
- Make sure you have all your quotation marks in place.
- Check out the MailForm site for the latest updates and improvements: www.mcfedries.com/MailForm/**MailForm.**

Frames Questions

How do I set up my frames without borders?

You need to add both FRAMEBORDER="0" and BORDER="0" to your <FRAMESET> tag, like so:

```
<FRAMESET COLS="25%,*" FRAMEBORDER="0" BORDER="0">
```

I have a frame with lots of links. Is there an easier way to specify the TARGET than adding it to every single <A> tag?

Yes! You can define a default target by including the <BASE TARGET> tag in the page header:

```
<BASE TARGET="YourFrameName">
```

Here, *YourFrameName* is the name of the frame that you want to use for all your links. It can also be one of the prefab frame names, such as "_top" or "_blank". After you put this in place, you don't need to use TARGET in your links (unless, of course, you want to use a different target for a particular link).

How do I change more than one frame from a single link?

The only way to do this is to have your link point to another frameset page. For example, suppose your original frameset page looks like this:

```
<FRAMESET COLS="100,*">
<FRAME SRC="menu.html" NAME="Left">

    <FRAMESET ROWS="50%,*">
```

```
    <FRAME SRC="one.html" NAME="TopRight">
    <FRAME SRC="two.html" NAME="BottomRight">
    </FRAMESET>

</FRAMESET>
```

This page sets up a frame on the left (named, boringly, "Left") and two frames on the right ("TopRight" and "BottomRight"). To change the two right frames in one fell swoop, set up your link to point to an identical frameset page that uses different SRC values in the "TopRight" and "BottomRight" frames:

```
<FRAMESET COLS="100,*">
<FRAME SRC="menu.html" NAME="Left">

    <FRAMESET ROWS="50%,*">
    <FRAME SRC="three.html" NAME="TopRight">
    <FRAME SRC="four.html" NAME="BottomRight">
    </FRAMESET>

</FRAMESET>
```

I don't want my site displayed in someone else's frames. Is it possible to prevent that?

Yes. Assuming your frames page is named "myframes.html", insert the following JavaScript into your page between the </HEAD> and <BODY> tags:

```
<SCRIPT LANGUAGE="JavaScript">
<!--
if (top != self)
    top.location.href="myframes.html"
//-->
</SCRIPT>
```

How do search engines index framed pages?

Here are some pointers about frames and search engines:

- Most search engines index only the frameset page (the one with the <FRAMESET> and <FRAME> tags). Therefore, be sure to include <META> tags in this page.
- Some search engines don't index <META> tags, so you might consider putting some kind of indexable content between <NOFRAMES> and </NOFRAMES>.
- If you want the search engine to index your "inside" pages, then it's also a good idea to include a link to those pages between <NOFRAMES> and </NOFRAMES>. This gives the search engine an entry point into the rest of your site.

◆ The problem with the latter suggestion is that surfers can easily end up in an inside page that lacks your framed navigation controls. However, you can use JavaScript to "reframe" the page. I have a script on my site that does just that: www.mcfedries. com/JavaScript/reframer.html.

Page Design Questions

Is it possible to determine the resolution of the user's screen?

Yes, using JavaScript's <SPAN STYLE="font-family: monospace">screen.height</SPAN> property. In the following example, the script checks this property and then replaces the current page with another page that's optimized (presumably) for the user's screen resolution:

```
<SCRIPT LANGUAGE="JavaScript" TYPE="text/javascript">
<!--

// Check for 640x480
if (screen.height == '480')
    location.replace('480.html')

// Check for 800x600
else if (screen.height == '600')
    location.replace('600.html')

// Check for 1024x768
else if (screen.height == '768')
    location.replace('768.html')

// Check for 1280x1024
else if (screen.height == '1024')
    location.replace('1024.html')

// Everything else
else
    location.replace('else.html')
//-->
</SCRIPT>
```

How do I create a stationary background that doesn't scroll along with the page text?

Add the BGPROPERTIES="FIXED" attribute to your <BODY> tag:

```
<BODY BGPROPERTIES="FIXED">
```

You can also do it with style sheets:

```
<BODY STYLE="background-image: url(http://www.wherever.com/whatever.gif);
             background-attachment: fixed">
```

Note, however, that both methods work only with Internet Explorer.

How do I center page text both vertically and horizontally?

You can use <CENTER> to center text horizontally, but there is no HTML tag for centering vertically. However, you can do it if you create a table for your entire page, and then use the VALIGN="MIDDLE" and ALIGN="CENTER" attributes within the main TD tag. Here's the skeleton:

```
<BODY>

<!--Set up a table for the entire window-->
<TABLE WIDTH="100%" HEIGHT="100%">
<TR>
<TD VALIGN="MIDDLE" ALIGN="CENTER">

<!--The real page text and stuff goes here-->
This text appears smack dab in the middle of the screen.

<!--Close the big table-->
</TD>
</TR>
</TABLE>

</BODY>
```

How do I provide users with an easy way to return to the top of a page?

Right below your <BODY> tag, add the following anchor:

```
<A NAME="top">
```

You can then send the surfer to the top of the page by including a link such as this:

```
<A HREF="#top">Return to the top of the page</A>
```

Appendix **C**

The CD: The Webmaster's Toolkit

As I've mentioned before, this book's whole purpose is to be a one-stop shop for budding websmiths. To that end, the text is geared toward getting you up to speed with this HTML rigmarole without a lot of fuss and flapdoodle. But fine words butter no parsnips, as they say (no, they really do), so you'll also find a complete "Webmaster's Toolkit" on the CD that's pasted into the back of this book. This toolkit is jammed to the hilt with handy references, files, and software that should provide everything you need to get your web authorship off to a rousing start. This appendix describes what's on the CD and tells you how to install it.

Accessing the CD's Contents

To get to the goodies on the CD, there are two routes you can take:

- ◆ Use your browser to open the file named index.htm in the main folder of the CD. This gives you a nice, clickable interface to everything that's on the CD.
- ◆ Open the CD and access the files directly.

Webmaster References

With over 100 HTML tags and over 100 style sheet properties in existence, there's a lot to keep track of. To help you out, I've create a few references that give you the full scoop on all the available tags, styles, and more. Here's a summary:

- **HTML tag reference**   This reference supplies you with the nitty-gritty on all the HTML tags. For each tag, you get a description of the tag, notes on using the tag, a complete list of the tag's attributes, browser support (including links to the appropriate Microsoft and Netscape pages, as well as to the corresponding official W3C page), and an example that shows the tag in action.

- **Style sheet reference**   This reference runs through a complete list of the available style sheet properties. For each property, you get a description of the property, notes on using it, a list of the property's possible values, browser support, and an example that shows how the property works.

- **The 216 "safe" web colors**   This page shows you all the 216 so-called "safe" web colors to use on your pages. ("Safe" means that these colors display well on almost all screens.) One table shows you the colors and another table shows you the corresponding RGB values.

- **The X11 color set**   This page runs through all the colors that have defined names (such as "Red," "Blue," and "Chartreuse").

The HTML Examples from the Book

Many of this book's chapters (especially those in Part 1, "Creating Your First Web Page") are sprinkled with examples showing HTML tags on the go. If you'd like to incorporate some of these examples into your own web work, don't bother typing your poor fingers to the bone. Instead, all the example files are sitting on the CD, ready for you to use. These example files are in the \Examples directory on the CD. Note, too, that everything is organized by chapter. The files for Chapter 1, "A Brief HTML Primer," are in \Examples\Chap01, the files for Chapter 2, "Laying the Foundation: The Basic Structure of a Web Page," are in \Examples\Chap02, and so on.

Web Graphics Sampler

Back in Chapter 6, "A Picture Is Worth a Thousand Clicks: Working with Images," you saw how a graphic or two can add a nice touch to an otherwise drab web page. Then, in Chapter 22, "Some HTML Resources on the Web," I mentioned a few spots on the web where you can find images to suit any occasion. But before you go traipsing off to one of these sites, you might want to check out what's on the CD. There you'll find hundreds of files that give you everything from simple bullets and lines to useful icons and pictures. There's even a section with some high-quality animated GIFs.

Programs for Web Weavers

The Webmaster's Toolkit is also loaded with a whack of software programs that can help you create better pages. The rest of this appendix presents a summary of the programs you'll find.

HTML Editors

Here's a list of the HTML editors that are in the Webmaster's Toolkit:

> **Page Pitfalls**
>
> Please note that most of the programs on the CD are demonstration versions of commercial programs. You can try out any program without charge, but of you want to continue to use a program, you need to purchase it from the vendor.

- ◆ **Dreamweaver**   This is an excellent, professional-quality HTML editor that's loaded with great features for churning out top-notch pages. It also boasts some impressive site management features, templates, and much more.

    CD site: /3rdParty/HTMLEdit/Macromedia/Dreamweaver/

    Website: www.macromedia.com/

- ◆ **GoLive**   This is an advanced HTML editor that's packed with features to make your webmastering life easier. It uses a "visual design" model for precise control, and also supports esoterica such as style sheets, Dynamic HTML, and XML.

    CD site: /3rdParty/HTMLEdit/Adobe/GoLive/

    Website: www.adobe.com/

- ◆ **HomeSite**   This is one of the best HTML editors on the planet. It has a great interface and more features than you can shake a stick at: a built-in spell checker, the ability to edit multiple documents at once, color-coded HTML tags, the ability to search-and-replace text across multiple files, and much more.

    CD site: /3rdParty/HTMLEdit/Allaire/Homesite/

    Website: www.allaire.com/

- ◆ **HotDog Professional**   This is one of the veterans of the HTML editor wars, and has emerged from the front lines better than ever. If you just want a good editor that doesn't offer a lot of unnecessary accessories, give HotDog a taste.

    CD site: /3rdParty/HTMLEdit/Sausage/HotDog/

    Website: www.sausage.com/

- **HTML Assistant** This is a decent HTML editor that gives you a graphical way to build your web pages. It includes a built-in spell checker as well as easy methods for creating forms and tables.

  CD site: /3rdParty/HTMLEdit/Brooklynnorth/HTMLAssistant/

  Website: www.brooknorth.com/

- **NetObjects Fusion** This is an extremely powerful editor that not only excels at regular HTML, but can also make it a breeze to create truly interactive sites that use JavaScript, Java, style sheets, and even dynamic HTML. It also features some amazing site management tricks (such as automatically updating links if you move or rename a page).

  CD site: /3rdParty/HTMLEdit/NetObjects/Fusion/

  Web site: http://www.netobjects.com

Graphics Software

Chapter 6 gave you the basics for adding images to your pages. Here are a few tools that help take some of the drudgery out of graphics work:

- **ACDSee** If you just need to take a quick gander at an image, ACDSee is the program to use because this utility excels in displaying image files. It's extremely fast, so it's perfect for sneak peeks. However, it can also do a bit of image manipulation, and it can convert graphics from one format to another.

  CD site: /3rdParty/Graphics/ACDSystems/ACDSee32/

  Website: www.acdsystems.com/

- **GIF Animator** This is a great program for creating animated GIFs. It's a snap to use (I gave you the basics in Chapter 11, "Making Your Web Pages Dance and Sing"), and it's crammed with cool features such as a banner-creation tool, transitions, and image optimization.

  CD site: /3rdParty/Graphics/Ulead/Gifanimator/

  Website: www.webutilities.com

- **LiveImage** Were you confused by my discussion of client-side image maps in Chapter 9, "Images Can Be Links, Too"? If so, then I suggest you check out LiveImage, which gives you an easy, graphical way to create client-side image maps without worrying about coordinates and other finicky stuff.

  CD site: /3rdParty/Graphics/Liveimage/Liveimage/

  Website: www.liveimage.com/

◆ **Mapedit**   This program gives you an easy, graphical method for defining server-side image maps (as opposed to the client-side image maps that I yammered on about in Chapter 9).

CD site: /3rdParty/HTMLEdit/Boutell/Mapedit/

Website: www.boutell.com/

◆ **Paint Shop Pro**   This is one of the best graphics programs on the market today. It supports all kinds of formats, offers great tools for creating drawings, makes effects such as drop shadows a breeze, and does much more.

CD site: /3rdParty/Graphics/Jasc/PaintShopPro/

Website: www.jasc.com

FTP Programs

I discussed using FTP to get your web handiwork onto your web host's server back in Chapter 8, "Publish or Perish: Putting Your Page on the Web." To help out, the CD boasts two of the best FTP programs around:

◆ **CuteFTP**   CuteFTP has a bizarre name, but it's an easy-to-use FTP program that gives you a no muss, no fuss way to fling files around the Net.

CD site: /3rdParty/FTP/Globalscape/CuteFTP/

Website: www.globalscape.com

◆ **WS_FTP Pro**   This program's easy interface and long list of features have made it one of the most popular FTP utilities on the Net.

CD site: 3rdParty/Ftp/IPSwitch/WS_ftppro/f_x86t32.exe

Website: www.ipswitch.com/

Audio Software

Lots of web designers like to add music to their sites to enhance their visitors' visits. The CD has some audio tools that can help:

◆ **Crescendo**   This is a plug-in that enables you to hear MIDI files.

CD site: /3rdParty/Audio/LiveUpdate/Crescendo/

Website: www.liveupdate.com/

◆ **Koan Plugin**   This music plug-in supports not only MIDI files, but also MP3 files, as well.

CD site: /3rdParty/Audio/Sseyo/Koanplugin/

Website: www.sseyo.com/

◆ **Koan Pro**   Use this program to create MP3 files to use on your website.

CD site: /3rdParty/Audio/Sseyo/Koanpro/

Website: www.sseyo.com/

Other Stuff

To wrap things up, the CD also contains the following miscellaneous tools:

◆ **CommNet**   This is a data communications application that seamlessly integrates Internet Telnet and modem dial-up and capabilities into a single, fast, full-featured, and easy-to-use application. CommNet supports both Zmodem and Telnet Zmodem file transfers and VT100/full-color PC ANSI and SCO ANSI emulations.

CD site: /3rdParty/FTP/Radient/Commnet/

Website: www.radient.com/

◆ **Drag & Zip**   This program is an add-on that gives Windows Explorer the ability to compress and decompress files.

CD site: /3rdParty/Other/Canyon/Drag&Zip/

Website: www.canyonsw.com/

◆ **TextPad**   This is a powerful replacement for Windows Notepad text editor.

CD site: /3rdParty/Textedit/Helios/Textpad/

Website: www.textpad.com

◆ **UltraEdit**   This is a great text editor that understands HTML (for example, it uses color coding to distinguish tags from regular text), enables you to work on multiple files at once, supports macros, and has lots of other powerful features.

CD site: /3rdParty/Textedit/IDMComp/Ultraedit/

Website: www.idmcomp.com/

◆ **WinZip**   For faster service, many of the Net's files and documents are stored in a "compressed" format that makes them smaller. After you download a compressed file to your computer, you need to "uncompress" the file in order to use it. WinZip is a handy little utility that makes it a breeze to uncompress any file. You can also use it to compress your own files if you'll be shipping them out.

CD site: 3rdParty/Other/Nicomak/Winzip/

Website: www.winzip.com/

Legal Stuff

By opening this package, you are agreeing to be bound by the following agreement:

This software product is copyrighted, and all rights are reserved by the publisher and author. You are licensed to use this software on a single computer. You may copy and/or modify the software as needed to facilitate your use of it on a single computer. Making copies of the software for any other purpose is a violation of the United States copyright laws.

This software is sold *as is* without warranty of any kind, either expressed or implied, including but not limited to the implied warranties of merchantability and fitness for a particular purpose. Neither the publisher nor its dealers or distributors assumes any liability for any alleged or actual damages arising from the use of this program. (Some states do not allow for the exclusion of implied warranties, so the exclusion might not apply to you.)

Index

X-Y-Z

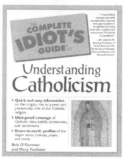

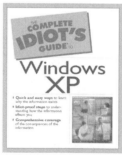